Old Before Their Time

Old Before Their Time is the deeply personal story of a 35-year scientific investigation of the effects of childhood sexual abuse on child development and adult outcomes. The startling conclusion is that early childhood trauma accelerates biological aging of the body and the mind.

The reader will gain a comprehensive perspective on the many ways in which maltreatment embeds itself in a child's mind, body, and behavior and is expressed across generations. It concludes that the prevention of child maltreatment is the single most powerful target for the prevention of mental illness, and for reducing premature death from common illnesses.

One in five women and one in eight men report a history of child sexual abuse. As adults, victims often have questions about how it has affected them. *Old Before Their Time* provides answers as well as recommendations to improve child protection and treatment services which impact millions of children and families every year. Written for a general science reader, this engaging book is well-referenced for professionals who work with children or adults with histories of child maltreatment.

Frank W. Putnam, MD, is a child and adolescent psychiatrist. Recipient of numerous awards, he is internationally recognized for his research on the psychobiological effects of child maltreatment.

"Dr. Frank Putnam is one of the world's greatest scientists in the area of child abuse, which the Centers for Disease Control has called the largest public health problem in America. Starting with his work at the National Institutes of Health, he and his team have meticulously followed over 100 sexually abused girls over a time span of more than 30 years and measured their (and their children's) mental health, physical, hormonal, emotional, and cognitive development. Their stunning research findings form the bedrock for our understanding of the pervasive long-term effects of early abuse, as well as providing a guide to effective intervention. His research work then led Dr. Putnam to implement a stunningly effective intervention program across three adjacent states, which should be a model for prevention and treatment around the country.

This is a riveting story detailing the science of child abuse, the incredible political complexities of studying this dark aspect of our society, and the (sometimes malicious) resistance of the mental health field to fully and realistically deal with its devastating consequences. It is a must read for anyone interested in understanding and alleviating human suffering."

—**Bessel van der Kolk**,
Author of the #1 New York Times bestseller The Body Keeps the Score

Old Before Their Time

A Scientific Life Investigating
How Maltreatment Harms
Children and the Adults
They Become

Frank W. Putnam

Routledge
Taylor & Francis Group

NEW YORK AND LONDON

Designed cover image: Getty Images

First published 2026
by Routledge
605 Third Avenue, New York, NY 10158

and by Routledge
4 Park Square, Milton Park, Abingdon, Oxon, OX14 4RN

Routledge is an imprint of the Taylor & Francis Group, an informa business

For Product Safety Concerns and Information please contact our EU
representative GPSR@taylorandfrancis.com. Taylor & Francis Verlag
GmbH, Kaufingerstraße 24, 80331 München, Germany.

ISBN: 9781032974835 (hbk)
ISBN: 9781032974828 (pbk)
ISBN: 9781003593928 (ebk)

DOI: 10.4324/9781003593928

Typeset in Caslon
by KnowledgeWorks Global Ltd.

To the generations of subjects, students, staff, and scientists who contributed to the success of the Female Growth and Development Study (FGDS).

Thank you

CONTENTS

ABOUT THE AUTHOR

Frank W. Putnam, MD, is a child and adolescent psychiatrist, professor of psychiatry at the University of North Carolina at Chapel Hill and former professor of pediatrics at Cincinnati Children's Hospital, Ohio. He spent 20 years as a research scientist at the National Institute of Mental Health in Bethesda, Maryland. The recipient of numerous awards and honors, Dr. Putnam is internationally recognized for his work on dissociative disorders, altered states of consciousness, the psychobiological effects of child maltreatment, and treatment of post-partum depression. He is author/co-author of over 200 scientific publications and three books.

PREFACE

This personal account is centered around the Female Growth and Development Study (FGDS), which officially began in 1987 and continues today. The FGDS follows approximately 80 sexually abused girls, initially aged 6–15 years at enrollment, and an equivalent number of statistically matched comparison girls into adulthood and beyond – for over 35 years as of this writing. The FGDS is a longstanding collaboration, primarily of the late Dr. Penelope (Penny) Trickett, PhD, Dr. Jennie Noll, PhD, and myself.

The scores of scientific publications from this study are widely scattered across time and diverse academic journals, such that only dedicated scholars could piece it all together. In addition, there are important integrative insights bridging the separately published scientific results that are inevitably missing from the individual papers and presentations.

Among ourselves, we have always thought that the FGDS deserved a book to pull together everything that we learned. But a book is not an easy endeavor and, despite discussions at various time points in the FGDS's history, there never was the perfect moment to write an inclusive summary. Life events, including Penny's death and my terminal diagnosis, have conspired to force my hand to write as definitive an account of this seminal research program as possible – although some important lifelong outcomes remain to be determined.

A consequence of what we learned from the FGDS is a greater involvement in child maltreatment prevention efforts on all our parts. In particular, I have embedded lessons into the FGDS narrative from my experiences across related domains, such as maltreatment forensics, state and national child protection policies and politics, and treatment approaches. The purpose of this book is to bring together and integrate not only the scientific lessons of the FGDS, but the larger picture of the causes and lifelong personal and societal consequences of child maltreatment as well as to identify opportunities to intervene in what is arguably the single most preventable, universal risk factor for serious mental health disorders, costly medical diseases, and social dysfunction in the United States.

Frank W. Putnam, MD
Stuart, VA
February 6, 2025

ACKNOWLEDGMENTS

During the course of my career, there were many people who helped me find my way forward and facilitated the important work of preventing child maltreatment. First and foremost are Penelope (Penny) Trickett (d. 2016) and Jennie Noll with whom I shared the precarious project of prospectively following the lives of ultimately hundreds of sexually abused and comparison research subjects and their offspring for decades. Only Penny and Jennie can truly appreciate how touch-and-go it was at times. I would like to thank William (Bill) Harris for his perceptive insights, political acumen, and generous support keeping the project running through lean times. Lisa Amaya-Jackson, Judith Herman, Richard Loewenstein, David Rubinow, and Bessel van der Kolk are long-time supporters who provided encouragement and advice during difficult moments. There are many others, too numerous to name, who made important contributions to this work. I trust they know who they are.

Thank you all.

PROLOGUE: A PARKING LOT EPIPHANY

Life changed for me one spring evening in 1985, as I walked out of the National Institutes of Health in Bethesda, MD, to the parking lot along Wisconsin Avenue. I had just seen a nine-year-old girl and her foster mother in the outpatient clinic. Ten years out of medical school, I had recently concluded a clinical psychiatry research fellowship at the National Institute of Mental Health (NIMH). As a result, I had decided to concentrate my research on multiple personality disorder (MPD), later renamed dissociative identity disorder (DID).

The young girl I'd just seen had immediately glommed onto my leg when I came into the room. If I didn't know better, I might have foolishly attributed her excited response to my rapport with children. The foster mother assured me, though, that she did this with anyone and everyone she had never seen before.

Despite her inappropriate attachment to strangers, Jodie (pseudonym) was hyperalert, reacting – sometimes startling – to sounds and voices in the hallway outside the interview room. Buzzing around the room, making bizarre faces in the observation room one-way mirror, aggressively looking at my notes as I wrote, she was hyperactive, intrusive, emotionally labile, and, by history, hypersexual.

The county banned her from school buses because she was molesting other children. On occasion, she even groped adults. She masturbated herself to sleep at night. The foster mother was especially worried, because now she was developing prominent breasts.

At recess, a teacher's aide was assigned to continually monitor her. Jodie could explode at the slightest provocation violently attacking much larger children. Although never considered smart, her scholastic abilities, fund of knowledge, and reasoning fluctuated dramatically day-to-day, sometimes even hour-by-hour. No one could be sure of when she genuinely forgot something that she had learned or when she was being oppositional.

At that point in time, neither psychiatry nor psychology had good ways of characterizing Jodie, or what was going on with her. No single diagnosis covered her or many of the other children I had been seeing. But by now I had seen enough children like Jodie to know that she was not unique. There were plenty of disturbed children like her – or worse.

Walking to my car, I kept thinking about the wide range of disturbed behaviors and seemingly biologically dysregulated bodies that I was seeing as I evaluated children for possible dissociative disorders. These troubled children did not fit with the little that I had learned about child development during my adult psychiatric training.

The very disturbed children, coupled with the distressed and overwhelmed responses of those charged with their care and wellbeing, convinced me that something terrible was happening to these children. But whatever it was, I wasn't in the position to do much about it. Tenuously holding a minor staff psychiatrist job – which was renewed for only one year at a time and always at the very last minute – I could conduct my own research only after I first recruited subjects for research on schizophrenia at the NIMH satellite program located at St. Elizabeths Hospital in Anacostia, MD. I cautioned myself that I already had too many projects at various stages to undertake yet another.

The St. Elizabeths research unit never stayed full for long. At full capacity, ward dynamics, patients, and staff combined, would decompress the toxic overcrowding by scapegoating a patient leading to an elopement or discharge. And then I'd have to drop everything when Lew, the clinical director, would get on my case to recruit new patients to fill the empty beds. He wanted the research unit kept full, regardless of the glaring hole in the bucket.

I had taken on this Sisyphean job because I was interested in a weird psychiatric condition, known then as multiple personality disorder and now called dissociative identity disorder. Almost by accident I found a case of MPD, misdiagnosed as bipolar disorder, during my clinical research fellowship. That led to the discovery of additional cases and my fledgling efforts to start a research program to investigate this mysterious condition.

The multiples – some of the most amazing people I have ever known – all told me that they'd been this way since childhood. Usually at some point in early adolescence they discovered that other people were not like them, and they learned to disguise their multiplicity.

As adults they might appear successful in their public lives, but in private they paid an immense price. At some point, many would psychologically implode from the ongoing wars in their heads and end up in the mental health system, usually diagnosed as having schizophrenia or bipolar disorder. On average, they spent seven years misdiagnosed and treated for psychiatric and neurological disorders they didn't have, before their dissociative disorder was identified.

If what my MPD research subjects and patients were telling me about their childhoods was accurate, I reasoned, I should be able to find children with multiple personality disorder. That's how I started seeing children. I circulated my behavioral profile of child dissociative symptoms to child protection units, foster care agencies, and child therapists in the DC metropolitan area. It seemed a long shot. My library research had not turned up any child cases in the modern psychiatric literature.[1] I figured that I might get one or two referrals for evaluation. Over the following years I received well over a hundred.

Most of those children weren't pathologically dissociative in my opinion, but they were emotionally disturbed, behaviorally disorganized, and seemingly biologically dysregulated. A few most likely did have an early stage of multiple personality disorder.[2]

But at that transcendental moment in the parking lot, I really didn't understand what I was seeing. Many different things seemed to be wrong with these children. But I couldn't sort out what were causes and what were the effects. Not yet trained in child and adolescent psychiatry or having children of my own, I knew little about normal child development or child psychopathology.

Walking to my car in the twilight of that spring evening, one thought kept looping in my head: "Something terrible happened to these children."

It was then that I had the sudden blinding realization that despite the confusing array of symptoms and disturbed behaviors that I witnessed in these referred children, the common thread was their histories of child abuse.[3] At that moment I had my first deep glimpse into how maltreatment hurts children and the adults that they become.

Gently mocking myself for having just received my "calling," I stood quietly for a few minutes, transfixed by a profound sense of purpose. At the core of my being, I knew that this was what I was supposed to do. Ending child abuse was to be my life's work.

Even today, memory of that moment in the parking lot remains remarkably fresh, retaining its power to inspire and sustain me despite difficult times.

While the epiphany in the parking lot would jump-start my quest to understand the profound biological and behavioral dysregulation of maltreated children, I would come to appreciate that a steady stream of scientific findings on the one hand and supportive collegial relationships on the other (leavened with a dash of serendipity, and baked in a high degree of optimistic persistence) were essential to sustaining me on what would prove to be a long, sometimes painful, journey.

In psychiatry, especially in psychoanalysis, attempts are often made to "reverse engineer" the cause of a particular form of psychopathology. That is, to start with symptomatic adults and deduce the early childhood life events and developmental pathways that led to their mental problems.

My experiences with adult MPD cases convinced me that it was not possible to retrospectively reconstruct how they became psychologically organized as an "us" as opposed to an "I." A prospective, longitudinal approach from childhood forward was necessary. Together with my colleague, Dr. Penelope Trickett, I would embark on the multi-decade Female Growth and Development Study (FGDS) of the biological, psychological, and social effects of severe child maltreatment (specifically incest) on young girls as they grew up and became mothers (and even grandmothers).

Ultimately, many others would join us as graduate students and co-investigators. Together we were able to identify biological and behavioral mechanisms by which early childhood trauma embeds itself within an individual's mind and body and is expressed over the lifespan. Today, the FGDS continues to reveal just how deeply and profoundly childhood trauma shapes an individual's life course.

At times I would be blindsided by the vehemence of pushback to our research findings, even more so when the venom was directed at me. Resistance to acknowledging the widespread existence and brutal realities of child maltreatment was something survivors going public, and their advocates, often faced. It came from multiple directions at once. There were aggressive legal attacks by defense lawyer/accused parent organizations such as the "False Memory Syndrome Foundation," there was the rampant hysteria whipped up by the true believers in the existence of international satanic cults, and there were the frustrating dismissals – and even outright disdain – from the mainstream mental health establishment.

Science was my salvation. My initial efforts led to an appreciation of the centrality of systematically describing the clinical phenomenology of a mental disorder coupled with the necessity of measuring the underlying pathological processes. Creating diagnostic tools and interventional models that framed mental health problems along continuums rather than as dichotomous all-or-nothing psychiatric "diagnoses" proved critical to broadly communicating the contributions of childhood trauma to a wide range of mental, medical, and social problems.

In my day-to-day work with the many professions and systems involved in child mental health and family violence prevention, I would gain a deeper understanding of the multi-layered social and political complexities confounding coherent policies and coordinated action. Working across diverse public health, legal, and political domains, I found that aggressively challenging widespread but misleading stereotypes is essential to improving awareness and increasing an acceptance of the role of childhood trauma in adult mental health problems. While my colleagues were (usually) helpful, my patients and our research subjects taught me the most. Especially the children.

Since that life-changing moment in the parking lot, I have had other deep glimpses into the enduring carnage wrought by childhood abuse. Now, as I face a terminal illness, this book is a final effort to share my insider's look at the trials and tribulations, challenges and rewards of working within a complex, multi-institutional, sometimes dysfunctional child protection/mental health world to protect children and to enhance their wellbeing.

Notes

1. Eventually, scouring the nineteenth-century psychiatric literature, thanks to the National Library of Medicine, I found several case reports and even one case series of what sounded like dissociative children.
2. Years later I received independent confirmations of my childhood dissociative disorder diagnoses in several instances (including Jodie).
3. While the role of maltreatment in these children's behavior problems seems obvious now. At the time, it was rarely seen as a contributing factor by their caretakers or therapists. Most foster and adoptive parents were only vaguely aware of the child's trauma history and rarely knew even general details. I learned to ask foster parents to contact their foster care agency to get whatever details were on record.

ABBREVIATIONS

A-DES	Adolescent-Dissociative Experiences Scale
AACAP	American Academy of Child and Adolescent Psychiatry
AAP	American Academy of Pediatrics
ACE	adverse childhood experience
ACTH	adrenocorticotropic hormone
ACYF	Administration for Children, Youth, and Families
ADHD	attention deficit hyperactivity disorder
APA	American Psychiatric Association
APA	American Psychological Association
AR	alternate response
BEB	Behavioral Endocrinology Branch
BMI	body mass index
BSC	Board of Scientific Counselors
CAC	child advocacy center
CANNet	Child Abuse and Neglect Network
CAPTA	Child Abuse Prevention and Treatment Act
CCRC	Crimes Against Children Research Center
CDC	Child Dissociative Checklist
CFTSI	child and family traumatic stress intervention
CpG	cytosine-phosphate-guanine
CPS	child protective services

CPTSD	complex post-traumatic stress disorder
CRH	corticotrophin-releasing hormone
CSA	child sexual abuse
DA	district attorney
DES	Dissociative Experience Scale
DICA	diagnostic interview for children and adolescents
DID	dissociative identity disorder
DISC	Diagnostic Interview Schedule for Children
DSM	*Diagnostic and Statistical Manual of Mental Disorders*
DTD	developmental trauma disorder
ECS	Every Child Succeeds
ECT	electroconvulsive therapy
eECS	electronic Every Child Succeeds
EEG	electroencephalogram
EMR	electronic medical record
EMT	emergency medical technician
EndCAN	National Foundation to End Child Abuse and Neglect
ER	emergency room
FDA	Food and Drug Administration
FGDS	Female Growth and Development Study
HFA	Healthy Families America
HPA	hypothalamic-pituitary-adrenal
ICU	intensive care unit
IOM	Institute of Medicine
IRB	Investigational Review Board
IV	intravenous
JFS	Jobs and Family Services
LDP	Laboratory of Developmental Psychology
MECA	Methodology for Epidemiology of Mental Disorders in Children and Adolescents
MEG	magnetoencephalography
MPD	multiple personality disorder
MPD/DID	multiple personality disorder/dissociative identity disorder
MSMA	multi-site meta-analysis
NAMI	National Alliance on Mental Illness

NCA	National Children's Alliance
NCANDS	National Child Abuse and Neglect Data System
NCS	National Children's Study
NCTSN	National Child Traumatic Stress Network
NFP	Nurse Family Partnership
NICHD	National Institute of Child Health and Human Development
NIH	National Institutes of Health
NIMH	National Institute of Mental Health
NRC	National Research Council
NSSR	New York School for Social Research
OCTF	Ohio Children's Trust Fund
ODJFS	Ohio Department of Jobs and Family Services
OMB	Office of Management and Budget
PBS	Public Broadcasting Service
PCAA	Prevent Child Abuse America
PCIT	Parent Child Interaction Therapy
PSANE	Pediatric Sexual Assault Nurse Examiner
PTSD	post-traumatic stress disorder
RA	research assistant
RDoC	Research Domain Criteria
SMR	sexual maturity rating
SRA	satanic ritual abuse
STD	sexually transmitted disease
TF-CBT	Trauma-Focused Cognitive Behavior Therapy
TOP DD	Treatment of Patients with Dissociative Disorders
TTRC	Trauma Treatment Replication Center
UCLA	University of California at Los Angeles
USC	University of Southern California
VP	vice president

1

MULTIPLE PERSONALITY DISORDER

Choosing Biological Psychiatry

During morning rounds in 1976, Patty (pseudonym) was weepy, help-less. Tightly curled in a fetal ball, she pulled a pillow down over her head. When the attending psychiatrist asked about her state of mind, she responded weakly from beneath the pillow, "I just want to die. Please let me die."

She'd been like this for several weeks, refractory to antidepressant medication and what passed for psychotherapy in daily sessions with me.

In the hallway, the attending psychiatrist told me that she, Patty, was going to need electroconvulsive therapy (ECT). As an intern taking a psychiatry elective, I was directed to write the special orders and pro-gress note to prepare Patty for a series of ECT treatments starting the next day.

My rounds took longer than usual. I postponed writing the ECT orders and note to attend a lecture and when I returned to complete the paperwork, I was shocked to see Patty in the dayroom bullying a group of cowering patients into exercising. Strutting up and down, angrily barking nonsensical commands and obscenities, she harangued fellow patients like a deranged drill sergeant. The nursing staff stood back watching, agape in amazement.

DOI: 10.4324/9781003593928-1

1

"Really makes you believe in biological psychiatry," a fellow intern observed.

His remark remained with me as I witnessed rapid, occasionally violent, shifts in mood and mental state in psychiatric patients (and others) over the course of my training.

In addition to rapid switches from depression to mania and back again, patients went into catatonic states, in which they became frozen statues in the blink of an eye. On the Veterans hospital wards, dangerous flashbacks to Vietnam would be triggered by seemingly innocuous stimuli – a sound, a gesture or even a smell. In other patients, something minor that they saw or heard or just thought about, could elicit an overwhelming panic attack.

In the late winter of 1979, as the end of my residency in adult psychiatry drew near, I pondered my next steps. Recently divorced, I felt free but rootless. A novel I was writing, *Paths*, based on my experiences treating Vietnam war veterans, was well advanced and was the most compelling focus in my life. I needed time to finish it.[1]

Although I was promised a junior faculty position at the Yale School of Medicine, New Haven, CT, upon graduation, I was too uncomfortable with the dogmatic psychoanalytic orientation of the department of psychiatry to start a career there. To fit in, I'd have to acquiesce to an orthodoxy I didn't believe in.

I'd seen too many rapid shifts in mental state to believe in psychoanalytic psychiatry. There had to be something else going on. A research fellowship in biological psychiatry could buy time to figure out what I wanted to do with my life. And I could finish *Paths*.[2]

The center of the growing biological psychiatry movement was the NIMH (National Institute of Mental Health) Intramural Research Program located on the National Institutes of Health (NIH) research campus in Bethesda, MD. A fellow resident, Dennis Langer, MD, left Yale early for a fellowship at the NIMH. He suggested I come to Bethesda and interview. Dennis tipped me off on the topics I was likely to be asked about, which involved theories about excesses, deficits, and imbalances in various neurotransmitters, the chemical messengers that connect one neuron with another.

Driving down from New Haven, CT, to Bethesda on a Friday in early 1979, I spent the weekend on Dennis's living room couch reading his collection of scientific papers in preparation for Monday's interviews. One of his roommates, John Nurnberger, MD, PhD, had been in my Indiana University combined medical and graduate degree program. Together, they quizzed me over beers.

Offered a two-year (extended to three years) clinical research fellowship in the psychobiology section of the biological psychiatry branch, under Robert M. Post, MD, I landed in the heart of the biological psychiatry revolution that was aggressively supplanting psychoanalysis as the dominant approach to mental illness.

At that time, biological psychiatry was a scientific movement seemingly brimming with promise to unravel the secrets of the mind and the nature of mental illness. Brain imaging technologies were rapidly coming online thanks to refrigerator-sized laboratory computers, improved analog to digital hardware, and brain mapping algorithms. Biochemical assays were being developed for the neurotransmitters and hormones that bathed the brain and circulated in the blood. A variety of miniaturized monitoring devices, such as wearable activity and heart monitors and core temperature probes, were becoming available to track circadian rhythms.

By the time I arrived, biological psychiatry was firmly entrenched at the NIMH and increasingly impacting the field through publications and funding to university research programs. For another couple of years, one would encounter the residue of prior psychoanalytic research in the form of stacks of psychotherapy session notes bundled with reels of audiotape or boxes of videotape piled precariously high on closet shelves. But demands for space soon emptied the closets and storerooms. Trash barrels full of psychotherapy process notes and tapes were consigned to the incinerators.

Years later I would witness the "neurogenetic psychiatrists" dump gallons of frozen urine, plasma, and spinal fluid collected by the biological psychiatrists, as the field of psychiatry pivoted to yet another scientific paradigm.

The "gold" of one psychiatric research paradigm transmuted into the dross of the next.

Discovering Multiple Personality Disorder (MPD)

As an NIMH clinical research fellow, one of my duties was to conduct a weekly psychotherapy group with rapid cycling bipolar patients. This was an extremely frustrating experience, in that mutely depressed patients one week could be clamorously manic the next. Continuity was hard to come by – greatly impairing appreciation of cause-and-effect relationships between behavior and its consequences.

One patient, Joan (pseudonym), was different. She remained continuously, bitterly depressed. Relentlessly suicidal, she required resuscitation after two near fatal attempts.

Remarkably, on rare occasions and only for brief stints (15 minutes or less), Joan revealed a witty and socially engaging side. This infrequently seen persona led her to be diagnosed with rapid cycling bipolar disorder. Yet, everyone – doctors, nurses, and even the other patients – regarded Joan as somehow different; and, in staff meetings, half the time seemed to be devoted to discussing her care. Still, nothing seemed to help her.

Joan also differed from other patients in that she had a classic, non-neurologic, "hysterical" paralysis from the waist down. She went everywhere in a wheelchair, including to my weekly group therapy session. Numerous examinations demonstrated that there was no neurological cause for her paralysis. Attempts to discuss her pseudo-paralysis with her were met with vehement anger and self-destructive acting out, such as hunger strikes and mutism, effectively ending further inquiries. Indeed, Joan radiated a silent rage that kept everyone at a distance.

One day in group therapy, I witnessed a brief appearance of Joan's witty persona. By now having seen numerous mood swings, catatonic states, traumatic flashbacks, temporal lobe seizures, and panic attacks, I knew that whatever Joan's change in mental state was, it was none of those. Her switch was something very different. Struggling to conceptualize it, I speculated that perhaps Joan suffered from multiple personality disorder (MPD).

MPD was a much maligned, hotly disputed diagnosis. Throughout my training I witnessed acrimonious debates among senior psychiatrists and psychologists about the existence and nature of MPD.

As a senior medical student, I attended a grand rounds[3] given by Cornelia Wilbur, MD, Sybil's therapist.[4] During the question-and-answer session, a psychologist stood up. "I could make someone a multiple personality," he claimed.

Dr. Wilbur responded that she had been psychoanalyzed and had dealt with her feelings of grandiosity and omnipotence. She knew that she couldn't create a multiple personality. I didn't find her answer a compelling defense for the existence of MPD.

Later I joined the group selected to have lunch with Dr. Wilbur. She described some of her MPD cases in ways that I judged were too subjective, and I was left feeling dubious about the reality of MPD.

Yet, grasping for an explanation of Joan's momentary transformations, I wondered if maybe she could have MPD. I convinced her skeptical primary psychiatrist, Ed Silberman, MD, to at least inquire about this possibility. We were amazed when Joan confirmed the diagnosis by letting us meet some of her dissociative identity states, including one that could walk.

While I enjoyed a modicum of acclaim among our research group for having made this rare diagnosis, which was instrumental in successfully changing our treatment of Joan, I doubted that I'd ever see another MPD case in my career[5].

Shortly thereafter, I encountered two more cases of MPD that changed my opinion of how common, but unrecognized, this mysterious condition was.

First year clinical fellows were required to be on night and weekend call to cover the NIMH psychiatric research wards. In addition, on-call fellows might be paged to consult on psychiatric emergencies on other NIH inpatient units. One night, I was paged about a psychiatric problem on a neurology research ward. A large male patient (Mr. B.) was going berserk.

With trepidation, I went to the neurology unit located a few floors above my ward in the giant NIH clinical center. A quick history from the nurses included his lifting up and slamming down an incredibly heavy hospital bed as well as splitting the top of a bedside table with a karate chop. He had not, however, directed his rage at people.

Paradoxically, it was clear that the nurses were fond of Mr. B. They emphasized that he was polite and gentle when he wasn't in one of these mental states. He carried a diagnosis of intractable temporal lobe epilepsy, although the neurologists found only minor, non-specific EEG (electroencephalogram; brain wave) abnormalities. The possibility of pseudo-seizures was noted on the chart.

Mr. B. was a powerfully built, middle-aged man. Seated in an arm-chair, he was friendly but bewildered. Politely addressing me as "sir," he spoke slowly with a notable stammer. His short crewcut and upright bearing gave him a military demeanor. He didn't recall slamming down the bed or breaking the bedside table. He expressed consternation that he was often told about doing things that he couldn't recall.

In addition to amnesia for recent events, he shared past examples that he'd been told about including fighting off police and firemen attempting to rescue him after an automobile accident and receiving Marine Corps medals for acts of bravery during the Korean War that he didn't recall.

On the mental status exam there was no impairment in short-term memory or cognitive functions. He reported hearing an internal voice – which he called "my inner mind" – on occasion. The voice gave him advice or commented on situations. Generally, he found the voice helpful.

After several months of exposure to Joan's dissociative identity states, there was a familiar feel to what I was hearing and seeing with Mr. B. I arranged to videotape a more formal interview during which he was hypnotized for part of the time. While he was under hypnosis, I met four distinct identity states that demonstrated marked changes in mood, posture, handedness, and speech, including absence of his stammer. One of these identity states was a frightened child that sucked its thumb – a regression that appeared incongruous in this robust man.

I continued to see Mr. B. over the next several weeks. He was weaned off his considerable doses of anticonvulsants with no change in his "sei-zures," which had not been seizures at all, but switches among dissocia-tive identity states. It became apparent that triggers for the activation of one particular dissociative identity state named "Rage," were interactions in which Mr. B. felt that a fellow male patient on the ward was being mocked or belittled. That patient wore a football helmet to protect his neurosurgical dressings from intense epileptic seizures. Mr. B. believed that some people ridiculed his friend for wearing the helmet.

I met Mr. B.'s family, who shared numerous examples of his "forgetful-ness." In one episode, he woke everyone around midnight on Christmas

Eve saying that he smelled gas. He led them outside and then went back into the house. After waiting for several hours in the cold for Mr. B. to return, his wife went back into the house. She found him asleep in their bed. He had no memory of the incident.

On discharge, I referred Mr. B. to a psychiatrist near his home in Kentucky, who said that he had worked with several MPD cases. That was my first awareness that there was an informal network of therapists who quietly treated MPD patients. On follow-up a year later, Mr. B. had returned to work (previously he was on disability), but he remained as dissociative as before. His family, now interacting directly with his identity states, reported that he was functioning reasonably well.

Shortly thereafter, another clinical research fellow, Richard Loewenstein, MD, diagnosed a third MPD case at the NIMH. We published a clinical report chalking up our encounters with so many cases of this exceptionally "rare" disorder, to working at an institution that specialized in obscure disorders and treatment resistant cases as part of a high-risk/high-reward research strategy (Putnam et al., 1984).

In retrospect, I realized that I'd seen at least three other cases during my psychiatry training – all of whom I had misdiagnosed as having partial complex seizures, although their brain waves only showed nonspecific temporal lobe abnormalities. It was becoming apparent to me that this "rare" condition might be a lot more common than realized.

Our relatively minor publication elicited a remarkable number of letters and phone calls from psychiatrists, psychologists, and mental health therapists treating similar cases, often seeking consultations and referrals. Tapping into this loose network, I began to look for ways to investigate this mysterious condition.

The 100 Cases Study

Undertaking an unsupported research program with little to no budget and limited resources, I had only my time to make use of. And even that wasn't under my complete control. But I did have something else, an ability to teach myself complicated things.

One of those things was computers. Being comfortable with computers and programming at multiple levels made all the difference in my career. I could collect data, analyze it, and make figures, tables, and graphs to communicate the results. I could write and revise scientific papers, even entire books – because I had computer skills.

Many of my fellow clinical research fellows were given research assistants (RAs) and secretarial time, so they never had to enter data, analyze it, or make charts and graphs themselves. Because I wasn't doing bipolar research, I was last in line for services. Anything for me in the RA or secretarial pipeline got pushed back or forgotten when Bob, Jim, Ed, or Tom needed something for a scientific meeting.

By necessity, I learned to do everything for myself. My first acquaintance with computers had come toward the end of college – a little Fortran punch card programming on the IBM-1620 that filled the basement of the Wesleyan University observatory. But I didn't get what computers could do for me. I did not see them as something I needed in my life, only as interesting machines.

In graduate school I learned machine language and assembler coding while working with Professor James Randall, PhD, on a PDP-12 computer, measuring autonomic nervous system changes in meditating subjects. He was intensely proud of that computer, as if it were his firstborn. The personal computer of its day, the PDP-12 was as stout as a refrigerator, had a tiny video screen, and tea saucer-sized reels of magnetic tape to store programs and data. (Decades later, a PDP-12 was included in a public display of early scientific computers in the NIH clinical center.)

I went to medical school and completed my internship and psychiatry residency and didn't see another computer for about eight years – until I arrived at the NIMH. On Bob Post's psychobiological research ward, there was a single IBM typewriter computer terminal that only the senior research assistant knew how to use. There was no video screen. You typed commands and saw the results on reams of fanfold paper (it was a remote terminal for an IBM-360 mainframe computer located about a block away in the division of computer resources and technology).

The text editor (Wylbur), with which one issued commands and wrote programs, was column oriented – everything had to be in the correct column or the program crashed. There were 80 columns to a line. You couldn't see exactly which column the typewriter printhead was aligned with, so there would be frustrating searches for a comma or backslash in the wrong column or similar minor syntactical errors requiring painstaking proofreading to find and fix. It was on this crude typewriter computer terminal that I first appreciated what computers could do for me.

I had a great mentor in Julie, who was my best friend for many years. Divorced, with college-age kids, she was older than me, with a timeless soul and an ageless, smiling face. A project manager for a genetics research group, Julie was a master at analyzing data and troubleshooting statistical programs.

As a first step to gaining a more comprehensive clinical profile of MPD, I sought to clarify the clinical phenomenology. What were the defining characteristics of this mysterious disorder?

Tapping into the loose network of MPD therapists, I connected with Ralph Allison, MD, a forensic psychiatrist who had written several books about his MPD cases and briefly published a newsletter for therapists. Ralph graciously shared with me his defunct newsletter mailing list, which he'd kept on handwritten 3 × 5 note cards. I also created my own mailing list from reprint requests for our three cases paper. Julie helped me create a questionnaire (a 25-page booklet) that I drafted on that primitive typewriter computer terminal and printed in volume on the mainframe computer (see Figure 1.1).

One of the first actions of President Reagan following his inauguration in 1981 was to sign the Government Paperwork Reduction Act, which specified that before a government employee could ask ten or more US citizens a question, the Office of Management and Budget (OMB) had to approve it. I needed an OMB approval number before I could mail out my questionnaire.

The OMB was clueless about MPD and questions about hallucinations, fugues, and amnesias – but they were also justifiably uncomfortable with their new responsibility of policing scientists. So, I was able to resolve their concerns without difficulty.[6]

I mailed copies of the questionnaire with an enclosed, postage-paid return envelope using the NIH government franking privileges. As the returns came back, Julie helped me enter and clean the data set. Then I started learning to write statistical programs to analyze the data. Julie knew all the tricks and provided me with examples that I could adapt.

Whenever there was a problem, she knew how to solve it. (You really only learn statistics when you have a data set that you care about.)

My first attempt at an MPD scientific paper had involved a quantitative review systematically comparing nineteenth- with twentieth-century case reports.[7] It was written in longhand on yellow legal tablets. I have legible handwriting, so transcription was not difficult. But it took the secretaries months to get a formatted draft back.

My submission came back from the journal with generally positive reviews, but also with many suggested revisions and clarifications before I could resubmit. However, because I had to wait my turn for secretarial time, I was unable to make the requested changes and resubmit a typed and formatted draft within the 30-day allotted time.

That's when I knew I needed my own word processor.

At that time there were few choices. I was on the verge of buying a "Trash 80" (Radio Shack TRS-80), a major purchase for me, when IBM announced its first personal computer. Sight unseen, I placed an order and was told that it was one of the first 50 sold in the US. Next, I bought a 300-baud modem and, after many frustrating attempts, programmed communications software to work on the NIH IBM mainframe from home.

Working from home at night and at weekends, I started to write up the results of the multiple personality questionnaire study. By today's standards it was a long, slow slog, but at the time it seemed miraculous. That paper, *The Clinical Phenomenology of Multiple Personality Disorder: Review of 100 recent cases*, eventually published in 1986, became a classic (Putnam et al., 1986).

Most importantly, the results have since been replicated many times over across different countries and diverse cultures. The 100 cases study essentially doubled the number of MPD case reports in English at the time and represented the first systematic effort to delineate a clinical profile to aid clinicians in the diagnosis of this mysterious condition[8].

While writing a section of the 100 cases paper, I might realize that there was another analysis that needed to be done. I'd exit the word processor, dial up the mainframe, write the statistical program, submit it to the job queue, wait for it to run, troubleshoot the inevitable errors, rerun it – rinse and repeat – until eventually I got the answer. Then I could start writing again.

This process could take a whole weekend when the analyses were complicated, or the programming errors subtle. But in the days before computers, the turnaround would have taken weeks to months just waiting for a research assistant to get around to doing one of my many analyses on a hand calculator. Most importantly, having done it all myself, I understood what was entailed and potential errors or problems. Moreover, I found it incredibly exciting. I had the best MPD data set in the world and there was so much to ask it.

When preparing a presentation for a scientific meeting, we first took our data to the art department, where the data points were laboriously plotted on graph paper by hand. These plots were then taken to photography where they were turned into 35 mm slides known as "blue isolettes" – white lines and lettering on a blueprint-like background. Stacks of 35 mm slides were the PowerPoints of that era. I traveled to scientific meetings with my talks preloaded in a Kodak carousel slide tray carefully padded and packed in the center of my suitcase.

It usually took three to four weeks to prepare for a professional meeting, unless, of course, you were one of the big guys. Then you went to the front of the line – or at least closer to the front depending on your size. An upcoming major meeting would cause that line to become impossibly long for a little guy like me.

The major function that my IBM PC lacked was the ability to make graphs or figures. A plug-in graphics card was rumored to be in the works, but even if I could create graphs on the video screen, I had no way to print them.

Then I learned about another computer at NIH, the DEC-10. The DEC-10 could plot graphs, producing elegant pen-drawn graphics – in multiple colors if you wished – that were ready for the photography department. By skipping the art department bottleneck and showing up in photography early with camera-ready DEC-10 computer plots, I cut my wait time by more than two-thirds.

Now, with this collection of computers, I had it all – and I was off and running. Since then, computers have continued to play an ever greater empowering role in my work, both research and clinical.

DEPARTMENT OF HEALTH AND HUMAN SERVICES
PUBLIC HEALTH SERVICE
ALCOHOL, DRUG ABUSE, AND MENTAL HEALTH ADMINISTRATION
NATIONAL INSTITUTE OF MENTAL HEALTH

OMB No. 0930-0082
Approval Expires
2-29-83

MULTIPLE PERSONALITY DISORDER -- CLINICIANS' QUESTIONNAIRE

INTRODUCTION

The phenomenon known as Multiple Personality Disorder (MPD) has long occupied a controversial postion in the field of psychiatry. This questionnaire is an attempt to collect systematic data on the presentation, diagnosis, past history, phenomenology, treatment, and outcome of Multiple Personality Disorder.

We request that the responding clinician select, and report in this questionnaire, a single case that meets the diagnostic criteria for Multiple Personality listed in Diagnostic and Statistical Manual of Mental Disorders, Third Edition, American Psychiatric Association, 1980 (DSM III). The current DSM III criteria are:

A. Within the individual exist two or more distinct personalities, each of which is dominant at a particular time.

B. The personality that is dominant at any particular time determines the individual's behavior.

C. Each individual personality is complex and integrated, with its own unique behavior patterns and social relationships.

CONFIDENTIALITY

To ensure that each case is counted only once, even if more than one clinician should report on the same patient, we are asking for the patient's initials and birth date. They will not be made public, and no case will be published individually in this study. The information in the body of the questionnaire will be used for statistical tabulations only.

Identifying information for the responding clinician is requested for the purpose of possible later contact for a follow-up questionnaire.

Clinician's Name: ______________________

Address: ______________________
(Street)

____
(City) (State) (Zip)

Telephone: ______________________
(Area code) (Number)

Professional Degree: ________ Specialty Training: ______________

----[001-009]------- ---------[011-016]---------

Serial Number: [ ][ ][ ][ ][81333] Date Questionnaire Filled Out: [ ][ ] [ ][ ] 19[ ][ ]

[017-019] ----------[020-025]--------

Patient's Initials: [ ][ ][ ] Patient's Birth Date: [ ][ ] [ ][ ] 19[ ][ ]
(Month) (Day) (year)

INSTRUCTIONS

Please fill out the questionnaire according to the instructions given with each question or group of questions. Your answers should be limited to data on a single patient whom you know well. The questionnaire is designed to be computer-coded; however, there is room for limited comments on some questions. The last page is reserved for any comments, observations or thoughts that you wish to share on any aspect of Multiple Personality Disorder.

Send to: Frank Putnam, M.D.
Bldg. 10, Rm. 3 S 239
National Institute of Mental Health
9000 Rockville Pike
Bethesda, MD 20205

ADM 582
2-82

Thank you.

Figure 1.1 Title and instructions page of the 100 Cases Clinician's Questionnaire.

Source: Author.

Researching Multiple Personality Disorder

Skepticism of MPD dates back well over two centuries to the beginnings of modern psychiatry at the Salpêtrière Hospital in Paris. Under Philippe Pinel (a zoologist by training), the Salpêtrière led the movement to treat mental illness humanely, including freeing patients from their shackles.

By the late nineteenth century, under the leadership of Jean-Martin Charcot, psychiatrists, psychologists, and neurologists at the Salpêtrière were intensively investigating a mental condition known as "hysteria" – a common neuropsychiatric diagnosis of the time. Today, most of these cases are diagnosed as dissociative disorders.

Widely considered the father of modern neurology, Charcot conducted dramatic weekly demonstrations of hysterical symptoms for audiences of hundreds of tourists and curious Parisians. Following his death in 1893, former disciples rejected Charcot's neurological theories of hysteria, attributing hysterical and dissociative symptoms to increased psychological suggestibility or even deliberate deceptions by patients "to please" their doctors. These two critiques – that hysteria and the dissociative disorders reflect either increased suggestibility, wittingly or unwittingly shaped by overly fascinated psychotherapists, or alternatively the deliberate deception of credulous doctors by manipulative patients – remain core criticisms of MPD/DID (dissociative identity disorder) to this day.

The NIMH research group I joined specialized in rapid cycling bipolar disorder. At any given time, there were between 12 and 20 bipolar patients, mostly women, on our research ward. They repeatedly switched between mood states of profound depression and raging mania over intervals of days to weeks. Some spent years on the 3 West research ward, during which time we investigated the biological changes across scores of their switches. We tried to disrupt these mood swings with experimental medications or physiological interventions such as sleep deprivation or continuous physical activity. From these studies, a number of medications, collectively known as "mood stabilizers," were identified.[9]

Borrowing this approach, I began looking for psychophysiological differences among the identity states of MPD patients as if they were akin to the radically different mood states of bipolar patients. I was looking for repeatable behavioral and biological markers that could reliably differentiate the MPD dissociative identity states from each other as well as distinguish MPD cases from normal individuals attempting to simulate the disorder.

If I found that the MPD identity states had distinct biological signatures that could not be faked by simulating subjects, I could disprove the core criticisms made by skeptics.

While not the first to attempt this approach, the technology and resources available to me at the NIMH were superior to earlier efforts. Tapping into the loose network of MPD clinicians, I recruited therapists to bring their patients to the NIMH to participate in a battery of research tests.

To take maximum advantage of my limited access to any given NIH laboratory's technology or expertise, I scheduled two to four MPD subjects and their therapists for a week or more at a time. Many of the multiples were thrilled to meet other people like them. Complementary identity states (often the child alters) would hang out together while waiting to participate in an experimental session. There were inevitable frictions between a few others, but for the most part it was manageable chaos. The real problems occurred with their therapists, who could become competitive about who knew more about MPD or had a patient with the greatest number or the most unique identity states.

This one-upmanship was my first insight into the competitive dynamics around "special" patients that infused the MPD therapist community.

The battery of tests included cognitive measures, especially memory tests probing the amnesias that MPD subjects reported for the activities of some identity states. There were psychophysiological tests such as electrodermal and cardiac responses to various stimuli, as well as a variety of brain imaging technologies including EEG, MEG (magnetoencephalography), auditory and visual evoked potentials, regional cerebral blood flow, and spectrum analyses of the voices of different identity states.

With their therapists' help, we selected three to five dissociative identity states that were identifiable by distinctive mannerisms and speech, able to maintain "control" of the body through an experiment, and comfortable with the laboratory setting.

Simulating normal control subjects (including some semiprofessional actors) were asked to create and name three to five "imaginary identity states" with distinctive attributes, such as age and gender, as well as physical differences, such as height, weight, eye/hair color, handedness, and personal differences (such as favorite hobbies, colors, music, and foods) (Putnam, 1986). They were encouraged to practice and refine these "imaginary identity states" outside of the laboratory whenever possible.

Typically, each MPD identity and simulating control imaginary state was tested in a randomized order on four or more occasions spaced at least a day apart. Research assistants, working blind to whether a subject was a multiple or simulating control, administered the tests treating every named identity state (MPD or imaginary) equally. However, with a little experience most research assistants could tell the real MPD cases from simulating subjects.

Statistically we computed measures of the similarity or dissimilarity among a subject's identity states and also compared overall performance between the two groups. In certain experiments, such as the ability to keep highly similar lists of words separate, the MPD identity states outperformed the imaginary identity states of the simulating controls. On other measures, the controls outperformed the MPD subjects. In some experiments – for example, the progressive habituation of startle responses across identity states to repeated blasts of a noxious noise – both groups performed equally.

It was clear that, on some tests, individuals psychologically organized as MPD identity states performed significantly differently from simulating control subjects. The MPD identity states differed from each other in ways that the imaginary identity states of the simulating control subjects could not duplicate. However, deep down (at the autonomic nervous system level) there are psychological and biological continuities that span their amnestic boundaries. Despite what they may say or feel, the dissociative identity states of an individual with MPD/DID are not as separate and unique as different people.

Individual MPD identity states showed remarkable consistencies across multiple spaced trials. The controls' imaginary identity states on the other hand, with one notable exception, did not show distinct differences from each other that were consistent over repeated trials. The one exception was during hypnosis (Putnam et al., 1990). As my studies progressed, I offered simulating control subjects an option of choosing either one of two traditional altered states of consciousness, hypnosis or deep relaxation, to add to their repertoire of imaginary identity states.

Control subjects choosing hypnosis (and scoring well on standard hypnosis measures) were able to create and sustain a discrete state of consciousness that was significantly different from their "normal" state and their imaginary identity states. These hypnotic states were, however, psychophysiologically distinct from the MPD identity states. If nothing else, my research convinced me that individuals psychologically organized as an "us" were fundamentally different from simulating controls.

Indeed, MPD/DID is another form of the human condition.[10] It becomes "pathological" when it seriously interferes with a person's welfare and functioning.

There was not, however, a single unique psychophysiological or brain activity signature that reliably diagnosed an individual as having MPD. The lack of definitive diagnostic tests is true for the vast majority of psychiatric disorders.

The MPD research subjects, all patients of other therapists, were initially accompanied by their therapists to NIMH for testing. Later, after I got to know some research subjects better, they returned alone. I spent down time between experiments with them individually and in groups, learning about their lives – from their childhoods to the present.

They all reported being multiple for as long as they could remember. It was only late in childhood or early adolescence that they understood other people were not like them. As they became aware of their differences from other people, especially the amnesias and disremembered behavior, they developed strategies to disguise and compensate for their dissociative experiences and blend in as best they could.

In the spring of 1982, as my research fellowship drew to a close, I took a hard look at what I had learned from two-and-a-half years studying this unusual human condition. I wanted to pursue several phenomena further. But first I was going to have to take a real job, one that would allow me as much access as possible to the wealth of technology and expertise available at the NIH.

Dr. Richard (Dick) Wyatt, MD, chief of the NIMH Adult Schizophrenia Research Branch, located on the grounds of St. Elizabeths Hospital in Anacostia, MD, had apparently been keeping his eye on me. He offered me a staff position recruiting subjects for his research studies. As long as Dick's research beds were full, I could pursue my own scientific research program on whatever I liked.

The Dissociative Experiences Scale (DES)

In the 1980s, as far as biological psychiatry and behavioral psychology were concerned, the unconscious mind did not exist. The basic argument went: *If you cannot measure it, then you cannot talk scientifically about it. And if you cannot talk scientifically about it, then the unconscious mind does not exist.* Old school psychoanalysts, nonetheless, continued to encounter the unconscious mind daily in the form of dreams and Freudian slips of the tongue. But in the highest psychiatry and psychology scientific circles, mention of the unconscious mind was *verboten.*

One day, Dr. Dianne Chambless, PhD, of American University, Washington, DC, invited me to present a psychology colloquium on dissociative disorders for students. (I had participated in a PBS (Public Broadcasting Service) series on abnormal psychology for college students and that exposure led to invitations to present to college and graduate students at local universities.) I loved talking with psychology students before they were too warped by Skinnerian doctrine to see the mysteries of our unconscious mind. It felt delightfully subversive, for me, a scientist at the National Institute of Mental Health, to show up with my colored pictures of brain activity patterns of the different identity states and talk about the "mind" – unconscious and all.

This was at a time when multicolored brain scans were especially novel. And, although we didn't – and still don't – understand a lot about what these colorful brain images represent, the visual differences are nonetheless seen as convincing. Perhaps more so than they deserve.

I have little recollection of what I said except that at the end of the presentation the students' questions centered around the implications of an unconscious mind. Feeling pleased by my swipe at conventional wisdom, I was surprised when a young lady stopped me on my way out.

"Your real problem," she said, "is that you need a scale to measure dissociation."

She was right. I had been thinking about developing a measure to quantify dissociation. It was needed to jump-start the scientific investigation of dissociation, the pathological process underlying MPD. Once we could reliably and validly measure dissociation, we could begin to correlate it with measures of behaviors and biology. Then we could start to make real progress toward understanding how to diagnose and treat pathological forms of dissociation, such as MPD/DID.

But dissociation was not an easy process to define, much less measure. As a scientific subject, dissociation was stuck in the "great man" stage of scientific development. There were venerated authorities – both historic and contemporary – who promoted a range of definitions and theories. But their knowledge was derived from the individual patients they treated. Their definitions and treatment principles were subjective interpretations of clinical experiences – oftentimes based on a single case.

How could the rest of us decipher what was broadly true and what was unique either to them or their patient(s)?

The field of dissociation needed to move beyond the great man's opinion stage to the *terra firma* of scientific foundation. As a first step, we needed to be able to measure validly dissociation in people in general, not just psychiatric patients, to understand more about its nature – and to determine when it was pathological and when it was normal.

Although I had ideas about how to measure dissociation, it remained a challenging undertaking. During my NIMH research fellowship on the bipolar unit, I had attempted to develop an anger and irritability scale to augment the depression and mania measure collected by the nursing staff. My anger scale didn't get very far, but that nascent effort acquainted me with the formidable problems of proving that a psychological scale actually measures what it claims to measure.

In short, psychological scales need to be both reliable and valid. The essence of reliability is that the scale always gives the same score whenever it measures the same thing. It is a ruler made of steel, not rubber. It doesn't stretch or shrink from measurement to measurement.

Sticking with the analogy, validity is when that steel ruler measures a "foot" and the length of that "foot" equals the gold standard ruler that defines a "foot." In measurement science, there are empirical metrics that quantify the reliability and validity of psychological scales, which are referred to as the scale's psychometric properties.

Based on conversations with MPD research subjects and patients, I concluded that the best way to quantify dissociation was to ask people to rate how frequently certain unusual experiences, generally considered dissociative, occurred in their daily lives. These included episodes of amnesia for complex behavior, fragmentation or profound alterations in their identity or sense of self, experiences of depersonalization and derealization, and periods of intense absorption. Scores above an empirically determined threshold would be indicative of pathological dissociation.

The young woman who made this prescient observation was Eve Bernstein (now Eve B. Carlson, PhD), at that time a first-year graduate student in psychology at American University. Just starting her master's degree research, Eve was already looking for a topic for her doctoral dissertation. After a couple of additional conversations, the development of a reliable and valid self-administered measure of dissociation became Eve's PhD dissertation project, although she had to finish her master's thesis first.

The Dissociative Experiences Scale (DES) is the product of our collaboration (Bernstein & Putnam, 1986; Carlson & Putnam, 1993). It has proven to be both reliable and valid and is used in literally thousands of peer-reviewed scientific publications. Now there are a half-dozen validated dissociation measures available, which generally correlate highly with the DES. In aggregate, these measures have taught us a great deal about the psychology and neurobiology of dissociation.

In particular, they have firmly established the causal linkage between traumatic experiences and increased levels of dissociation – primarily amnesias, identity fragmentation, depersonalization, and derealization.

Consequentially, in many studies, subjects are divided into high and low dissociators based on their DES or other dissociation scale scores. High scorers, i.e., highly dissociative individuals, differ from low scorers with the same diagnoses in both biological and psychological responses to laboratory experiments as well as effectiveness of current treatments for dissociative disorders and PTSD (Brand et al., 2019). In recognition of the accumulating evidence that traumatized people with high levels of dissociation are fundamentally different from those with low levels, the latest version of the *Diagnostic and Statistical Manual of Mental Disorders* (*DSM-5*) (American Psychiatric Association, 2022) includes the clinically important distinction: "*PTSD – with dissociation.*"

I learned a lot from the DES – not only about dissociation, but also about the nature of psychological measurement and how a psychological measure is used, misused, and abused in the real world. Later we created a dissociation scale for children aged 5–12 years (the Child Dissociative Checklist, CDC) and one for adolescents aged 12–18 years (the Adolescent Dissociative Experiences Scale, A-DES) to capture the full range of developmental differences (Putnam et al., 1993; Armstrong et al., 1997). The CDC and A-DES are derived, in part, from the behavioral checklists I originally circulated to identify possible dissociative children and adolescents.

Beyond what these measures taught us about dissociation as a psychobiological process and a psychiatric disorder, they provided a larger lesson about how to influence a scientific field. Simply put, one of the most powerful things one can do is to provide scientists with good tools.

From the first, I gave the DES away to everyone who wanted it. Initially, I copied, assembled, and mailed packets (fortunately I worked at NIMH and postage was free) with the scale and relevant articles, all over the world. Later, Lisa Connelly created a CD containing the dissociation scales, scoring instructions, age norms, an extensive bibliography, and selected research papers, which was mailed upon request. Lisa had a world map on her office wall with pins marking the exotic places where copies of our dissociation scales were sent.

The DES is free and in the public domain – as are all my measures. Unfortunately, today I see many investigators or their university's intellectual property lawyers copyrighting scales and measures that they have created – often with federal funds, which should make them public domain. Maybe there are a few bucks to be made, but most of these copyrighted scales and measures will never be used routinely, because they cost too much. The larger takeaway is that if you want to influence a clinical or scientific field – create good tools and make them as widely and inexpensively available as possible.

Male Multiples

"I've got this great idea," the caller said. Founder and editor-in-chief of numerous journals on child maltreatment, family violence, and related topics, the caller frequently had "great ideas" about what I should be working on for him. I made that mistake only once.

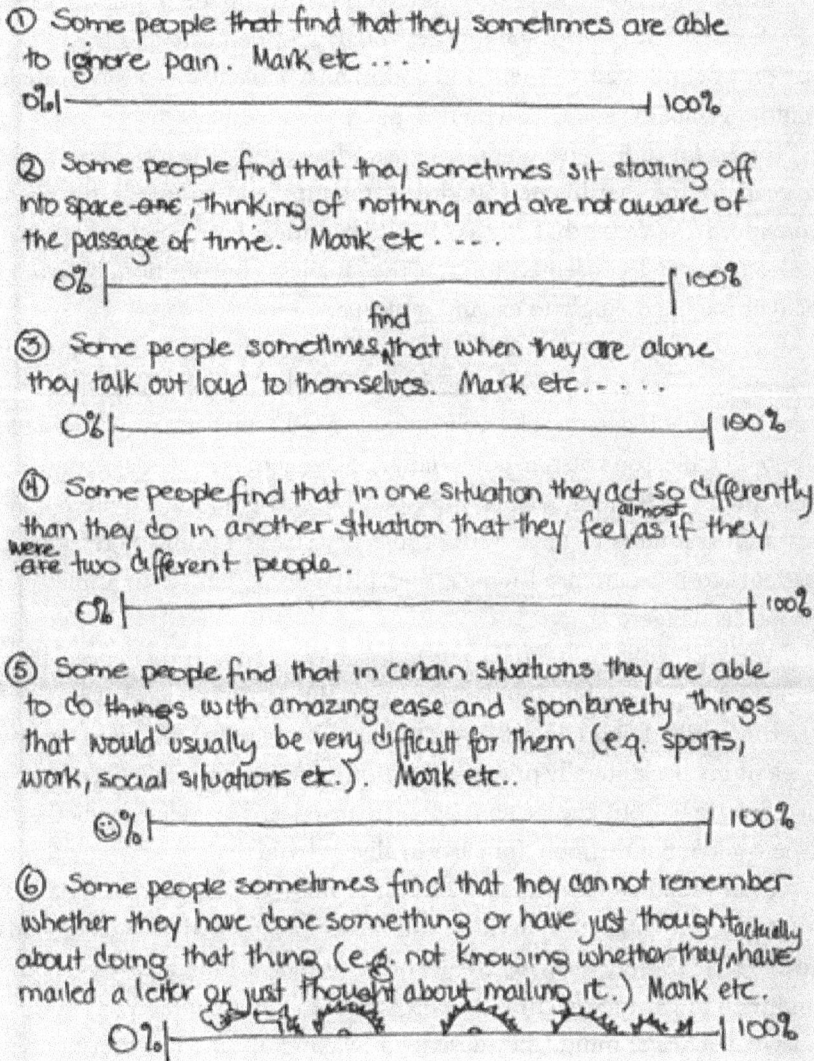

Figure 1.2 An early draft of the DES in my handwriting.

Source: Author.

"We should do a study of male multiple personality disorder patients. Nobody has done that. You find them. I have a new graduate student who can test them," he enthused. "She can …."

At the pronoun "she," I balked. There was absolutely no way that I was going to refer adult male MPD cases to a female graduate student.

Although I have had positive interactions with male multiples, some of whom were accomplished professionals and dedicated to the elimination of child maltreatment and community violence, as a group, male multiples include some extremely dangerous individuals.[11]

The editor didn't give up on his great ideas easily. The more he sought to reassure me that his new graduate student could handle it, the more convinced I became that it was a really bad idea. From past experience, I also knew if I consented to even the smallest contribution, he would badger me unceasingly to expand its scope.

Richard Loewenstein and I were working on a paper combining our male MPD cases. I had already decided that I was not going to do another study focused exclusively on male MPD subjects. Some were too unpredictable, too volatile, potentially too dangerous to work with. After a couple of stalking incidents, I decided I wasn't going to expose female research assistants to male MPD subjects nor was I going to refer male patients to inexperienced female therapists. Some female multiples can be just as dangerous.

Working with male MPD research subjects, I had experienced their explosive unpredictability in the laboratory. But more frequently I encountered it while doing clinical consultations. On occasion, the hairs on the back of my neck literally prickled in a visceral response to an aura of menace radiating from the person. More than once, I wondered whether I would get out of the room (or jail cell) alive if I said or did the wrong thing.

Briefly, I interacted with an FBI unit profiling serial killers and rapists. Watching videotaped interviews and reading transcripts, it was obvious to me that several were highly dissociative men who sexually assaulted and then killed their victims, usually women, in depersonalized and dissociated states of mind. They described "waking up" and discovering they had killed someone or that someone they were involved with was dead. And they might have only dream-like memories of the events.

When I drew the FBI unit director's attention to evidence of pathological dissociation in some of the interviews, he said he didn't believe in "psychology" and dropped me from the cases. I was okay with it, because I was starting to have nightmares about the things I heard.[12]

Indeed, those who investigate horrendous, unsolved serial crime cases would benefit by considering the possibility that the perpetrators suffer from a dissociative disorder. Unfortunately, some therapists, entranced with this exotic disorder, blame heinous actions by MPD/DID patients on a "bad" identity state, excusing the person as a whole from responsibility for their criminal behavior.

In the long run, this doesn't work out well.

Making Enemies

In my efforts to disseminate a more accurate clinical profile of MPD and validate a free tool (DES) to screen for pathological dissociation, I didn't realize I was making enemies. Powerful enemies. Enemies who began to systematically attempt to discredit me and my work.

It was not a strictly personal vendetta, as these MPD deniers attacked anyone and everyone whom they viewed as a threat to their control over public perception of the reality and nature of child sexual abuse (which is the primary cause of MPD/DID). The devastating effects of their behind-the-scenes campaign against me would culminate years later.

In the beginning, when I responded to attacks on the credibility of dissociation as a psychological process and MPD as a psychiatric disorder, I naively thought I was engaging in traditional academic debate.

Paul McHugh, MD, then chairperson of the Johns Hopkins department of psychiatry, was a major opponent of the diagnosis of MPD. An influential figure in the psychiatric world at that time, McHugh spent much of his career attacking psychiatry in general and psychoanalysis in particular. He also advised and represented the Catholic Church in its public relations and legal responses to the priest child sexual abuse scandals (Heaney, 2021).

As a leading skeptic of child sexual abuse, McHugh created venues in which to publicly attack MPD. As one of the few researchers producing scientific data about MPD and child abuse, I had a large bullseye on my back. Using his connections, McHugh engineered debates between us (and others), both in person and in print. I responded to the nominally neutral invitations to debate with him in service to the field. When I showed up, I found that the format had been structured to my disadvantage – e.g., even though I am an equal co-author on this publication, somehow the journal left my name off this citation (McHugh, 1995).

Although many personal anecdotes about this well-organized professional denial of child maltreatment come to mind, they are difficult to substantiate and fail to convey the much larger picture of an ongoing war against publicly acknowledging that terrible things are being done to children.

When I was professor of pediatrics and director of a child abuse forensic evaluation center at a major children's hospital, I got another look at this nefarious pushback through the eyes of pediatricians who were viciously attacked in court, slandered in the media, and even physically threatened for testifying about the maltreatment of children. Although the specifics were different between the attacks on psychiatry and pediatrics, the basic legal arguments are essentially the same.

In the instance of psychiatry, the lawyers and their hired-gun "expert witnesses" attacked the legitimacy of trauma-related diagnoses such as dissociative disorders or complex PTSD. In the case of the pediatricians, the lawyers and experts attacked diagnoses such as battered child syndrome and shaken baby syndrome (abusive head injury). In all instances, testifying doctors were attacked professionally and an attempt was made to make them look incompetent and anti-parent. In place of the doctors' diagnoses, the expert witness teams for the defense would attempt to substitute their own "diagnoses," such as "temporary brittle bone disease" (which has no scientific foundation) for battered child syndrome and "false memory syndrome" to explain the delayed recall of traumatic memories.

For both psychiatry and pediatrics, these expert witness teams are part of a larger network of child abuse deniers. From discussions with foreign colleagues, it is apparent that similar organized pushback occurs in many countries. In some countries, the judicial system is clearly on the side of the deniers. Clinicians reporting child abuse risk loss of their livelihood and even time in jail.

One can speculate on the motives behind this aggressive denial of child maltreatment – especially sexual abuse.

Once, at an in-person debate in Chattanooga, TN, I asked McHugh why he didn't believe the allegations of child sexual abuse by priests, given the then tens (now hundreds) of thousands of priest sexual abuse victims identified worldwide.

McHugh replied to the effect that it was "inconceivable" that a priest would do something like that to a child. Adding, that if a priest did in fact do that, the congregation would run him out of town[13].

If only it worked that way!

Transitioning to Children

Taking my adult MPD research subjects and patients at their word that they had always been an "us," I reasoned that I should be able to find children with multiple personality disorder.

Starting in about 1983 and lasting well into the 1990s, I circulated a series of checklists among DC- and Baltimore-area family welfare agencies, child protective services, foster parent organizations, and child therapists. This series of checklists (periodically revised) covered unusual, problematic, and possible child and adolescent dissociative behaviors. I asked to be referred children (accompanied by a legal guardian) who showed some or many of the checklist behaviors. As I began to see an increasing stream of children, I arranged for many to receive psychological testing.

Predictably, most of the children had serious behavioral problems. Jodie was typical of many, but by no means all, of the disturbed children who I saw.

At the other end of the behavioral spectrum was a smaller group, mostly young teenage girls, who seemed spacey or tranced out most of the time. Caretakers described them as quietly retreating into fantasy realms at the slightest stress or social demand. They were detached, depersonalized, emotionally shut down, and living in worlds of their own creation.

If one could get them to talk about their imaginary worlds, which was rare, they described bejeweled palaces with rainbow-flowered gardens in magical kingdoms inhabited by mythical beings such as unicorns and fairies.[14]

But there was a dark side to these imaginary worlds—the teenagers inflicted punishments on themselves. Frequently they performed self-mutilation, almost ritualistically, to atone for some real or imagined transgression, or to "punish" a therapist or caretaker, or just to "feel real." Often, a foster parent or hospital staff would discover a hidden, carefully curated, self-mutilation kit containing razor blades, broken glass, needles, BIC lighters, and other implements of self-torture. In the hospital, they broke CDs or glassware to replace sharp objects confiscated by staff. Their bouts of self-mutilation often occurred in the evening or at night.

Their suicide threats, gestures, and attempts led to repeated psychiatric hospitalizations. As inpatients, they waged relentless passive aggressive struggles with ward staff over minor infractions of rules and privileges. Academically they were erratic, performing well on occasion, while drawing a blank at other times. Their clinical course was characterized by a sawtooth pattern. Promising improvement would suddenly catastrophically crash. Later we would come to understand the impact of family stress and revictimization on their fluctuating clinical course (Myrick et al., 2013).

All the disturbed children had sleep problems galore. They were up at night doing strange things that frightened their caretakers, who locked their own bedroom doors. They had perplexing memory problems, often vehemently denying doing things that they had just been observed doing. They might suddenly become physically disabled with puzzling somatic complaints that didn't fit known conditions.

Socially these children were disasters. Other children intuitively recognized their weirdness and shunned them. A substantial portion were hypersexual, appearing older and more physically and behaviorally advanced than their peers. Seemingly oblivious to the shocking impropriety of their actions, they impulsively groped other children and, frequently, adults.

In addition to being exquisitely emotionally labile, caretakers described examples of "mixed" emotions and self-sabotaging behavior whereby the child appeared to be trying to be good, yet couldn't help but do the "wrong" thing. Other times they exhibited competing emotional states – rapidly alternating between happy and sad, angry and frightened, silly and serious.

Some foster parents said that the child's emotional states waxed and waned so dramatically ("I never know where he's at") that it was impossible to predict how they would react to even minor stress. Others reported being able to predict the child's behavior from a distance by observing their body language. Jodie's foster mother said, for example, that she could tell how Jodie would react to something by the way she walked and the pitch and speed of her speech.

After scores of evaluations and consultations for child and adolescent behavior problems, I found myself struggling with some important, but vaguely defined questions about what was happening to these children. My questions comprised two broad categories – the nature of their behavior problems and the mechanisms of their apparent biological dysregulation.

The overriding question was: What accounted for the enormous variability in symptoms and behaviors I was seeing? There was not a simple, single, straightforward child abuse syndrome. Rather, things seemed terribly wrong in many ways across many domains. It was also becoming clear to me that there was very little we, as healing professionals, could do to help. In fact, we couldn't even agree on what to call these disturbed kids.

Impelled by my epiphany, I would spend my career seeking to make sense of what I saw – and trying to do something about it.

During the mid-1980s, knowledge about child maltreatment was highly siloed. In total, there were approximately a thousand research and clinical articles in English, widely scattered among an array of professional journals. Data on incidence and prevalence of child maltreatment were just starting to accrue. Noting that 90 percent of juvenile delinquents had child abuse histories, President Reagan's Health and Human Services secretary, Margaret M. Heckler, expressed alarm at an annual 10 percent increase in reported maltreatment cases, then totaling an estimated 1.5 million children. She also pointed to early evidence of an intergenerational cycle of family abuse and violence which she described as a "Like father like son – like mother like daughter" syndrome.

One question that was repeatedly raised by my peers when I presented research on the connection between child maltreatment to later mental health problems was: "How do we know children with MPD and other psychiatric diagnoses didn't cause their maltreatment?"

In other words, perhaps their mental disorders came first, provoking maltreatment by overwhelmed parents (I found this version of the old "blame the victim" argument especially enraging).

Other scientists naively urged me to conduct studies of maltreated children using their "non-abused" siblings as normal control subjects.

This "littermate control" strategy may be useful for rat research, but it fails grievously with children. Growing up in a home with child maltreatment or domestic violence profoundly affects every family member, whether a direct victim or not.

In a telling exchange at one professional meeting, Harvard psychiatrist Joe Biederman summed up academic child psychiatry's position. Claiming to have isolated a gene that accounted for attention deficit hyperactivity disorder (ADHD), he contemptuously dismissed my question about whether he had controlled for child abuse saying, "No! And I don't control for flat feet either."

There was another highly emotional controversy that profoundly affected the credibility of child abuse research. Could children be believed? Indeed, could you even believe adults? After all, Freud had claimed that fantasies of sex with one's parents was a "normal" developmental process.[15]

A number of sensationalized preschool and daycare alleged sexual abuse cases – most notably the McMartin preschool case – were recurring headline news. Some of the allegations of the children, for example that witches were flying through the air, or there were tunnels and dungeons under the schools, were either incredible or easily disproven. Nonetheless, passionate "believe the children" advocates righteously attacked anyone who questioned the credibility of children.

Closely tied in the public mind to these preschool cases, were claims made by a relatively small group of adult MPD and sexual abuse patients who said that they were raised in blood-drinking, baby-eating, human-sacrificing, satanic cults. These horrific tales, told by a relatively few patients, but vigorously vouched for by their therapists, were dividing the child abuse treatment community as well as estranging mental health from law enforcement, which did not find physical evidence of such satanic abominations. (Of course, in the eyes of true believers, the failure of police to find tangible evidence of satanic ritual abuse, SRA, only meant that they were part of the conspiracy.)

Within the trauma therapy world "SRA survivors" increasingly appeared as presenters in the continuing education programs sponsored by local and regional hospitals that were popular in that era.

"SRA survivors" told graphic tales of horrendous physical and sexual abuse. Being impregnated by satanic worshipers during unholy rituals and later forced to eat their newborn babies alive was a common theme. Vast numbers of babies and virgins were allegedly brutally sexually violated, tortured, and then slaughtered – their remains creatively disposed of by traveling crematoriums disguised as conventional 18-wheel trucks or in vast pig farms that recycled SRA victims into hot dogs. Satanic worshipers posed as upstanding citizens by day, but were somehow (especially unlikely before the internet was widely available) linked in a huge, ultra-secret, international conspiracy by night.

Where were the bodies? Human remains are difficult to dispose of without a trace – especially on the scale that this was alleged to be happening. The high temperatures required for complete cremation would warp a truck frame and explode the tires. Fleets of refrigerator trucks would be needed to transport the numerous bodies to the pig farms.

One of the principal arguments made in support of the veracity of SRA accounts was that different patients were all telling similar stories. So, there must be truth to them – right?

Interested in the sudden increase in MPD cases being diagnosed in the US,[16] Professor Sherrill Mulhern, an anthropologist from the Sorbonne who studied cultural expressions of dissociation, tracked the most prolific SRA presenters from conference to conference, recording their presentations. At one conference a given presenter would represent herself as a therapist telling her patient's story. But at the next conference, the therapist would tell the same story as her own personal experience as an "SRA survivor." Some conference presentations involved panels of "SRA survivors" taking turns telling their horrific stories.

Over time, Professor Mulhern documented that SRA conference presenters frequently borrowed juicy details from each other, incorporating them into their own story in subsequent presentations. So, not surprisingly, "SRA survivors" were telling similar stories.

Although I had public arguments with "SRA survivors" and their therapists at conferences, there seemed little that could be done to thwart what appeared to be a growing satanic panic. And it was becoming part of the fair and balanced charade to include me as the lone skeptic on a panel – or if I was not present, some (usually grossly distorted) version of my position as a token rebuttal to the SRA presentations.

When Dr. Richard Krugman, MD, editor of *Child Abuse & Neglect*, offered me an opportunity to write a commentary on two papers he was publishing claiming to document satanic ritual abuse, I jumped at the opportunity to go on the record in a major journal. My commentary, "The Satanic Ritual Abuse Controversy," published in 1991, capped years of public and professional opposition to SRA allegations.

Savaging the two papers on the quality of their data and analyses, I also noted that they defy belief based on larger principles of human nature. To quote myself (Putnam, 1991)

> The picture of the alleged satanic cults that emerges from the two papers is not readily believable. On the one hand, they are said to be highly organized, multigenerational, international groups with membership turnover (e.g., the Young et al. subject whose family left the cult when she turned 11 (p. 186)) that practice highly codified religious rituals. On the other hand they are depicted as evil incarnate participating in violent cannibal rape orgies, which incredibly leave absolutely no trace of the blood and gore spilled. Equally incredibly, in the case of the Jonker and Jonker-Bakker paper, they were able to repeatedly lure large numbers of children away from their normal play or school activities, drug them and force them to participate in painful and disgusting rituals without anyone ever noticing that the children were missing or without the children protesting to their parents or teachers. Such total child crowd control is incomprehensible to anyone who has ever tried to herd a group of children through a museum or zoo.
>
> One must ask how can such large scale, violent, and bloody activities escape detection in every single instance where they have been alleged to have occurred? Authorities on criminal conspiracies note that the larger the conspiracy is and the longer that it is in operation, the more difficult it is to keep it a secret, particularly if members can leave the organization. Studies of real cults, e.g., Hare Krishna, Children of God, People's Temple, have shown that when such groups engage in violent or criminal

behavior they often implode and disintegrate in rapid order. How do the Satanists avoid this fate?

At about the same time, I organized a plenary panel to counter the increasingly numerous presentations on satanic ritual abuse that were occurring in the professional dissociative disorder scientific society, of which I was a co-founder. To quote, Richard Noll, PhD, one of the presenters:[17]

> At the invitation of psychiatrist and researcher Frank Putnam, then the Chief of the Dissociative Disorders Unit at the National Institutes of Mental Health, Noll was one of four members [Richard Noll, Sherrill Mulhern, George Ganaway, and Frank Putnam] on a plenary panel opening the 7th International Conference on Multiple Personality/Dissociative States in Chicago on 9 November 1990. In a ballroom filled with television cameras and more than 700 conference participants (including feminist intellectual Gloria Steinem, who was a firm believer in the veracity of "recovered memories" of satanic ritual abuse) the members of the panel presented, for the first time in a public professional forum, a skeptical viewpoint concerning SRA reports.

My memories of the panel are primarily of the uncomfortable moments at the end when, as moderator, I took hostile questions from an emotional audience. There were loud, angry conversations going on. People were standing up and shouting insults at us. I was accused of being a tool (at best) of the satanists. It was clear that many in the room concluded that I was a satanist (after all, I worked for the government, and the government was known to be part of the satanic conspiracy, because the CIA needed brainwashed SRA victims to carry out its nefarious activities). Richard Noll comments on the aftermath.

> Noll's participation on the panel was viewed by SRA believers as part of a deliberate disinformation campaign by Frank Putnam, who was skeptical of the reality of satanic cults. This set Putnam

apart from other prominent American psychiatrists who were
true believers ... According to an account based on interviews,
"conference attendees characterized [Noll] as a professional
expendable who had no idea he was being used. Through him,
they contended, Putnam could cast doubt on the contentious
issue of linking MPD to ritual abuse"[18]

As the conference continued over the next few days, I was repeatedly harassed. A few men "accidently" bumped into me and some women
pointedly left a room when I entered. I had threatening notes slipped
under my hotel room door and, one time, into my brief case during a
moment's inattention. Two men took turns menacingly following me
around – even out to dinner – deliberately letting me see that I was being
stalked.

But the longer-term outcome was that I essentially left the professional society I had co-founded. I returned to meetings only a few times
over the next decades, for presentations on research projects I played
a role in, such as Dr. Bethany Brand's PhD, TOP DD (treatment of
patients with dissociative disorders) study.

Our symposium and my commentary in *Child Abuse & Neglect* certainly did not end the SRA panic. Rather, hefty lawsuit settlements
dampened the true believers' public enthusiasm. Allegations of SRA still
occur, but of the well over 12,000 children evaluated by our child advocacy center (from 2000 to 2011) we never found a credible case. We
did, however, see children abused in the context of religiously sanctioned
punishment (for example, severely beaten with a rod – lest one spoil the
child – or sexually abused by a religious leader who assured them he was
fulfilling "God's will").[19]

Notes

1. *Paths*, which traces the recovery of a Vietnam war veteran, was written before the
   diagnosis of post-traumatic stress disorder (PTSD) became official in the *Diagnostic
   and Statistical Manual of Mental Disorders III* (*DSM-III*) (American Psychiatric
   Association, 1980). In addition to helping me deal with the disturbing stories I heard
   in therapy with combat veterans, writing *Paths* clarified for me a clinical picture of
   PTSD that would later help me to recognize the trauma underlying the symptoms
   and behaviors of sexually abused patients.
2. Didn't happen. *Paths* was overtaken by life events.

3. "Grand rounds" is a traditional medical meeting usually hosted by each and every department in a medical school and open to the public as well as all faculty. They are often held monthly.

4. Sybil refers to a famous US case of MPD that was popularized by a bestseller by Flora Schreiber and later a movie starring Joanne Woodard as Dr. Wilbur (Woodward also starred as an MPD patient "Eve" in an earlier movie.)

5. I contacted Dr. Wilbur, who interviewed Joan and helped us formulate a new treatment plan. In her consultation, Dr. Wilbur made a strong case that the "cause" of MPD was child abuse, often bizarre abuses. Although not the first clinician to draw this conclusion (some nineteenth-century case reports mention incest and physical abuse – although often cloaked in Latin to protect the less worldly), Dr. Wilbur was instrumental in identifying child maltreatment as a common factor across cases. Joan reported years of incest by her father. On long-term follow-up, Joan did well (see Putnam, 2016, p. 104).

6. About a decade later I proposed another questionnaire study, this time it was a no-go with the OMB. They were now comfortable controlling what government scientists could or could not ask US citizens.

7. I was fortunate to have an account at the National Library of Medicine which hunted down old MPD articles in defunct journals – and once even a hand cranked, silent film – for me to tabulate. This exercise ultimately informed the 100 Cases study questionnaire.

8. Submitting the 100 cases paper, I got my first hint of the editorial and reviewer pushback I would encounter the remainder of my career. Although, the journal's editor-in-chief, Daniel X. Freedman, accepted a previous paper immediately on submission with the stipulation that I was not to change a "single word," the rejection that I got back on the 100 cases paper consisted of a half-dozen sentences all questioning my sanity and morality. There was no critique of methods or results. Only a vicious *ad hominem* attack on my credulity. Fortunately, the same draft was reviewed appropriately and featured on the cover of another journal.

9. Although biological psychiatry has been criticized of late as producing little of lasting value, the mood stabilizers, some of which are anticonvulsants originally used to treat epilepsy, help many people with bipolar disorders smooth out their worst mood swings.

10. An analysis of a large, representative sample finds that about 4 percent of the US population suffer from pathological dissociation, the psychobiological process underlying dissociative disorders such as DID/MPD (Simeon & Putnam, 2022).

11. For example, Ted Bundy, the Hillside Strangler (Kenneth Bianchi), and the Ohio State rapist and murderer (Billy Milligan) – all of whom were diagnosed with MPD by psychiatrists familiar with the disorder who spent time with them after legal proceedings were concluded.

12. Most clinical research with MPD/DID describe samples of 8–9:1 female to male cases. A truism among dissociative disorder therapists is that the females are in the mental health system and males are in the criminal justice system. But definitive research supporting this belief remains lacking.

13. In multiple interviews, McHugh expressed his belief that Catholic priests were either morally incapable of abusing children or would be severely disciplined by the congregation including in an August 5, 2002 interview with New York Times journalist, Erica Goode. "No one thought the priests walked on water," he [McHugh] said, "and if any of them had laid a hand on us, our brothers and fathers would have turned up at the rectory and taken them out." https://www.nytimes.com/2002/08/05/us/psychiatrist-says-he-was-surprised-by-furor-over-his-role-on-abuse-panel.html

14. Listening to descriptions of their imagined worlds, I was reminded of the auto-biographical novel by Hannah Green (pseudonym for Joanne Greenberg), *I Never Promised You a Rose Garden* (Greenberg, 2022 (1964)) about her therapy with psychoanalyst Frieda Fromm-Reichmann at Chestnut Lodge in Rockville, MD. Ms. Greenberg was diagnosed as schizophrenic, but many experienced clinicians dispute that. Her fantasy world of Iria is reminiscent of the magical, but punitive, imaginary worlds described by these teenage girls.

15. Freud's Oedipal complex for boys and later psychoanalysis' Electra complex for girls.

16. Elsewhere, I argue that the rapid increase in MPD case reports in the literature was a result of improved clinical awareness resulting from research delineating the critical symptoms and behaviors – analogous to the rapid increase in diagnosis of battered child syndrome following a better clinically defined syndrome in the late 1960s.

17. https://en.wikipedia.org/wiki/Richard_Noll.

18. https://en.wikipedia.org/wiki/Richard_Noll.

19. Apparently demonizing someone as a baby-eating, blood-drinking, Satan-worshipping pedophile is the absolutely worst denunciation that can be made against another person. Today, however, the gruesome stories of the "survivors" are only hinted at. No one has stepped forward to tell a first-hand tale of the macabre tortures and sacrilegious abominations that they purportedly endured at the hands of twenty-first century satanists. Rather, now SRA allegations take the form of broad partisan smears. Despite the differences, both versions reek of the ancient "blood libel" an abhorrent anti-Semitic trope.

References

American Psychiatric Association (1980). *Diagnostic and Statistical Manual of Mental Disorders III* (3rd edition). American Psychiatric Association.

American Psychiatric Association (2022). *Diagnostic and Statistical Manual of Mental Disorders* (5th edition; Text revision). American Psychiatric Association.

Armstrong, J.A., Putnam, F.W., & Carlson, E.B. (1997). Development and validation of a measure of adolescent dissociation: The Adolescent Dissociative Experiences Scale. *Journal of Nervous and Mental Disease*, 185:1–7.

Bernstein, E.M., & Putnam, F.W. (1986). Development, reliability and validity of a dissociation scale. *Journal of Nervous and Mental Disease*, 174:727–735.

Brand, B.L., Schielke, H.J., Putnam, K.T., Putnam, F.W., Loewenstein, R.J., Myrick, A., Jepsen, E.K.K., Langeland, W., Steele, K., Classen, C.C., and Lanius, R.A. (2019). An online educational program for individuals with dissociative disorders and their clinicians: 1-year and 2-year follow-up. *Journal of Traumatic Stress*, 32:156–166. doi: 10.1002/jts.22370.

Carlson, E.B., & Putnam, F.W. (1993). An update on the Dissociative Experiences Scale. *Dissociation*, 6:15–26.

Greenberg, J. (2022). *I Never Promised You a Rose Garden*. Penguin. Originally published under the pseudonym Hannah Green (1964) by Holt, Rinehart and Winston.

Heaney, K. (January 4, 2021). The memory war. *New York Magazine*.

McHugh, P. (1995). Resolved: Multiple personality disorder is individually and socially caused hysteria (Debate section). *Journal of the American Academy of Child and Adolescent Psychiatry*, 34:957–963.

Myrick, A.C., Brand, B.L., & Putnam, F.W. (2013). For better or worse: The role of revictimization and stress in the course of treatment for dissociative disorders. *Journal of Trauma & Dissociation*, 14:375–389.

Putnam, F. (1986). The scientific investigation of multiple personality. In J.M. Quen (Ed.), *Split Minds Split Brains: Historical and Current Perspectives*. New York University Press, pp. 109–126.

Putnam, F.W. (1991). The satanic ritual abuse controversy. *Child Abuse and Neglect*, 15:175–179.

Putnam, F.W. (2016). *The Way We Are: How States of Mind Influence Identities, Personality and Potential for Change.* IPBooks.

Putnam, F.W., Guroff, J.G., Silberman, E.K., Barban, L., & Post, R.M. (1986). The clinical phenomenology of multiple personality disorder: Review of 100 recent cases. *Journal of Clinical Psychiatry*, 47:285–293.

Putnam, F.W., Helmers, K., & Trickett, P.K. (1993). Development, reliability and validity of a child dissociation scale. *Child Abuse & Neglect*, 17:731–740.

Putnam, F.W., Loewenstein, R.J., Silberman, E.J., & Post, R.M. (1984). Multiple personality disorder in a hospital setting. *Journal of Clinical Psychiatry*, 45:172–175.

Putnam, F.W., Zahn, T.P., & Post, R.M. (1990). Differential autonomic nervous system activity in multiple personality disorder. *Psychiatry Research*, 31:251–260.

Simeon, D., & Putnam, F.W. (2022). Pathological dissociation in the National Comorbidity Survey – Replication (NCS-R): Prevalence, morbidity, comorbidity, and childhood maltreatment. *Journal of Trauma and Dissociation*, 23:490–503.

2

THE FEMALE GROWTH AND DEVELOPMENT STUDY (FGDS)[1]

Angels in the Auditorium

What is one supposed to do with an epiphany?

Not long after my transcendental moment in the parking lot, I was up for a scientific review. Every three years the NIMH required us to present our research program to leading scientists chosen from outside institutions. They judged its merits and recommended whether it was worthy of future support. I thought it an enormous hassle and doubted that anyone would understand my work.

In my lowly station, it was a make-or-break deal. A negative review could end my research career. Also, I was an odd duck, trying by myself to study a controversial condition, MPD, that most reviewers only knew about from movies like the *Three Faces of Eve* or *Sybil*.

The scientist assigned to review me was Norman Garmezy, PhD (1918–2009), a developmental psychologist famous for his work on risk and resilience in children facing adversity. Norm was a prince of a man, one of the finest mentors ever to grace academia. At the time I had no idea who he was or that he was appointed to judge me. Years later, one of the secretaries in Building 15K, Jean, slipped me his handwritten review, which I was never meant to see. It was extremely kind and complementary. He was one of the few who understood where I was trying to go with my research.

36

DOI: 10.4324/9781003593928-2

There was another unknown angel sitting in the audience during my review, Hazel Rae. Hazel was the deputy scientific director for the NIMH Intramural Research Program. She had joined the NIH in the 1950s as a secretary in the typing pool. Hazel did not have any scientific training but had risen to become the NIMH deputy scientific director through a combination of interpersonal and organizational skills. Many of the institute's scientists thought she had some pretty nutty ideas. I found that Hazel intuitively understood stress and trauma. Outlasting many scientific directors, Hazel knew the institute's scientists, large and small, their programs, and their personalities.

Hazel, Jean, and ultimately many other women quietly supported our child abuse work at the NIMH, making things happen that were otherwise difficult or impossible for me to accomplish through standard channels. From them, I learned about quiet powers that secretaries, low-level administrators, research assistants, and even the cleaning staff can sometimes exercise from behind the scenes at a place like the NIH.

Hazel had recently sat through a similar triennial review of the Laboratory of Developmental Psychology (LDP).[2] There she heard a young developmental psychologist, Penelope (Penny) K. Trickett, PhD, present her research on physically abusive parents. As the only two NIMH intramural scientists studying child abuse, Hazel thought that Penny and I should get to know one another.

The LDP, directed by Dr. Marian Radke-Yarrow, PhD, studied the effects of maternal depression on child development and needed a psychiatrist for clinical backup. They frequently saw depressed mothers expressing suicidal (and occasionally infanticidal) thoughts, who needed evaluation on the spot. Clinical backup for Marian's maternal depression research was to be my "day job."

After my review, Hazel sent a note congratulating me and suggesting I connect with Dr. Trickett. She sent Penny a similar note. We agreed to meet in the clinical center cafeteria on the main NIMH campus on a Friday afternoon to get acquainted.

Penny was born in New York City and grew up in DC. She received a PhD from the New School for Social Research (NSSR) in Manhattan and started her child development research career at Yale, CT, under Edward Zigler, PhD (1930–2019), best known as the father of Head Start.

A chance remark about my hobby making stringed musical instruments, led to the discovery that Penny and I were both fans of Howard (Howie) Mitchell, a musician and instrument maker who had been Penny's high school physics teacher. I owned Howie's record album and had carefully studied a booklet he wrote detailing his craft building and performing on Appalachian dulcimers and psalteries. Sometimes small coincidences can solidify lasting bonds, making them seem inevitable.

Penny and I agreed that a prospective longitudinal study of sexually abused children (restricted to incestual sexual abuse) was needed to better understand – and therefore better treat – the effects of sexual abuse on child development.

Ours was a marvelously complementary partnership from the first. Penny understood developmental psychology research, and I had experience with biological and behavioral investigation. For about four months, Penny and I met weekly on Friday afternoons in a quiet corner of the clinical center cafeteria designing a research study. She was interested in the effects of incestual sexual abuse, as was I, believing it to be the worst form of maltreatment – a conclusion that is largely supported by current research (Briggs et al., 2021). Unfortunately, Penny's NIMH fellowship was ending, and she had accepted a job at a child development center in Baltimore, MD. We were therefore under serious time pressure to get something going before she left.

We roughed out a research design that called for following a sample of about 100 sexually abused girls, aged 6 to15 years, for at least three years (and hopefully longer). We would match the abused girls with an equivalent number of non-abused "comparison" girls who would serve as the baseline. To control for powerful non-abuse factors such as poverty, race, and family composition, the comparison group would be statistically matched to the abused group on age, race, family socioeconomic status, and whether the girls were living in homes with one or two parents/caretakers when they were enrolled.

The most powerful element of our research design was that it was "cross-sequential." The age span of 6 to 15 gave us a cross-sectional look at the impact of sexual abuse on girls of different ages. By following a cross-section of abused and non-abused comparison subjects forward through at least three timepoints (Times 1, 2, and 3) that were each a year or more apart, we could see if and how sexual abuse impacted subsequent psychological, social, and biological development, including puberty and hormonal changes.

Age 6 years was as young as we could go and still have reliable and valid measures for symptoms such as depression, anxiety, and cognitive measures, such as IQ. The youngest girls would be prepubertal and the oldest postpubertal, with the remainder falling somewhere in between. We were especially interested in the transition through puberty, because this is the time when the rate of serious mental health problems practically triples for girls.

The cross-sequential design with its repeated re-evaluations allowed us to focus on specific ages or developmental stages. For example, if we were interested in what was happening with 12- to 13-year-old girls, a time when many are having to first contend with increased sexual attention, we could combine the 12- and 13 year-olds from the first evaluation timepoint (Time 1) with the 9-, 10,- and 11-year-olds who would turn 12 or 13 at other evaluation timepoints (Times 2 and 3) during our study. At the end, we would have a large group of 12–13-year-olds to analyze; this larger sample provides more statistical power to detect key differences between abused and non-abused 12- to 13-year-old girls.

When we had a sufficient handle on the study design and a ballpark feel for the bare bones we needed in terms of subjects, resources, and funds, I approached my boss, the late Richard (Dick) Wyatt, MD, to ask his advice. He told me to contact a mysterious Dr. Garmezy and see what he would suggest. Surprised, as this was the first time I had heard about Dr. Garmezy, I did so. Dr. Garmezy, in turn, invited me to spend time with him at the Child Development Program at the University of Minnesota in Minneapolis.

While I was there, Dr. Garmezy listened patiently to our ideas about how to study the impact of sexual abuse on child development. Among his suggestions was to contact Dr. Robert Haggerty, MD, then president of the W.T. Grant Foundation in New York City. At the time I wondered if I was being passed off to yet another person who would, in turn, send me along to someone else. But it soon became clear that Dr. Garmezy was paving our way.

Penny knew more about the W.T. Grant Foundation and thought it was worth a try. Following my visit with Dr. Garmezy, she and I flew to New York for a meeting with Dr. Haggerty. As we presented our proposal, I doubted it would make sense to anyone who had not seen what Penny and I saw while working with abused children. At the end of our spiel, I tentatively stated one of the more controversial hypotheses drawn from our observations – that sexual abuse would accelerate the pubertal development of the abused girls.

Looking at me hard for a long moment, Dr. Haggerty said, "That has worried me for 20 years. As a pediatrician I've worked up a number of girls for precocious puberty and couldn't find anything wrong. But I knew some of them had been sexually abused."

He indicated that the foundation would welcome a proposal for review by the board.

Penny and I left the meeting in great spirits, but getting back to Washington proved a nightmare. After sitting on the runway at La Guardia for hours waiting for thunderstorms to pass, we barely caught the last train back to DC, arriving about 6.00 in the morning. Literally using our last quarter in the payphone, I called my fiancée Karen to pick us up. Exhausted, but buoyed by the success of our visit, Penny and I were giddy when Karen arrived at the station.

The prospective, longitudinal study of the effects of sexual abuse on females is known as the Female Growth and Development Study (FGDS). Penny and I started it with those first W.T. Grant dollars, and it continues today, more than 35 years later. We have faced extinction at numerous turning points, and yet, somehow, some way, someone comes through and keeps it alive. It has been over three decades since we saw our first subjects. We have also evaluated the children born to the original children. We have retrospective and prospective data on the mothers of the original children in our study. Three generations in all. These data paint a multigenerational picture of the devastation wrought by child sexual abuse (Trickett et al., 2011).

As Penny and I planned the FGDS, it was slowly dawning on those in mainstream psychology and, to a far lesser extent, in psychiatry, that childhood sexual abuse was far more prevalent than had been professionally or publicly recognized. And that it had serious, lifelong consequences. Still, there remained an appalling degree of pushback from the mental health establishment to even these basic facts. Many authorities continued to parrot the erroneous "statistic," unchallenged from one textbook edition to the next, that incest occurred only once in a million cases.

Existing research was largely cross-sectional, either looking at the acute reactions of sexually abused children or at the much later outcomes of adults, who retrospectively reported having been sexually abused in childhood. There were inconsistencies between these two perspectives and large gaps in knowledge about what happened between acute childhood reactions and later adult outcomes. Until the FGDS, no study had ever investigated how childhood sexual abuse affects the same individuals across multiple life stages.

Extant research was further muddied by the enormous variety of individual experiences – ranging from a one-time witnessing of a stranger flashing in public to years of brutal incest by a biological father – that were lumped together under the common heading of child sexual abuse (CSA).

To reduce this variability, we sought to restrict our sample to a tightly defined subgroup of sexually abused girls. Subjects were enrolled in the FGDS within six months of disclosure or discovery. All had suffered sexual abuse involving genital contact and/or penetration by a family member (parent, grandparent, older sibling, uncle, aunt, cousin, live-in boyfriend), as substantiated by child protective services (CPS). The non-abusing caretakers/legal guardians (usually the biological mothers, grandmothers, or adoptive or foster parents) provided informed consent in the children's presence. They shared the children's mental health histories and their own, and they completed questionnaires about the children and their home environments. The girls were given the opportunity to ask questions and signed informed assents. Each guardian and child were re-consented/assented at each new visit until age 18, after which the girls gave primary consent.

Figure 2.1 is the original conceptual model included in the funding request to the W.T. Grant Foundation. There are four blocks. The first block, "Trauma," is influenced by factors such as types of abuse, age of onset, duration, frequency, relationship to perpetrator(s), and use of physical threats or force. The child's "Acute Responses" (second block) reflect reciprocal interactions among psychological and physiological components. Certain positive and negative "Modifiers" (third block) in the child's family and environment shape the child's acute and, later, chronic "Outcomes" (fourth block) over time. One of these modifiers, the child's hormonal milieu, is related to pubertal stage, the timing of which, we theorized, was affected by the sexual abuse.

We hypothesized specific outcomes manifest both as impacts on the child's cognitive and coping capacities and as increases in the rates of specific mental health or behavior problems such as depression, anxiety, dissociation, and hypersexuality compared with the matched, non-abused girls.

The FGDS was the first research to rigorously specify a developmentally based model of how a form of child maltreatment (incestuous sexual abuse) produces the biological, psychological, and social outcomes that underlie an array of serious mental, medical, and public health problems.

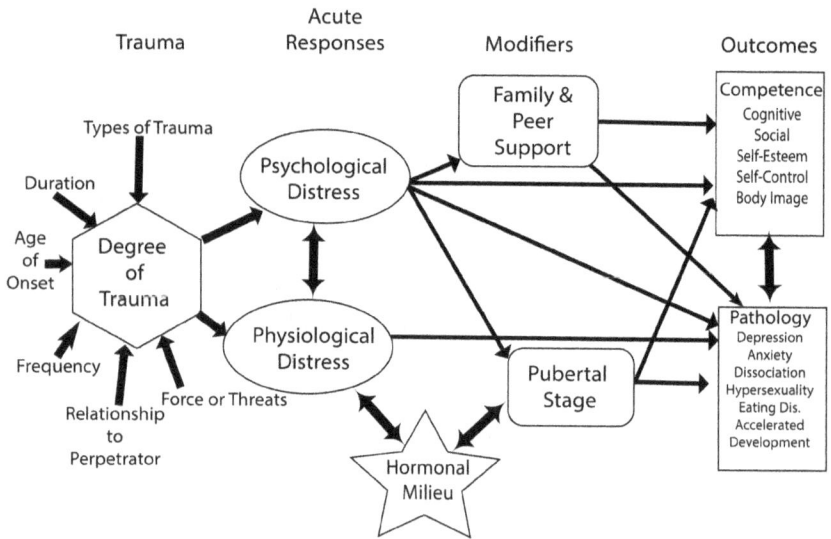

Figure 2.1 Original conceptual model included in the W.T. Grant Proposal.

Source: Trickett, P.K., Noll, J.G., & Putnam, F.W. (2011). The impact of sexual abuse on female development: Lessons from a multigenerational longitudinal research study. *Development and Psychopathology*, 23:453–476.

Walking Away from Adult Psychiatry

In leaving the St. Elizabeths Schizophrenia Research Branch for the Laboratory of Developmental Psychology located in Building 15K on the NIMH main campus in Bethesda, I was trading one day job for another – semi-sweetened by a vague promise that I could keep my research going in my spare time. But this transition involved far more than simply changing offices and clinical responsibilities. I was leaving the world of adult psychiatry for the more ambiguous world of child development and child mental health.

Some colleagues and friends were upset with my decision, especially at my reluctance to become more involved in the public and professional MPD controversies of the day. For me, getting quality training in child psychiatry and achieving board certification were paramount to being able to conduct my research. In July 1986, I started a fellowship in child and adolescent psychiatry at the Children's National Medical Center under the auspices of the George Washington University School of Medicine.

Shortly after starting my child psychiatry fellowship, Dr. Marilyn Benoit, MD, the training director, asked me to provide ongoing psychiatric consultation to City Lights, an alternative high school in the district. City Lights was created as part of the settlement of a lawsuit (Bobby D. v. Barry) against the DC government by the Children's Defense Fund, on behalf of children who were sent to out-of-state residential facilities because there was no local alternative – usually to Texas "schools" notorious for maltreating the children in their care.

In the words of the first director, Alice Tolmach, the at-risk adolescents served by City Lights were surrounded by human and social disaster, high rates of crime and violence, drug and alcohol addiction, chronic unemployment, suicide, and chronic medical and mental illness.

In other words, they were like many of America's children. What distinguished these children is that they all had been expelled permanently from DC public schools for disruptive or aggressive behaviors. Most had been convicted of a juvenile offense. They averaged three out-of-home placements – in foster or kinship care or a residential facility – typically, as a result of severe child abuse and neglect. Consulting with teaching staff on acting out and misbehaviors of City Lights students opened my eyes to what is now called systemic racism. There were humbling moments in which I had a flash of insight into the social chasms separating their lives from mine. For three years I spent two mornings a week working with some of the most severely traumatized adolescents I have ever seen. City Lights students showed me how painful a struggle it is to move forward in a world stacked against you.

Elsewhere, I tell the story of Reginald (pseudonym), an adolescent with multiple personality disorder, whom I treated at City Lights (Putnam, 1993). Over the years, people have come up to me at meetings and asked whatever happened to Reginald.

But I don't know, and the question always sends me back to the internet on another fruitless search for Reginald (who has a highly distinctive name). I confess I am haunted by memories of these young men and women, now grown old, wondering what became of them.

City Lights closed in February of 2009; the reason given was lack of funding.

Interviewed about the impact on her students, Principal Brenda Richards, said, "Without this kind of support, some of them will go back to the street. Sometimes, sir, it wasn't about the test, it was about staying alive, not being abused by your boyfriend, not doing illegal substances. It was about being cared for."[3]

You Can't Do That Here

The real possibility that the FGDS might be funded led me to the offices of the NIMH scientific director in Building 10. (As deputy scientific director, Hazel Rae had an office in the same suite. Maxine, Sue, and other women in the administration who were quietly helpful behind the scenes also worked there.)

I was there to ask the scientific director's permission for us to conduct our study. While the NIMH Investigational Review Board (IRB) had approved it (after considerable discussion), my new boss, Dr. Marian Radke-Yarrow, would not let me use any of her research space.

Marian was a developmental psychologist and chief of the Laboratory of Developmental Psychology. She received her PhD the year I was born. One of the recommendations from my recent scientific review was that I be assigned to Marian's lab, because she conducted research that was considered closest to my interests. For the first time, I was given control of a small research budget.

Marian and I were at loggerheads from the start. She tried to give me a closet for an office. I won that battle, but the war was on.

Marian's Laboratory of Development Psychology was in a grand old house. It was the former summer home of the Wilson family (as in Wilson sporting goods), who donated much of the land where the main NIH campus sits. The house, a stately stone and Tudor-style mansion, was built back when Bethesda was considered the country. Now known as Building 15K, the house sits on a small, sycamore-wooded hill overlooking Building 10, the enormous NIH clinical center.

A grand, circular staircase spiraled up to the second floor, dominating the 15K lobby. Offices were tucked away among the cozy niches and alcoves. There was a lovely walnut paneled library conference room. Every original room had doorbell-like pushbuttons for calling servants. Marian's office, the former master bedroom, had a white marble fireplace and French doors that opened onto a private terrace. A dumbwaiter shaft, now strung with computer networking cables, previously served the upstairs bedrooms. The servants' quarters, tiny airless cells with sloping ceilings and a single bathroom with an ancient, claw-footed, cast-iron bathtub, were in the attic. The attic was off-limits, as there were no fire escapes – in truth, the whole house was a firetrap.

The deep, dank basement was crudely partitioned into little rooms lined with government green filing cabinets containing decades of molding research records. Here, we were assigned the smallest, darkest, and dirtiest storage room.

Mysteriously there was an arched brick underground tunnel that led about 30 feet to a heavy, rusted, iron door. It opened onto the backside of a hill that is a Native American mound; you could find artifacts, if you knew where to look. Some staff believed the house was haunted, and they wouldn't work alone after dark.

Marian ran the place like a mausoleum. Everyone whispered and tiptoed – there was no show of emotion or spontaneity permitted. Early in my time there, I evaluated a young woman at the request of her parents. Somewhere they heard that multiple personality disorder could be mistaken for schizophrenia, their daughter's diagnosis. Grasping at straws (and unaware of the implications about their parenting), they came to see me for a second opinion.

The young woman, who was actively psychotic, sat in the lobby while I spoke with her parents in my office. She freaked out Marian and the 15K staff by arguing loudly with one of the accusatory voices she heard. Frightened staff barricaded themselves in their offices. The receptionist hid in the supply closet.

After the family was gone, Marian called me into her office and threatened to fire me if I ever brought "one of those people" into her building again[4].

Insolently I replied, "This is the National Institute of Mental Health, isn't it?" and walked out.

The only time Marian was nice to me was when Paul Newman came to visit while doing background research for a movie about mental illness on the American frontier. For Paul's sake, she lent me her office. Although I asked Marian to keep his visit a secret, every woman in the building, including Marian, just happened to have important business in the lobby when he arrived. Although I was worried about what he would think of the expectant women milling in the lobby, Paul came through the front door like he knew exactly what he would find.

But Marian was dead set against my bringing "those people," which included sexually abused girls and their non-offending parents or caregivers, into her building. She gave innumerable reasons why – little space, no parking, and interference with other research studies. I offered workarounds, but she rejected them out-of-hand.

Our grudge match came down to the scientific director's decision. When I stepped into his inner sanctum, I was immediately told two things. I could not do my study anywhere on the NIH campus and the NIMH would not pay for any of it. Marian won that round.

However, the W.T. Grant Foundation looked upon us favorably, and Penny and I received funding with which to look for space elsewhere. A social worker friend, Linda Blick, MSW, ran the Chesapeake Institute, a non-profit center for evaluating allegations of child abuse, primarily sexual abuse. Linda rented us space and we split the receptionist, utilities, and other shared expenses.

The Chesapeake Institute was housed in a dilapidated office building in Wheaton, MD. During the years we worked there, the half-vacant building became increasingly derelict. The parking lot behind the building was taken over by drug dealers. While waiting for research subjects, we watched from our third-story windows as they worked out of shiny black vans backed against the rear fence, poised for a quick getaway. A loud screeching of tires usually heralded the end of a transaction or the arrival of unwanted attention, often another black van.

As we prepared our research space in the rented Wheaton offices, several major life events occurred. For one, I came close to dying from a mysterious infection. My fiancé, Karen Thompson, and I had been bird watching in the marshes of Cape Cod and something bit me. After multiple hospitalizations, I ended up as an inpatient at Walter Reed Army Medical Center, partially paralyzed and deathly ill.

The doctors grew a tiny, highly motile, bacterium from my blood. They were delighted with their critter and, if it proved to be a new species, they promised to name it after me. Gleefully they told me that it killed the rats they injected it into. Crestfallen one Monday, they informed me that all the cultures had died over the weekend.

It was good practice for what I am facing now, as I write this. What I learned then proved true again when I was diagnosed with terminal cancer. In my work on child maltreatment, I'm doing exactly what I want to be doing and should be doing – despite whatever else is going on in my life. All I have ever asked was for an opportunity to do this important work. The epiphany in the parking lot continued to confirm my calling.

Karen and I married. She had lovingly cared for me throughout my prolonged illness and convalescence. If she could love me when I was a drooling, helpless mess, I knew that she was the one. We have two sons, Philip and Will, now grown men.

Forbidden to conduct our IRB-approved study on the NIH campus, we saw our first research subject in Wheaton in December of 1987, initiating our scientific quest to find out what terrible things were happening to sexually abused girls.

For about eight years we rented space at the Chesapeake Institute recruiting sexually abused girls and their non-offending caretakers from Washington metropolitan area child protection systems. With posters and handouts, we recruited the non-abused, age-, race/ethnicity-, socioeconomic-, and family constellation-matched comparison girls and mothers from social service and civic settings.

Courtesy of the supportive women in NIMH administration, we quietly tapped into various NIH research subject support funds and were able to reimburse our subjects for taxi and bus fares as well as compensate them for their time and inconvenience. Later, we lost the ability to pay for their time and travel, yet our subjects still returned again and again over 30+ years.

Data Is What They Are

As a result of what I had seen behaviorally and developmentally, I suspected that some of the abused children I evaluated for possible dissociative disorders were *biologically* altered in some fashion. Naively, I believed that if Penny and I could demonstrate that child sexual abuse caused critical biological changes – surely *then* people would understand that something terrible was happening to these children.

Only later would I learn the lesson that in the political arena, where the real power lies to make policy and allocate funds, *values trump scientific data*.

When we started our longitudinal study, the primary biological marker for stress was the hormone cortisol. Cortisol is secreted as the result of a biological chain of events in a neuroendocrine system known as the hypothalamic-pituitary-adrenal (HPA) axis. It starts in the brain, where stress stimulates the hypothalamus to activate the pituitary gland located at the base of the brain (once thought to be the seat of the soul) to make adrenocorticotropic hormone (ACTH). The bloodstream carries ACTH to the adrenal glands, which sit on the tips of your kidneys. The adrenal gland consists of two major parts, the cortex and the medulla. When simulated by ACTH, the adrenal cortex secretes cortisol into your blood. The adrenal medulla secretes the other major stress hormone, adrenaline.

Both hormones play critical roles in emergency responses. Cortisol acts to increase energy and to reduce inflammation and the effects of injury. That shocking electric jolt that rips through your body when some idiot almost crashes into you on the interstate, or when some other near disaster is barely averted, is a result of the surge of adrenaline that your adrenal medulla pumps out when you are seriously frightened or threatened. Without functioning adrenal glands, you're at risk of dying from even minor life stresses. As medications, cortisol and adrenaline (and related drugs) can be lifesaving in emergencies.

When we started working with children, biological psychiatrists were just beginning to measure cortisol and to correlate blood levels with stress in adults. Studying the parents of children with leukemia, John Mason found that the parents' cortisol levels rose and fell in sync with their emotional responses to relapses or improvements in their children's cancer. His work was among the first to show the close relationship between immediate stress and the secretion of cortisol. Related research was being conducted with Vietnam veterans with PTSD, who were showing extremely low levels of cortisol compared with normal subjects.

Penny and I decided to take three samples of cortisol over a 40-minute period to see if there were differences in the stress responses of the sexually abused versus the comparison girls. The stress being the insertion of a small intravenous (IV) needle, called a butterfly catheter. We drew a blood sample initially as a baseline and again at 20 and 40 minutes. We also collected blood for other hormones related to puberty and the menstrual cycle. (At that time the only reliable cortisol test required blood; today we can measure cortisol in saliva, which makes this type of research much easier for everybody.)

The abused girls showed increased stress responses. Their baseline cortisol started significantly higher and increased at a faster rate than the comparison girls. The abused girls' cortisol levels remained elevated at 40 minutes, long after the comparison girls had dropped below their baseline. These early cortisol results were the first strong evidence that we were on to something important – and they reinforced my determination to continue the FGDS, whatever the cost.

In contrast to the Vietnam veteran studies, however, the sexually abused girls were showing higher, not lower, resting levels of cortisol. Presenting these data at scientific meetings, experts in the audience repeatedly told me that I had to be wrong. Everyone "knew" (based on the Vietnam veteran research) that cortisol was lower in people who had been traumatized.

One of the fundamental rules I've learned as a scientist is that "*data is what they are.*" (Former students can vouch that I said this often.) When your data turn out differently than you expected, when they go against your cherished hypotheses or flout conventional wisdom, you must accept them for what they are. Data can be wrong. You may have an error in your experiment or a malfunction in your instruments. But, until you find a definitive cause for the unexpected results, you must accept your data for what they are. Then work to understand *why* they are that way. Conversely, should your data – oh happy day – be too good to be true, you owe them the same degree of close inspection.

During this time, we were joined by Dr. Michael DeBellis, MD, a clinical research fellow working in another laboratory at NIMH. Mike was interested in our cortisol findings and had access to more sophisticated tests of the HPA axis. Using an injection of corticotrophin-releasing hormone (CRH), the hormone that the stressed brain sends to activate the pituitary gland, Mike was able to artificially stimulate the HPA axis as if the person were experiencing an emergency.

George Chrousos, MD, a world-renowned expert on cortisol and stress, also helped us immensely. Together, we were able to study a subsample of our abused and comparison girls. Again, we found that the abused girls had higher levels of cortisol, even though the intermediate hormone, ACTH, was lower in these girls. Less ACTH was still producing more cortisol in the abused girls (DeBellis et al., 1993).

This study required subjects to collect all their urine for three days in a row. Mike was terrific at persuading teenage girls to turn in jug after jug of pee – which we could independently assess for completeness by measuring creatinine levels. Again, we found that the sexually abused girls secreted more cortisol over a 24-hour period than the comparison girls. We also found that they had higher levels of adrenaline in their urine.

As always, *data is what they are.*

Eventually, other laboratories replicated our finding that abused children have higher levels of cortisol. The field is far more sophisticated now than it was in 1987 when we began. But our basic findings have passed the most important test – independent replication by other scientists.

We now know that the natural daily (circadian) rhythmic secretion of cortisol, starting with a big squirt in the morning when you wake up, is seriously dysregulated in traumatized children as young as pre-schoolers. Stabilizing interventions such as therapeutic foster care can normalize this HPA dysregulation, returning these children to a natural rhythm.

We also know that high levels of cortisol are bad for developing brains; they result in the loss of large numbers of brain cells in critical regions. There are plenty of animal experiments that prove this. The pattern of animal brain cell loss fits with human brain imaging findings. Some of the critical brain regions damaged by excessive cortisol in animals are significantly smaller in abused children.

We do not know exactly how high levels of cortisol result in the death of brain cells. The best evidence suggests that excess cortisol interferes with the neutralization of toxic by-products produced by the metabolism of certain brain neurotransmitters, the chemical messengers that link individual neurons together into networks and circuits.

One of the FGDS's major contributions to understanding the effects of child abuse on the HPA axis is the finding that throughout adolescence the abused girls' baseline cortisol levels steadily decreased until, by age 18, their resting cortisol levels were significantly lower than the matched comparison girls (Trickett et al., 2010). Now, finally, the sexually abused girls looked like the Vietnam veterans. This finding has yet to be independently replicated, because no one else in the world has prospectively followed the serial cortisol levels of a group of sexually abused and matched comparison subjects from childhood into adulthood.

In those early years at scientific meetings and public conferences, when I presented on the biological effects of sexual abuse, I would frequently be surrounded at the podium afterward by women who urgently wanted to tell me something. The message was that I had confirmed for them what they intuitively knew – their childhood sexual abuse had changed their bodies.

Obviously, I cannot vouch for their individual experiences, but there is now indisputable evidence that child abuse can forever change a developing child's body, brain, and even their genes. Many of the children I evaluated for a possible dissociative disorder truly had something terrible happening to them.

The Strange Man

During my efforts evaluating children for possible dissociative disorders, I thought I saw something else happening. I was constantly surprised by how much older the abused children looked and acted when compared to my nebulous impression of how they should look and act for their age. It was as if these children were maturing sooner or faster than they should be – but was it their behavior or their bodies? Indeed, was this even happening at all?

This question – does sexual abuse accelerate puberty – has been raised by a number of researchers and doctors, and it was *the* question that bothered Dr. Haggerty for so many years.[5] But it is a complicated research question. What exactly *is* puberty and how do you know when you get there?

It turns out that puberty is not so much a single event as a long, complicated process that develops, and sometimes even temporarily recedes, over multiple years. Puberty is associated with dramatic changes in behavior and observable changes in the body, especially the development of what are known as "secondary sex characteristics." In girls, these include the development of breasts and pubic hair. Facial hair and changes in voice are among the more obvious markers for males. In both, the ultimate outcome is fertility.

As a result of these physical, sexual, and behavioral changes, the world relates to the pubertal child differently than before. Most conspicuously for girls, there is a point where older boys start "noticing" them in ways they may find confusing, intrusive, and even frightening. Men and older boys may make sexual comments about their bodies and try to touch them or act in ways that are uncomfortable or disturbing. Peers, female and male, may joke about their physical maturity and make humiliating remarks.

There is extensive research documenting that early pubertal maturation is, in general, not a positive thing for young girls. In our society, early maturing girls are less likely to finish high school, more likely to get pregnant as young teenagers, and more likely to use cigarettes, alcohol, and illicit drugs at earlier ages. The predatory type of older male who is drawn to these girls introduces them to these things. If sexual abuse causes earlier maturation, either physical or behavioral, it further increases the risk that these girls will not do well in life. Given evidence that the age of puberty is declining for females in general, these outcomes take on added importance.

Despite our meager resources, we had our subjects' biology reasonably well covered. What we needed were clever (and economical) ways to study their behavior. After all, their behavior is what first led me to wonder if abused children were being biologically altered. The girls seemed sexualized, not only in physical appearance, but in their interactions with adults. Penny had observed similar disturbing behaviors in her research. But we needed more than shared impressions. We needed replicable strategies to quantify what we were seeing.

Together with a graduate student, Ruth, we devised a method that would allow us to observe the responses of each girl (abused and non-abused) to "a strange man" (an unfamiliar male psychologist). The "blinded" male psychologist (he was not told if the subject was a sexual abuse victim or a matched comparison subject) would engage in a standard eight-minute "warm-up session" that was videotaped and later coded by "blind" raters, who also estimated the child's apparent "age."[6]

The raters were looking for 54 specific behaviors drawn from the anthropological literature on courtship. We were looking for both approach ("come hither") and avoidant ("keep your distance") body language. The raters coded behaviors deemed: coy and submissive, preening and flirtatious, pouting and negative, and physically revealing such as legs apart and showing their tongue. We were especially interested in the non-verbal gestures the girls exhibited to a young adult male they were meeting for the first time. These 54 behaviors were statistically collapsed into three basic factors that could be calculated for each child: "wariness," "affiliativeness," and "coyness."

"The Strange Man" scenario, as we came to call this part of our study, was the first test a girl experienced when she joined the FGDS, so she was as uncontaminated by us as possible. After an informed consent process with her mother or guardian, and her own informed assent, the girl and her guardian were led down a hall to a room with a male psychologist to begin.

After the guardian left (we videotaped this parting and their later reunion to assess their relationship), the male psychologist sat the child down at a small table in the far corner of the room that had a selection of age-appropriate books, magazines, and drawing materials. Returning to the larger testing table in the middle of the room, he told her that she was early and he had to finish something else first. In the meantime, she could read, play, or draw at the testing table, at the small table, on the floor, or anywhere she liked.

The psychologist (Rob Weinstein, PhD, debuted the role of "The Strange Man" first, followed by Bill Saltzman, PhD) then became "busy" putting labels on file folders and filling them with the various measures that would later be given to the child. All the while he casually engaged in a "getting to know you" type of conversation on topics such as school, sports, hobbies, or best friends.

Some of the sexually abused girls exhibited surprisingly forward behaviors. What we could see from studying the videotapes was that the girls were using these seemingly sexually provocative behaviors as social icebreakers and rapport builders *rather than as sexual advances*. But I highly doubt some males would consider that distinction important.

Ruth received her PhD and, as is unfortunately all too often the case, moved on in her life without publishing the results beyond the mandatory *Dissertation Abstracts*. I was miffed, although I could understand her wish to "never see the #*&%@! thing again" having myself taken over a year to make the very minor changes requested in my neuroscience thesis before its final acceptance.

But she left us stuck. As a result of our intensive work, we believed that we knew something about the nature of these "sexualized" behaviors – and, therefore, perhaps a way to address them that might protect sexually abused girls from attracting the older predatory males who seem able to spot them from blocks away. But the research wasn't published in a peer-reviewed journal, and therefore our knowledge did not officially exist and could not, for example, be easily built on in grant applications.

However, that wasn't the end of the story. Over a decade later, Soyna Negriff, PhD, took up the provocative non-verbal behavior question once again. This time we had much more outcome data to bring to bear on the question, because we had seen the subjects multiple times and had rich information about their lives. Most were now young adults, many with children of their own.

We again found significant group differences in non-verbal behaviors that predicted negative outcomes (Negriff et al., 2010). Most notable was the coyness factor. Girls who scored high on the coyness dimension simultaneously displayed a confusing mixture of "come hither" and "stay away from me" non-verbal behaviors. They might open their mouths showing their tongues in a provocative fashion while at the same time tightly crossing their legs.

Coy behaviors exhibited by girls – primarily a subset of sexually abused girls – in the first eight minutes of our 35+-year study prospectively predicted much earlier consensual, non-abusive sexual intercourse. In addition, they predicted a lifetime pattern of relatively risky sexual behaviors – such as a greater number of partners, a greater number of high-risk partners, risky sexual practices, and increased risk of early teenage pregnancy, as well as an increased risk of sexually transmitted diseases.

We now know, both from the prospective, longitudinal FGDS and from many retrospective studies, that girls who were sexually abused in childhood are more than twice as likely to be raped and sexually victimized as adults. I believe that misunderstood non-verbal social behaviors such as the coy demeanor play a role in revictimization. Thus, coy behaviors provide potential targets for protective interventions in sexually abused girls.

Although we've piloted a few ideas over the years, we've never had the chance to really use what we know to develop an intervention that protects sexually abused girls from a lifelong pattern of further victimization. This fact is crucial: trauma is cumulative. The more traumas a person experiences the more likely they are to have serious mental health and medical problems. A history of trauma is not a guarantee that it will happen again, but it is an enormous risk factor.

Once we know that a child has been traumatized, then we must do everything we can protect that child from being retraumatized – especially sexually victimized. Addressing coy behaviors – for example by teaching the "affiliative" behaviors associated with healthy outcomes in our study – may be one approach to protecting sexually abused children from further victimization. Virtual reality seems like a promising venue in which to try to do this.

The Mathematics of Child Maltreatment

While attending a computer trade show with programmer friends, I discovered a software program called *Extend*™, that was the answer to my dreams. I had been struggling to code mathematical simulations of the biological and psychological effects of trauma using the highest-level programming language, *Pascal*, in which I was conversant. *Pascal*, however, was clunky at iteratively solving sets of coupled differential equations to plot multidimensional "developmental" trajectories.

My primary resource was my time, and programming in *Pascal* was taking far too much of it (although I did gain important insights when a simulation finally worked). Simulations that had taken me many evenings and weekends to code, compile, troubleshoot, and run in *Pascal* could be cobbled together in literally hours with *Extend*™.

One of the goals of my simulations was to gain a better understanding of what I called the "mathematics of maltreatment." Could one calculate the severity of an individual's abuse and its likelihood of producing certain outcomes? Insights were being gleaned from analyses of the FGDS data. But computer simulations would enable me to systematically change parameters to test combinations of factors (Gonzales et al., 1999).

My clinical observations and research convinced me there were complex interrelationships among children's abusive experiences, family environments, and behaviors – and, later, their adult outcomes. Could I figure out which interactions were key and therefore focus treatment and prevention on these points of leverage?

Much of what people, both lay and professional, assume they know about the effects of incest and other horrendous recurrent abusive experiences is what I came to call the "shattered mirror" notion of child abuse and trauma. Book jackets and movie posters of autobiographical accounts of child abuse often portray the traumatized survivor reflected in the shards of a broken mirror or as a fractured face or shattered silhouette.[7] The abuse is frequently analogized to a bomb exploding within, psychologically blowing the person apart.

But the reality of child sexual abuse, especially incest, is far, far, far more complicated. If each episode of abuse were an explosion, the typical incest survivor would be reduced to mental moon dust. In the FGDS the "average" incest survivor was sexually abused once or twice a week for about two years – or roughly 100 to 200 times – something most of us find incomprehensible.

While recurrent incest in early childhood does lead to fragmentation in the survivor's sense of self – as exemplified by psychiatric diagnoses such as borderline personality disorder (BPD) and MPD/DID – these mental divisions are a result of repeated trauma interfering with a young child's developmental task of unifying "personality" (Putnam, 2016).

Trauma or adversity interferes with a child's ability to integrate different self-experiences into a coherent personality. Abuse does not, as many believe, blow to bits individuals who have achieved a reasonably unified sense of self.[8]

Figure 2.2 plots the beginning, duration, and end (to the best of our knowledge) of the incestual sexual abuse of the girls in the FGDS. Each line represents an individual victim's history. Each line begins at the age (x-axis) the child was at her first known sexual victimization and ends at the age of her last known episode. Solid black lines indicate sexual abuse with penetration – for example, penile or digital. Gray lines indicate sexual abuse without penetration – for example, oral-genital contact or perpetrator masturbation. The dashed vertical lines represent the average age at the beginning (7.5 years) and ending of the incest with a mean duration of about two years.

Note how few cases actually fall between the average beginning and ending dashed vertical lines. This is a good example of how an "average" that includes very different groups can be misleading. Also note, that although we saw all children within six months of their disclosure and child protective services (CPS) substantiation, the abuse might have occurred years earlier, reflecting delays in the child's disclosure.

The FGDS sexual abuse subjects in Figure 2.2 are stratified by perpetrator based on a hierarchical cluster analysis of abuse characteristics (age of onset, duration, perpetrator, severity, multiple perpetrators, and physical violence). The victim's relationship to her abuser(s) proved to be the most informative grouping variable.

The incest experiences of the first group, "Other Relatives," were primarily of short to medium durations, but often involved physical violence and coercion. The second group, "Other Father Figures," typically

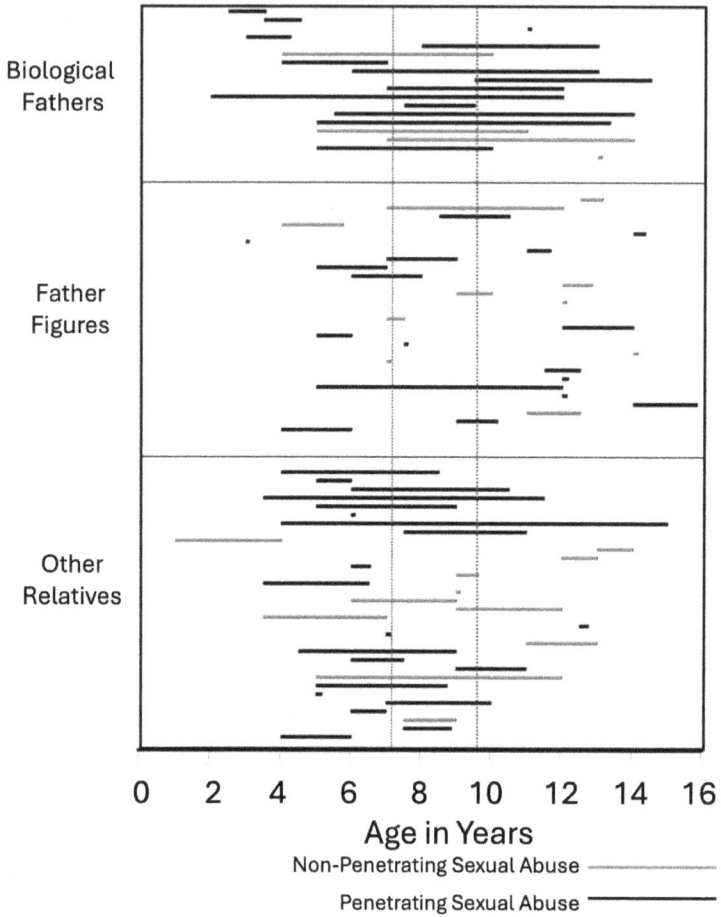

Figure 2.2 Age of onset, duration, and last known incest experience by perpetrator category.

Source: Trickett, P.K., Noll, J.G., & Putnam, F.W. (2011). The impact of sexual abuse on female development: Lessons from a multigenerational longitudinal research study. *Development and Psychopathology*, 23:453–476.

involved stepfathers and maternal live-in boyfriends. The onset of sexual abuse generally occurred at older ages and lasted for shorter durations but usually involved considerable force and coercion.

The third perpetrator group, "Biological Fathers," was characterized by early onsets and long durations. This group used the least violence and intimidation. In many respects it was the most confusing for survivors, in that sexual abuse often began before a young child could appreciate the inappropriate nature of the acts and relationship. For outcomes such as degree of dissociation it was the most damaging.

While victims in all three groups shared many outcomes, there were often significant differences in degree. We and others have observed "sleeper effects," that is, abused children who appeared to be the least disturbed at Time 1 could be the most disturbed a year later at Time 2 and vice versa.

There is another, virtually unquantifiable, parameter that would have to be included in any mathematical model of incest – fear and anxiety about the next episode. Given that most incest victims are repeatedly sexually assaulted, often hundreds of times, there is the factor of what happens between episodes of molestation.

Patients and research subjects frequently told me their pervasive fear and anxiety about the "next time" was agonizing. Continuous, exhausting vigilance was required to avoid being caught alone by the offender(s). Given their easy access and often parental power and control over their victims, perpetrators are constantly setting up situations in which to molest their prey.

Sometimes victims initiated episodes of abuse to have a modicum of control over when and where they occurred. This was an understandable adaptive strategy to manage the inevitable, yet it often increased survivors' sense of complicity and guilt. No survivor should feel guilty for this.

In later years, when students and fellows approached me with elaborate strategies to quantify childhood trauma, I shared what I learned from my simulations and analyses: simply tallying the types of abuse and adversity a person has experienced is more informative than elaborate models that attempt to weight different traumas. Yet, while simple summation types of "trauma scores" are useful in looking at health risks in large samples, they have serious limitations when applied to an individual.

When it comes down to the person in front of you, their precise degree of trauma is incalculable. An individual's trauma story should be respected whether they score a one or a ten on a given scale.

We can make general statements based on trauma scale scores, but they only apply in general. Well-meaning efforts to screen people for trauma with scales and checklists can be useful in opening discussions of how certain events have affected their lives and behavior. But they don't tell us what each person needs to heal or how to end the intergenerational cycle many are trapped in.

For that to happen, we must listen carefully to each and every one.

Notes

1. The name was chosen to mask the purpose of the study in the medical record. No reference to child abuse was included in the medical chart. Subjects were given consecutive identification numbers based on enrollment date. A separate key distinguishing the sexual abuse from the comparison subjects was restricted to authorized investigators.
2. The NIMH intramural organizational hierarchy consisted of "units" embedded within "sections" embedded within "branches" or "laboratories." The last two having essentially equivalent organizational status.
3. http://www.washingtoncitypaper.com/blogs/citydesk/2009/02/27/the-last-morning-at-city-lights-public-charter-school/.
4. Known as an "anthropological psychologist," Marian Radke-Yarrow was often critical of mothers, especially as a source of accurate information about their care-taking behaviors. In a controversial article that upset the child behavior research community, Dr. Radke-Yarrow (and co-authors) opined that maternal reports of their child's or their own behavior "… as measures of family variables, are flimsy bits gleaned by approaches at least one or two steps removed from the actual functioning." Radke-Yarrow, M., Campbell, J.D., and Burton, R.V. (1964). Reliability of Maternal Retrospection: Preliminary Report. *Family Process*, https://doi.org/10.1111/j.1545-5300.1964.00207.x
5. Although our study started in 1987, we weren't the first to advance this hypothesis in print. A physician assistant, later Dr.Ph., Marcia Herman-Giddens, published a paper in 1988 proposing that sexual abuse accelerated puberty based on observations from her medical practice.
6. Typically, the abused girls were blindly estimated to be one to two years older than their chronological age. Only rarely were they estimated to be younger. The comparison girls were usually estimated to within less than a year of their chronological age and were more often estimated to be younger than their actual age.
7. Indeed, the abstract cover art on the *Journal of Trauma and Dissociation* looks like broken glass.
8. The popular but misleading belief that trauma "explodes" a person's personality is a conflation of the identity fragmentation characteristic of early onset, chronic child abuse by caretakers and the "shattered assumptions" outcomes in adults, who have their sense of safety and justice destroyed by a single traumatic experience. The adults describe an acute painful loss of innocence about the world, replaced by paranoia, anxiety, and depression. They, nonetheless, retain a unified sense of self.

References

Briggs, E.C., Amaya-Jackson, L., Putnam, K.T., Putnam, F.W. (2021). All adverse childhood experiences (ACEs) are not equal: The contribution of synergy to ACE scores. *American Psychologist*, 76:243–252. https://doi.org/10.1037/amp0000768.

DeBellis, M.D., Chrousos, G.P., Dorn, L.D., Burke, L., Helmers, K., Kling, M.A., Trickett, P.K., & Putnam, F.W. (1993). Hypothalamic-pituitary-adrenal axis dysregulation in sexually abused girls. *Journal of Clinical Endocrinology and Metabolism*, 78:249–255.

Gonzales-Heydrich, J., Steingard, R.J., Putnam, F.W., Beardslee, W., & Kohane, I.S. (1999). Using "off the shelf" computer programs to mine additional insights from published data: Diurnal variation in potency of ACTH stimulation of cortisol secretion revealed. *Computer Methods and Programs in Biomedicine*, 58:227–238.

Negriff, S., Noll, J.G., Shenk, C.E., Putnam, F.W., & Trickett, P.K. (2010). Associations between nonverbal behaviors and subsequent sexual attitudes and behaviors of sexually abused and comparison girls. *Child Maltreatment*, 15:180–189.

Putnam, F.W. (1993). Dissociation in the inner city. In R.P. Kluft & C.G. Fine (Eds.), *Clinical Perspectives on Multiple Personality Disorder*. American Psychiatric Press, pp. 179–200.

Putnam, F.W. (2016), *The Way We Are: How States of Mind Influence our Identities, Personality, and Potential for Change*. IPBooks.

Trickett, P.K., Noll, J.G., & Putnam, F.W. (2011). The impact of sexual abuse on female development: Lessons from a multigenerational longitudinal research study. *Development and Psychopathology*, 23:453–476.

Trickett, P.K., Noll, J.G., Susman, E.J., Shenk, C.E., & Putnam, F.W. (2010). Attenuation of cortisol across development for victims of sexual abuse. *Development and Psychopathology*, 22:165–175.

3
HARD TIMES

The Site Visit

In 1990 it was time to reapply for funding to continue the Female Growth and Development Study (FGDS), our prospective, longitudinal child sexual abuse study. In the meantime, the W.T. Grant Foundation underwent a leadership change. Dr. Haggerty retired and Dr. Beatrix (Betty) Hamburg, MD, was now foundation president. In April, Dr. Hamburg arrived for a site visit along with Dr. Richard Udry, PhD, as a consultant. Dr. Udry was an expert in population science with some experience in menarche (when girls first menstruate). He was not an expert on child maltreatment nor on the HPA axis. The foundation program officer, Lonnie S., accompanied them.

We were ready. Despite working in a rundown building in Wheaton, MD, the NIH transportation and research subject compensation funds for which our study was eligible (thanks to the NIMH women administrators) helped us recruit about 90 percent of the proposed sample of sexually abused and comparison girls. To ensure a steady flow of new subjects, Penny and I (and after Penny married and moved to California, Karin Helmers, RN, PhD, our nurse, and I), would visit child protection service teams in the Washington, DC, metropolitan area including surrounding counties in Maryland and Virginia. (In the US, most CPS teams are organized at a county or city level.)

DOI: 10.4324/9781003593928-3

We tried to visit each CPS agency about twice a year to describe the study and remind workers to inform families about the opportunity to participate. Turnover of child protection investigators is extremely high, making it necessary to repeatedly visit agencies to inform new workers as well as remind veterans about the project. The best strategy was to recruit an advocate on a CPS agency's staff to approach prospective families (thank you, Carol).

In cases of substantiated familial sexual abuse, we asked CPS workers to give the family a page-long description of our study. If the family was interested in learning more, they could sign a consent form allowing us to contact them with further information. In all, 11 CPS agencies referred cases to us.

After a short tour and a meet-and-greet with our staff and students, the W.T. Grant team sat in stony silence through a series of presentations by Penny, me, and our graduate students. Many of our preliminary analyses showed large differences between the sexually abused and non-abused comparison girls. The pernicious effects of incest were undeniable.

The abused girls had more mental health and behavior problems, engaged in more risky behaviors, and had fewer positive coping skills. We were also finding major differences in their biological stress responses – most notably in the HPA axis. Truth be told, we thought we had done very well – and we were positioned to do even better as the girls matured over the next three years.

Surprisingly, the W.T. Grant team seemed uninterested in what we thought were some rather incredible biological findings. Dr. Udry kept asking us about our hypothesis that sexual abuse might accelerate the pubertal development of girls. Although this question had troubled Dr. Haggerty for years, it was one of our more speculative hypotheses, based on clinical observations that the sexually abused girls appeared and acted "older" than their reported ages.

To test for accelerated physical maturation, we were Tanner-staging (otherwise known as sexual maturity rating or SMR) the abused and matched comparison girls yearly to see if the two groups started and progressed through puberty at the same rate. At the time of the W.T. Grant site visit, however, we did not have sufficient data to either prove or disprove our hypothesis, as most subjects were still maturing.

After a scrumptious takeout lunch from a local Thai restaurant, the site visit team asked us to leave the room so that they could meet alone. Puzzled (as they knew we had additional presentations planned), I anxiously paced the Chesapeake Institute's reception area waiting for them to emerge. Over an hour later, Lonnie, the program officer came out and informed me that they needed a taxi to the airport. The site visit was over.

We heard from the W.T. Grant team about a week later. They were not going to renew our grant. The reasons they gave didn't make much scientific sense and primarily focused on our hypothesis about accelerated puberty. I read the rejection letter to our staff and graduate students, answering their anxious questions as best I could. But I didn't have any real answers about what we were going to do next.

I remember going afterward to a local donut shop for a cup of coffee with Karin Helmers and just staring out the window. It was a cold, gray, rainy day. There are only a few other times in my life that I recall feeling so bleak.

Subsequently, I learned that the W.T. Grant team had always intended to kill the study, irrespective of our results. It was part of Dr. Hamburg's change of direction for the W.T. Grant Foundation. It was no longer funding research on child abuse.

In our publications and presentations, we have always given W.T. Grant credit for initiating the longitudinal research project. Without the startup funding that they provided, the FGDS would likely not have happened. Years later I located Dr. Haggerty, long retired, and sent him a sampling of publications from the FGDS. I wanted him to know how grateful we were for his initial support. I received a gracious email in reply.

Guerrilla Science

We were flat broke. Our staff hadn't been paid for more than a month, but they showed up every day to test subjects. Remember, we were trying to see every child, sexually abused and comparison, and their non-offending guardian, every year. At each of the evaluation time-points, we spent six to eight hours, usually spread out over a couple of days to weeks, testing the child and interviewing the guardian, typically their mothers.

Between our graduate students' class schedules and the families' erratic availability, there was a continuous scheduling and rescheduling of evaluations to coordinate in addition to staying current on data entry and analysis. There was plenty to do just to keep the study running. But finding money was now the most critical task.

Penny and I considered the possibilities. To keep things going, we needed about $3 million. In the short run, we needed $50,000 to buy enough time to write a grant application for the $3 million – assuming we got funded on our first submission.

I was actively talking about the study and our preliminary findings to various people and organizations – including many women's groups. At some point, I spoke about the effects of sexual abuse at the monthly lunch meeting of a women's business organization. During my presentation, I mentioned that our study had lost funding and was in the process of shutting down.

Afterward, as I spoke with the women gathered around the lectern, one of them asked if $30,000 would help.

"Absolutely," I said (at this point we had nothing).

She explained that she was the executor of her mother's estate. The will specified that the money should go either to children or animals. She much preferred that it go to children and quickly made good on her donation. I was able to pay our staff and the Chesapeake Institute the back rent. Shortly thereafter, Penny came through with a bridging grant from the Smith Richardson Foundation for $25,000.

Somewhere in the series of moves that followed from our financial and political problems, I lost the woman's name. I have always wanted to thank her in person – she saved the FGDS.

But even with the donation and a bridging grant from the Smith Richardson Foundation, we were still living on a shoestring budget and dependent on graduate students for free labor. We needed expensive laboratory supplies for the hormone studies: vacutainer tubes, pipettes, reagents, butterfly IVs, syringes, alcohol swabs, Band-Aids, gloves, and dry ice.

Fortunately, the NIH campus, especially Building 10, the giant clinical center, was rich for the picking. The surplus laboratory equipment parked in the hallways to make room for the latest state-of-the-art machines would have outfitted many world-class laboratories. The NIMH deputy scientific director, Hazel Rae, once remarked that the cost of the chemicals poured down the drain every day would more than pay for our entire study.

The solution to our needs was obvious … liberation!

When laboratory supplies ran low, I dressed selected staff in my collection of white doctor's coats, and we toured the NIH clinical center. As we wandered around various labs, it was amazing how the much-needed supplies found their way into those deep lab coat pockets.

Of course, we didn't fool everyone. One wonderful laboratory manager, aptly named Candy, used to subtly point out opportunities to purloin essential supplies or steer us toward items we didn't even know we needed, but would later prove useful. As always, the women at the NIH understood what we were about and helped us in little and big ways.

I justified our scrounging as "guerrilla science." We were living off the land, had the support of the people, and were seeking to revolutionize an understanding of the terrible things that happened to children.

You're Fired!

Although Marian and I observed a fragile armistice in Building 15K, mostly by avoiding each other, the NIMH Intramural Research Program was undergoing a dramatic transformation as acting scientific director, Michael Brownstein, MD, PhD, briefly took the reins. At the top of Mike's agenda was ridding the NIMH Intramural Research Program of "dead wood." I was on that hit list along with Tom Insel, MD, who, ironically, would later become the longest-serving NIMH institute director, the scientific director's boss.

In the scientific director's suite of offices once again, I waited nervously to be summoned and fired (he had already fired Tom, so I knew what awaited me).

The FGDS was going well, especially when one considered the conditions under which we were working. It was still too early, however, to have sufficient data to publish definitive findings.

Slowly recovering from my mysterious illness, I was also extra busy making up for lost time with my child psychiatry fellowship. Daily, I bounced between our research site in Wheaton, my office in Building

15K on the NIH campus in Bethesda, and various child psychiatry placements and hospital clinics in downtown DC. I was driving from one to another in metro traffic, but finding parking was always the real hassle. I spent two mornings a week as a psychiatric consultant to City Lights, an alternative school for adolescents who were permanently expelled from the DC public schools for behavior problems. Those children taught me a lot.

In the meantime, my co-principal investigator, Penny Trickett, married John Horn, PhD, a nationally renowned statistician. Penny moved to the University of Southern California (USC) in Los Angeles, where she accepted a named professorship in the department of social work. Penny and I were learning to communicate through this revolutionary new medium called email. It was a godsend, allowing us to connect easily, despite the coastal time zone differences, as well as exchange working drafts of our papers and grant proposals.

The FGDS attracted quality graduate students from local universities, who took the lead on sub-studies such as the "Strange Man," the "Mother-Daughter Etch-A-Sketch task," and "Hypnotizability and Traumatic Memory." Graduate students were invaluable, because we did not have the means to hire as many research assistants as we needed. Most graduate students used FGDS data for their degree research requirement.

So, overall, the FGDS was going well. If I were fired, literally everything would be lost for everyone involved.

Brownstein did not waste any time. He fired me as I was sitting down in the chair in front of his desk. Even when it's expected, a gut punch still hurts.

I figured I had nothing to lose. There have been a few moments in my life when everything was on the table. In those moments, I was surprised by my boldness and the courage of my convictions. This was one of those times.

Settling into the chair, I challenged Mike on what he knew about child sexual abuse and its contribution to mental illness, my work in particular, the strength of our study design, our hypotheses, and our findings to date. When he wavered, I pushed him harder. I wanted him to understand what was at stake. I was determined to convince him that the effects of child sexual abuse were a legitimate scientific undertaking, a burning public health issue, and worthy of NIMH resources. Remarkably, and to his credit, Mike responded to the scientific questions. We had a stimulating discussion about what could be happening biologically to these children.

About 30 minutes later, I left the scientific director's office, not only with my job back, but with two new research assistant positions to be paid for by the NIMH. I did not ask for these positions. Mike spontaneously offered them.

Marian, who had already reassigned my office, did not welcome my sudden reversal of fortune.

All Variance is Not Created Equal

Variance is a statistical concept that scientists use to quantify the amount of a given outcome that they can explain by an antecedent factor(s). For example, about 60 percent of the variance in the heights of adults can be accounted for by the heights of their parents. Taller parents tend to have taller adult children and shorter parents tend to have shorter adult children. (The remaining 40 percent of variance in the heights can be accounted for by other things such as diet, health, environment, and lifestyle, further complicated by interactions among genetic and environmental factors about which we know little.)

At the NIMH we routinely received emailed copies of the press releases touting our institute's "discoveries." One day, reading the latest press release, I learned that an NIMH study had, reportedly, discovered a gene that accounted for about 10 percent of the variance in a self-report questionnaire (Spielberger State-Trait Anxiety Scale) measuring anxiety. The press release included enthusiastic quotes from the newly appointed, permanent NIMH scientific director, Steven Paul, MD, my boss's boss, attesting to the monumental importance of this breakthrough.

Shortly thereafter I ran into Steve in the hallway outside of his suite of offices.

"Saw the press release about the anxiety gene," I opened. "You know, we can account for over 30 percent of the variance in the Spielberger with just a trauma history."

"Oh?" Steve replied. "But this is real science."

This was but one of the many instances in which I witnessed scientific bias toward genetic data over clinical data, despite the fact that clinical studies usually feature larger samples, are better controlled, and account for more variance on the same measures. Steve's prejudice became official policy in the early 2000s when the NIMH institute director, Tom Insel, stopped funding almost all the research on human behavior, redirecting the funds to neurogenetic studies. Research on behavioral and environmental contributions to mental illness and addictions took a huge hit of around half-a-billion dollars annually, from which it has never recovered.

Infatuation with neurogenetic "discoveries," coupled with denial of the powerful influences of childhood experiences and adult lifestyle, too often influence funding and policy decisions in research and treatment. This is a mistake. While as yet, we can do little about changing people's genes, we can do a great deal about changing their behavior.

A history of child maltreatment is by far the single best predictor of a child's risk for major mental illness and poor medical health in adulthood. No known gene or combination of genes comes close to accounting for the same percentage of variance. Child trauma is both preventable and treatable. But in comparison with the research dollars spent on the genetics of Zebra fish, the NIH, and the NIMH in particular, shortsightedly spends virtually nothing on child maltreatment research.

Time 4

After the lean years spent completing Time 3 evaluations, we were suddenly relatively well off. Always frugal, Penny and I had "carry-over" funds from the NIMH extramural grant that we scored (on the first submission) after losing the W.T. Grant renewal. In addition, we were awarded a grant for a Time 4 evaluation from the Administration for Children, Youth, and Families (ACYF). Penny had a career development (K award) grant to support her work, and I had my NIMH scientific investigator position, now as a unit chief in Marian's laboratory.

Unfortunately, the Chesapeake Institute (an early version of a child advocacy center/CAC), where we rented office and research space, was closing. A Red Line subway station was being built nearby, and rents were skyrocketing. It became increasingly difficult to sustain the

Chesapeake financially, because so much of the staff's time was wasted waiting at courthouses to be called to testify. There is no reimbursement for time spent testifying as a fact witness, and legal proceedings are frequently delayed, continued, or rescheduled at the last minute by one side or the other, complicating the social workers' control over their schedules.[1]

Ever productive, the FGDS published over a dozen scientific articles from the first three evaluations, including landmark research on stress hormone dysregulation and immune system dysfunction in the abused girls. We now had a strong track record with which to seek further funding and institutional support.

Thus, I revisited the scientific director and obtained permission to move the FGDS from the defunct Chesapeake Institute to Building 15K on the NIMH campus. Marian was livid. Her revenge was to assign us space in the dank, cockroach-infested basement and limit us to one reserved parking spot, which we zealously protected for our families.

Most importantly, in 1995, Jennie Noll, a newly minted PhD in developmental psychology and statistical methodology, joined the study. Creative and charismatic, as the Time 4 project manager, Jennie breathed new life, energy, and direction into the FGDS. From designing a logo and nurturing a powerful sense of shared mission across subjects, staff, and students to introducing new experimental protocols, Jennie took the study to new heights – and later saved it when things went south again.

Under Jennie's direction, the clammy basement rooms transformed into clean, colorful spaces for our subjects, who now averaged 18 years of age. We introduced new measures and added experimental protocols to further elucidate the biological and behavioral dysregulation detected during the first three evaluations.

In addition, we conducted systematic interviews with all subjects (abused and comparison) 16 years or older about their traumatic life experiences. These trauma interviews were especially enlightening. Previously we depended on a trauma history taken from a non-abusive caretaker (usually the mother) and a review of child protection records by a former CPS lawyer, Lisa Horowitz, JD, PhD, for details about their sexual abuse and other maltreatment.

We asked all the girls to select and talk about one of the most distressing event(s) of their lives. We kept the interview going for several minutes using neutral, non-leading prompts, while recording heart rhythms and videotaping facial expressions.

About two-thirds of the sexually abused girls described the sexual abuse as their most distressing experience. The remainder described the deaths of siblings, family, and friends. The comparison girls described deaths of family and friends, parental divorce, family conflicts, loss of pets, and conflicts with friends. However, a dozen of the comparison girls described previously unreported sexual abuse occurring after Time 1, which disqualified them from inclusion in the non-abused comparison group. Although these girls continued in the study as "Group 3", we recruited an additional 19 statistically matched, non-abused, comparison subjects to replace them.

The possibility – indeed, the high likelihood – that a subset of control or comparison subjects have covert child abuse histories that reduce between-group statistical differences is a common, but largely unacknowledged, confound in maltreatment research (Shenk et al., 2021).

The facial expressions of all subjects were videotaped during their "most traumatic experience" interviews. Later, the videos were blindly analyzed using a standard coding system for emotions. There were marked differences in facial expressions of the abused girls who talked about their sexual abuse and those who did not (Bonanno et al., 2002). Specifically, girls who acknowledged their sexual abuse histories showed more expressions of disgust, which psychologists regard as a primal emotion, whereas the facial expressions of abused girls who did not mention their sexual abuse were characterized by shame, a more complex emotion. The non-disclosers also exhibited more "false" or "social" smiling as opposed to genuine (Duchenne) smiles, which involve the eyes as well as the mouth. After this interview, all subjects aged 16 years or older completed a standard trauma interview.

In many respects, during the period of the Time 4 evaluation, which spanned 1995–1998, we saw the project running at its best. There was adequate funding, sufficient person power, a stable setting (important for both staff and subjects), and Jennie's strong, day-to-day leadership. The subjects were now old enough (averaging 18 years) that we were seeing meaningful adult mental and medical outcomes.

Assateague Island

We held an annual weekend retreat for staff and students to take stock of progress and plan for the coming year. For the first years we had rented a house facing Oyster Bay on Chincoteague Island on the Eastern Shore of the Delmarva Peninsula. After we lost funding, we used a small cabin that Penny owned on South Mountain in Virginia. When we secured Time 4 funding, we returned to Chincoteague for, what would prove to be, my last weekend staff and student retreat.

Assateague Island National Seashore is just across Oyster Bay from Chincoteague. It includes Assateague State Park, home to feral horses, including Misty, the wild pony made famous in the film *Misty* (1961). A wildlife sanctuary of extraordinary beauty, Assateague is a long thin barrier island. In addition to about 250 wild ponies (some of whom shake down visitors for snacks and nip if displeased with what is offered), there is a profusion of exotic birds and marine life. Cars are limited to a few roads. In addition to the nature trails, there are miles of pristine beach.

Assateague Island was familiar ground for me, in that years ago Julie and I spent considerable time there, usually canoeing across Oyster Bay from Chincoteague to areas inaccessible from the nature trails. Camouflaging the canoe in the bushes, we would head into the heart of the island. Once in the marshy forests, we followed trails made by the ponies, meandering between the boggy woodland and beach grass dunes. Frequently, we would come upon a bedding spot marked by a clearing of crushed grass just off a pony trail.

Once, we camped (illegally) in the dunes and woke around two in the morning to find ourselves surrounded by a ring of ponies standing quietly, looking at us. Later we watched them gallop in the silvery moonlit surf. For me, Assateague Island is a mystical place of ethereal beauty.

The Chincoteague rental house was constructed of heavy, dark timbers joined by pegs. An immense brick fireplace dominated the living room where we met as a team. Sitting in chairs or sprawled on cushions and pillows strewn around the floor, we reviewed our progress, critiqued scientific papers in preparation, and planned future analyses. Renting out-of-season, usually late fall or early spring, the weather was often wet and dreary, which only enhanced the austere beauty of the winter-burned marsh grasses and gray waves on Oyster Bay.

At various points, determined by weather and the group's mental fatigue, we would break and take walks along the beach or nature trails. Sometimes we walked as a group, but more often we dissolved into shifting pairs and small groups. Stretching our limbs, resolving our differences, and refining our goals, we wandered along the beach or down wooded trails, our chatter periodically hushed by lapses into contemplation of the natural beauty around us.

Penny and I would walk together for a while, making certain that we were on the same page. We would prioritize the next steps and always fret about future funding. At some point, usually as the winter or early spring darkness set in, various groups and pairs would turn back to the light and warmth of wine and dinner. Savoring the falling darkness, I would often be the last to return.

One especially cold and rainy day during my last team retreat, at the final break, I set off alone into the marshy forests of Assateague Island. Getting deliberately lost was something that I started doing years earlier. Carrying only a pocketknife, military lighter, compass, a couple of oranges or a baggie of nuts and raisins, and my belt canteen, I would head off into the woods alone on weekends.

I am not exactly certain how or why I started doing this, but I have always identified it with William Faulkner's story, "The Bear," from his novel *Go Down, Moses* (1942).

To first see Old Ben, the semi-mythological bear that Ike McCaslin hunts for years, McCaslin must strip himself of all his possessions – including hanging his pocket watch and compass on a bush – and become completely lost in the deep woods. Only then does Old Ben allow Ike a fleeting glimpse.

On these personal quests, my goal was to penetrate deeply into a forest, marsh, or swamp and become truly lost, then have to find my way out. Unlike Ike McCaslin, I would consult my compass if the day were cloudy or growing dark. Often, there would be a transcendental moment at some point in the journey. Indeed, it was these mystical moments I was seeking. On a couple of occasions, I feared for my life but survived.

On this day, I was aware of far more human activity than usual around me. Vehicles were rigidly restricted in the wildlife sanctuary, but I was hearing motors where they were not supposed to be. That was especially surprising given that the weather was terrible, a steady cold drizzle interrupted by heavy downpours.

It was foggy and growing dark as I came out of the scrubby maritime forest onto a gravel road in the middle of the island. A pickup truck pulling a horse trailer drove by. Further up the road, I could hear men shouting and horses whinnying.

No one paid attention to me as I came upon men in cowboy dress, some on horseback. They were aggressively trying to separate yearlings from their wild pony mothers. Pressed close together, the targeted mare and her yearling would circle defensively inside a larger fenced area into which they had been driven earlier. With much whooping and hollering the men attempted to insert themselves between the mare and her yearling.

The standoff would end when they managed to rope one or both, physically pulling them apart. The terrified, bleating yearlings were herded into a holding pen, while their frantically whinnying mothers were cut off and driven away by the horsemen. The audible anguish of the separated mare-yearling pairs was heartrending – although the men seemed impervious to it.

For much of the day our conversation at the retreat focused on whether we needed to measure the attachment status of the girls to their mothers. This late in the girls' development, I wasn't sold on the necessity of these data to our understanding of what was happening to the children, but I knew little about attachment at that time.

Here, standing in the pouring rain, I experienced the power of the attachment bond between mare and yearling, mother and child, at the moment that it was being brutally severed.

I watched until the last of the yearlings was separated from her mother and driven into the smaller holding pen, where, seeking comfort, she pushed in among the other skittish new orphans. The mares were driven away, although a few attempted to reunite with their offspring until the horsemen cut them off again. I wondered if the horses understood what was happening. Did they feel like traitors or masters of the wild ponies?

The rented house was warm, bright, and filling with delicious smells. Wine was allowed out now. I stoked the smoldering fire till it roared. At dinner we stood for a toast. With glasses raised, I affirmed my approval of the new attachment research project, noting that I had just witnessed the power of attachment (Kim et al., 2011; Kwako et al., 2010; Putnam, 2005).

"Refrigerator Mothers"

By adding a major focus on mother-child attachment to the FGDS for Time 4, we were stepping into a politically and emotionally charged arena.

In a little noted 1943 paper, Leo Kanner (1894–1981), later called the "father of US child psychiatry," is credited with identifying infantile autism as a disorder distinguishable from what was then called "childhood schizophrenia." By 1949, Kanner had turned his attention to the parents, focusing on what he perceived as their cold, emotionally distant relationships with their autistic children.

The popularization of his theory gave rise to the stereotype of the "refrigerator mother" (also known as the "schizogenic" or "schizophrenogenic" mother). The remote, unempathetic stereotype fits reasonably well with Freudian thinking about parental influences on child development. It was uncritically accepted and further elaborated on by prominent psychoanalysts including Silvano Arieti, Margaret Mahler, and Bruno Bettelheim.[2]

Tragically, over the next decades, many mothers and fathers of autistic and schizophrenic children were unjustly blamed and shamed as "refrigerator parents." Biological psychiatry, which began supplanting psychoanalysis in the late 1960s and early 1970s, gradually replaced this stereotype with the concept of biological brain diseases. Seminal research by Seymour Kety, MD, Thomas McGlashan, MD, and others strongly pointed toward biogenetic causes of autism, bipolar disorder, and schizophrenia. Biological psychiatrist, E. Fuller Torrey, MD, wrote a best-selling book, *Surviving Schizophrenia* (1983, 2019), that further exonerated parents of mentally ill children.

In addition, families of mental patients reacted against the stigmatizing stereotype of "refrigerator parents" by founding a non-profit organization, NAMI (National Alliance on Mental Illness) to advocate for medical approaches toward mental illness. Started in 1979 by mothers gathered around a kitchen table who "were tired of being blamed for their sons' mental illness," NAMI soon became a broad-based, grassroots advocacy organization with considerable influence in Congress and at the NIMH.

In its political and public outreach, NAMI understandably is vehemently opposed to any theories or data appearing to invoke or support the stereotype of "refrigerator parents." This inflexible position, however, poses a problem for those of us who work in the field of child maltreatment, which frequently finds parents responsible for grievous mental and physical harm to their children.[3] Furthermore, research on infant-caretaker attachment (bonding) unequivocally demonstrates the importance of parenting in child development. In longitudinal studies following infants and toddlers into adulthood, measures of the quality of infant-parent attachment prove to be strong, long-term predictors of an infant's later adult personality and mental health (Putnam, 2016).

Parenting matters a great deal!

As results from the FGDS were starting to be noticed, I received a call from NAMI headquarters in Arlington, VA. Someone there heard that we had biological findings related to mentally disturbed children.

"Would you come and present your research to NAMI staff and interested families?" the caller asked.

Although the phone call was unexpected, I was prepared. I knew of NAMI's phobic avoidance of anything that seemed to implicate parents in their children's mental illnesses. Schizophrenia researcher, E. Fuller Torrey, was a major NAMI spokesperson for the biological basis of mental illness. While stationed at St. Elizabeths Hospital, I had several lunchtime discussions with him about the misdiagnosis of multiple personality disorder as schizophrenia and the role of child abuse as a cause of MPD.

"You should understand that I am studying the biological effects of child maltreatment, primarily by parents," I warned the caller. It seemed best to put this fact on the table from the start.

"Oh," followed by a long pause. "Let me get back to you," followed by a dial tone. I never heard from NAMI again.

A group of US government scientists stationed at the NIMH Schizophrenia Research Program at St. Elizabeth's campus were commissioned officers in the US Public Health Service (a uniformed service entitled to all the privileges granted to branches of the military). On occasion we would meet for lunch at the Officer's Club on nearby Bolling Air Force base. Whenever Fuller, who was on the St. Elizabeth Hospital's staff, joined us, I looked for an opportunity to talk privately with him one-on-one about MPD and child abuse.

I hoped to convince him that child abuse should be the exception when it came to NAMI's vehement opposition to acknowledging parental contributions to their offspring's mental illness. I never knew what Fuller made of my efforts to clarify the differences between MPD and schizophrenia, or the etiological role of child maltreatment in MPD. He rarely commented on what I said and seemed politely unconvinced by my case.

What I took away from Fuller's sparse responses was how painfully damning the stereotype of "refrigerator parents" was for parents and family members of schizophrenic and autistic individuals. And how determined he and NAMI were to erase that offensive stereotype.

I understand. But not all parents are blameless.

Programs to improve parenting skills can be important interventions in the mental health and welfare of their children. We need to strike a balance, recognizing that some mental disorders are biological brain diseases, and some are outcomes of serious childhood maltreatment, traumas, and adversities.

We, as mental health advocates, clinicians, and scientists, must remain true to the science in assigning cause/blame for mental illnesses.

Data is what they are.

Gajdusek

The first, and only time, I saw Daniel Carleton Gajdusek, MD, he was in line in front of me attempting to renew his NIH parking sticker. Despite his protestations, the young woman at the service window refused to issue a new permit because he lacked a necessary signature. She kept calling him "mister," and badly mispronouncing his name.

A heavyset man, with a broad face and shock of graying hair combed low across his forehead almost touching his thick, black-framed glasses, he patiently corrected her.[4]

"My name is Guy-dah-skek." But to no avail; he left without the parking permit.

I was appalled. Dr. Gajdusek was a scientific legend. Winner of the 1976 Nobel Prize in Medicine (shared with Baruch S. Blumberg, MD, PhD), the story of Dr. Gajdusek's research with South Pacific cannibals was a famous medical tale.

Trained in pediatrics and an amateur anthropologist, Gajdusek lived among the Fore Tribe in New Guinea in the late 1950s. Investigating a debilitating and ultimately fatal neurological disease, which the Fore Tribe called Kuru, he discovered that Kuru was an infection spread when members of the tribe ate the brains of deceased relatives as part of a funeral ritual. The infectious agent proved to be not a bacterium, virus, fungus, or parasite, but a little understood entity called a prion. Prions are infectious proteins, now known to be responsible for several progressively fatal human brain diseases as well as mad cow disease, wasting disease in deer, and scrapie in sheep and goats.

In 1995 I gave a public talk at the NIH presenting findings from the FGDS. (I also gave a clinical center grand rounds in July 1997.) Afterward, a group of junior-looking people approached me as I was leaving the auditorium. Clearly distressed, they began telling me about a child sex trafficking ring on the NIH campus that they alleged was connected with Dr. Gajdusek's laboratory. Unsure of how to respond, I asked them to speak with me privately.

A few days later I met with two of them in my Building 15K office. They told me that Dr. Gajdusek brought young boys from Polynesia to the US under the pretext that he was paying for their education. Some of the boys lived with him, and others lived with his friends. On the surface this appeared a noble philanthropic activity (in fact, he received a humanitarian award in 1987). In reality, the boys were sex slaves. As proof, they brought copies of pages from Gajdusek's personal journals (that, surprisingly, he made available to certain members of his staff) and from scientific publications in which he described witnessing sexual activities between men and boys of the Fore Tribe.

I was shocked, although by this point, I had no illusions about what some men are capable of. Uncertain of what I could do, because, at best, the alleged child sex trafficking ring was only hearsay, I shared what I was told with an FBI agent and, separately, with a Montgomery County assistant district attorney. I also left a message on the county child protection hotline but received no return call.

Recognizing the adverse publicity that would ensue if it was discovered that a child sex trafficking ring was being run out of the National Institutes of Health, I attempted to bring what I heard to the attention of my administration. Recently reprimanded for not following the chain of command on another issue, I reluctantly approached my immediate boss, Dr. Marian Radke-Yarrow. We did not have a good working relationship and over the years, she had shown little understanding or concern about the impact of sexual abuse on children. Listening with a growing scowl, Marian made it clear that once again my work was causing her problems. Taking the documents that the informants had given me, she said that she would talk to "someone" about it.

After waiting a couple of weeks without hearing back, I asked Marian if she had followed up on what I had told her. She had, and the bottom line was that I should mind my own business! My allegation, whatever it was, did not involve our institute (NIMH), which was not going to get involved in another institute's affairs. There was likely an innocent explanation for it anyway. I was instructed not to tell anyone else.

Not sure how to proceed, I asked for the documents back. Marian said she left them with the person she met with. I considered the options and consoled myself that I had tried to warn the NIH and that I had shared what little I knew with the proper law enforcement authorities. I would stay alert for future opportunities, but for the moment I had done what I could.

Unfortunately, I do not have a record of when these events occurred relative to Gajdusek's indictment. My guess (based in part on the reaction from the assistant district attorney) is that Dr. Gajdusek was already under investigation when I made my report.

The official history is that an allegation of sexual abuse had been made by one of the child victims, who had reached adulthood. In April of 1996, Gajdusek was arrested, charged with sexual abuse of the foster and adopted children that he had brought to the United States over the years. While accounts vary on the number of children (29 to 56), most were young boys. Virtually overnight, all the children available to testify against Gajdusek disappeared. Someone paid their overseas airfares and arranged for their immediate departures.

Consequently, Gajdusek faced only one count of child sexual abuse. The day before he pleaded guilty, the NIH permitted him to resign – and thus remain eligible for his federal pension. Sentenced to 30 years in prison, Gajdusek served only one year. Immediately upon release from the Frederick County Adult Detention Center on April 29, 1998, a limousine picked him up at the prison gate and whisked him off to Dulles airport. He flew to Paris, thereby avoiding his sex offender status in the US. Gajdusek lived in Europe until his death in December of 2008, where, despite remaining an active pedophile, he was hailed as an esteemed scientist.

Gajdusek received a "special deal" made possible, in part, by the sudden disappearance of all his victims. It is not difficult to find other famous, powerful or wealthy men, who have sexually victimized many children or women, but served minimal or no jail time after plea-bargaining down to a single count.

The infamous case of Jeffrey Epstein comes to mind. Epstein was a billionaire who kept teenage girls as sex slaves and also provided them as "gifts" to the rich and famous, whom he flew to his private Caribbean island near St. Thomas, on his jet airliner dubbed the "Lolita Express."

Despite reports that the FBI identified more than 40 underage victims in Florida alone, Epstein was charged with a single count of soliciting prostitution from a minor. He served only 13 months of an 18-month sentence. While serving time, the judge allowed him to spend up to 16 hours a day, six days a week, at his Palm Beach mansion. And while on probation, he was permitted extensive unsupervised stays on his island.

You cannot get a more special a deal than that, although it was reported that Epstein was upset that his lawyers conceded too much.

Much later, the Epstein case intersected with national politics, and he was rearrested. He allegedly died by suicide while awaiting trial in a secure New York jail. However, it is speculated that Epstein was murdered to prevent his testimony, given that he was friends with two former US presidents, English royalty, and ultra-wealthy businessmen.

The most flagrant recent example of a "special deal" for a prominent man, is the case in which the Pennsylvania Supreme Court overturned comedian Bill Cosby's criminal conviction for sexual assault, based on an unwritten "promise" made by a former prosecutor who guaranteed Cosby immunity from all future prosecution. More than 60 women came forward with allegations against Cosby, none of whom were informed about this "special deal." To add insult to injury, the US Supreme Court refused to accept an appeal of the Pennsylvania Supreme Court's decision. These two Supreme Court decisions, made without input from those affected most, uphold the inviolability of "special deals."

I have wondered whether the Gajdusek affair played a role in my sacking at NIMH shortly thereafter. Just when it seemed we were finally receiving recognition for our research on the effects of sexual abuse on child development (the NIH director's office had involved me in an official response to an inquiry from the US Congress about the status of NIH research on child abuse, which was read into the Congressional Record), we were suddenly, brutally closed down and repeated attempts were made to destroy the FGDS.

Did my efforts to report what I heard about Dr. Gajdusek anger someone high above me?

What I do know is that Gajdusek's retirement pension "special deal" had to be approved at the very highest levels of the NIH – and, likely, even higher.

Humiliation and Exile

There was a new NIMH institute director, Steven Hyman, MD, and it was clear from our first meeting that he didn't like me – and, perhaps, was even out to get me. When we were introduced, the first thing Hyman said to me was, "What do you think of Judy Herman?"

I had the highest regard for Judith Herman, MD. Her breakthrough book, *Father-Daughter Incest* (1981), breached mainstream psychiatry's wall of denial about the prevalence and perniciousness of incest. Twice, I had written letters to Harvard supporting her promotion to full professor. Hyman made it clear that he did not feel the same way about Judy.[5] On another occasion, he crossed the street to avoid meeting me and did it in a highly conspicuous manner. There was no doubt about his message. My understanding is that Hyman was acting on behalf of an academic old boys' network that could be traced back to Paul McHugh.

It was a time of enormous, disruptive change within the NIMH Intramural Research Program. Marian was retiring and her laboratory of developmental psychology, my administrative home for the prior decade, would be eliminated. I was reassigned to the Behavioral Endocrinology Branch (BEB) under Dr. David Rubinow, MD. The BEB was up for a three-year scientific review, and I was among the presenters.

Although I thought my presentation went well, the review was devastating. I was as terrible a scientist, mentor, and leader as one could imagine. It was full of *ad hominem* attacks and devalued our research on child sexual abuse as a mere social problem, not a legitimate scientific one. The review concluded, "Given no clear indication of the vision and future scope of the program as well as the driving hypotheses (and priorities), the recommendation is that the project should be phased out."

Instantly I became a pariah, shunned by many in the NIMH – although a few remained loyal and provided covert assistance with the transfer of the FGDS to Jennie Noll. Hyman now had the political cover to declare my work worthless and cut off my resources. So be it. This time I knew I was finished at the NIMH and, unlike the previous time, explaining my research was not going to cut it.

Outside colleagues attempted a write-in campaign to reverse his decision. While well intended, it only enraged Hyman, who sent orders for me to call it off. I was counseled by a few people to go public – to take my plight to the *Washington Post* – and make a big media stink. I knew that would not work, and I did not see this as the end of the road. I wasn't ready to throw myself on my sword.

The final section of my rebuttal, which was never acknowledged, began: "We regard the BSC's [Board of Scientific Counselors] decision not to support further research on the effects of sexual abuse as yet one more obstacle to be dealt with on the long road to completing this study."

Anticipating the futility of my rebuttal, I requested and took our obsolete computers, data files, and notebooks, so we could continue the FGDS at another site. Later, I would be harassed by NIMH administration until I returned the computers – only to be immediately junked, because they were many generations behind.

Jennie saved our longitudinal study, if not single-handedly, it would have certainly failed without her. Penny and I played supporting roles, and we were lucky that the University of Southern California owned a building in Washington, DC, where we could rent [cheaply for downtown DC] a small suite for the Time 5 evaluation.

Between evaluations of Times 5 and 6, however, the USC building was sold. We were again homeless. Fortunately, through her connections, Jennie was able to move the study to the Catholic University of America, Washington, DC, for Time 6. There she expanded it to include the children born to the original sexually abused and comparison subjects, who were now in their 20s and early 30s. Later, for Times 7 and 8, Jennie led the FGDS from Cincinnati Children's Hospital, OH, and then from Pennsylvania State University, University Park, and was funded by the National Institute of Child Health and Human Development (NICHD).

During this difficult period, Penny and I had several phone conversations about our concerns for Jennie's career. We knew she was an incredible scientist, but because she worked in DC, Jennie was mostly unknown in her home department at USC. Despite her brilliance, productivity, and dedication, she would be overlooked for promotion solely for that reason – never mind the inevitable craziness that pervades the typical course of academic ascendancy. Although Penny was a tenured professor at USC, there was only so much she could do to advance Jennie's career.

For a while, things only got worse and worse for me. Hyman continued to heap on the humiliations. I was prohibited from having contact with NIMH research subjects – the reasons were never specified – and officially banned from every government committee and work group I served on. Years later, when I was asked to be an outside ethics consultant on a contentious NIMH internal debate involving research with maltreated children, the scientist who came to me for advice began by asking me what it was I had done that was so terrible.

I was damaged goods on the job market. People knew I had been killed off but not why. There was a terrible taint about me. At one point, the National Library of Medicine was hosting a film series that portrayed certain medical or mental disorders, followed by a discussion led by an NIH researcher with expertise on the condition. The series director invited me to be the discussant for the *Three Faces of Eve* (1957), staring Joanne Woodard (who also played Dr. Cornelia Wilbur in *Sybil*, 1976).

Just days later, the film series director called again to "dis-invite" me. Terribly embarrassed, he explained that Hyman had called and told him to replace me with Paul McHugh.

As always, the Building 15K secretaries were wonderful. They ordered sturdy boxes and helped pack my office. We shared Marian-stories as we worked.[6] I numbered the boxes and kept a list of the contents on my Newton (remember those?). They arranged to truck the 50 or so boxes to my home, where I loaded them into a cramped loft over my garage.

At a time when my peers were reaping the benefits of years in the laboratory and assuming leadership positions of power and resource, I was crawling around a dingy garage loft with a flashlight looking for the box with the right number.

I felt a failure. I had failed my staff, who had stood by me, at times working even when I couldn't pay them. I had failed the subjects, who had given of their time and endured the discomfort of blood drawings and stress tests. I had failed the students who had put in long hours without pay, including evenings, weekends, and holidays, to test the FGDS subjects. Everyone remained wonderfully supportive and never suggested that I should have done better by them.

Nonetheless, I felt terrible.

For an hour or so each day I worked on a novel (never published) titled *Institute*, in which a rogue government agency sneaks criminal DNA into gene therapy experiments that were conducted at the NIH. The story centered on a small band of enterprising scientists, technicians, and nurses, who survive in increasingly desperate conditions in a quarantined clinical center, while criminal DNA zombies roam the halls and grounds. Outside the perimeter, the Army keeps everyone from escaping. And, of course, the whole NIH campus might require nuking, if it looks like the mutant zombie, gene-therapy virus is in danger of escaping.

Not entirely coincidently, the bad guys had names suspiciously like the people who did me in. Not especially imaginative – but therapeutic.

I also remember walking back and forth to the NIH with my laptop in the blue backpack Karen gave me – just enjoying a sunny day. David Rubinow, my immediate boss, protected me as best he could. He understood the importance of the work. Although I made perfunctory appearances at the NIMH, my primary focus was on saving the study. David gave me the freedom to do this.

What I could not know then was that getting killed off by the NIMH was the best thing that could have happened to my career.

Notes

1. As director of a CAC during the 2000s, I determined that at any given time, about a third of our medical and social work staff were on call to testify in court. Personally, I received about two subpoenas a week just because my name was on the chart. Fortunately, we had memos of understanding with local judicial systems permitting our staff to remain at the hospital doing their jobs until absolutely the last minute. We also recorded staff depositions at our center. Nonetheless, staff time spent in court was still a big money loser for our center.
2. Bettelheim committed suicide after he was found to have falsified his credentials, plagiarized others' work on fairy tales, and emotionally and physically abused children at his therapeutic school.
3. My experience recruiting young adult subjects for the St. Elizabeth's Schizophrenia Research Program was that their parents cared deeply about their children's mental health and would do anything that they could to help them.
4. Actually, Gajdusek's impatience with being told "no" was legendary, so his forbearance with this impertinent young woman was an exception (see, e.g., Asher with Oldstone, 2013).
5. I asked Judy to speculate on why Hyman (whom she has never met) appeared to dislike her so much. Her best guesses were: (1) she was a feminist and studied incest, which she identified as a manifestation of patriarchal power; (2) Judy made clear that establishment psychiatry gravely and deliberately underestimated the prevalence of incest; and (3) she was a member of a women's committee of the American Psychiatric Association (APA) that initiated research into the sexual exploitation of patients by psychiatrists (primarily male), which she considers analogous to incest. The APA board of directors opposed this research, which was funded by private donations.
6. For many years, at the biennial meeting of the Society for Research on Child Development there was an invitation-only dinner for survivors of Marian's lab, where former fellows, post-docs, and junior investigators from different eras shared their traumatic experiences at her hands.

References

Asher, D.M., with Oldstone, M.B. (2013). *D. Carleton Gajdusek: A Biographical Memoir*, National Academy of Sciences website. https://www.nasonline.org/directory-entry/d-carleton-gajdusek-91uiu3/.

Bonanno, G.A., Keltner, D., Noll, J.G., Putnam, F.W., Trickett, P.K., LeJune, J., & Anderson, C. (2002). When the face reveals what words do not: Facial expressions of emotion, smiling, and willingness to disclose childhood sexual abuse. *Journal of Personality and Social Psychology*, 83:94–110.

Faulkner, W. (1942). *Go Down, Moses*. Random House.

Herman, J.L. (1981). *Father-Daughter Incest*. Harvard University Press.

Kanner, L. (1943). Autistic disturbances of affective contact. *Nervous Child*, 2:217–250.

Kim, K., Trickett, P.K., & Putnam, F.W. (2011). Attachment representations and anxiety: Differential relationships among mothers of sexually abused and comparison girls. *Journal of Interpersonal Violence*, 26:498–521.

Kwako, L.E., Noll, J.G., Putnam, F.W., Trickett, P.K. (2010). Childhood sexual abuse and attachment: An intergenerational perspective. *Clinical Child Psychology and Psychiatry*, 15:407–422.

Putnam, F.W. (2005). The developmental neurobiology of disrupted attachment: Lessons from animal models and child abuse research. In L.A. Berlin, L. Ziv, L. Amaya-Jackson, & M. Greenburg (Eds.), *Enhancing Early Attachments*. Guildford Press, pp. 79–99.

Putnam, F.W. (2016). *The Way We Are: How States of Mind Influence Our Identities, Personality and Potential for Change*. IPBooks.

Shenk, C.E., Rausch, J.R., Shores, K.A., Allen, E.K., & Olson, A.E. (2021). Controlling contamination in child maltreatment research: Impact on effect size estimates for child behavior problems measured throughout childhood and adolescence. *Development and Psychopathology*, 34:1287–1299. doi:10.1017/S0954579420002242.

Torrey, E.F. (2019 [1983]). *Surviving Schizophrenia* (7th edition). Harper Perennial.

4

FROM THE LABORATORY
TO THE FRONT LINE

The National Child Traumatic Stress Network (NCTSN)

I was at a think-tank-type weekend retreat in Cape Cod, MA. Still raw from my recent public savaging by the NIMH institute director, Steven Hyman, whereby my research program was terminated and my privileges and prerogatives severely curtailed, I listened for most of the first day. Towards the end, I started to come out of my defensive shell and contribute to the group.

Feeling isolated and powerless, I believed that most of the participants probably knew of my humiliation, if not the politics behind it. I was only present, because the meeting organizer, Dr. Bessel van der Kolk, was a close friend and understood my situation. I didn't know what I could contribute or if it would be considered tainted.

But something special was happening. Most of those present were veterans of numerous think-tank/retreat-type meetings as well as special committees, consensus conferences, tabletop exercises, and other venues designed to bring experts together to strategize about policy and problems. And, as seasoned participants, they knew that often nothing meaningful or enduring comes out of these academic exercises.

This meeting was starting to feel different. People were excited. There was an awareness of how precious our mutual synergy was. Scheduled

DOI: 10.4324/9781003593928-4

work breaks were ignored; we wanted to keep going. We continued meeting after we officially adjourned and then broke up into smaller groups. I didn't get to bed until late.

The next morning began again with an early breakfast. Although we were at the seashore and a walk to the ocean took less than five minutes, no one stepped outside except to shuttle back and forth between the sleeping quarters and conference center. I don't recall even looking out of the conference room windows. All the action was inside.

A shared vision was emerging – a vision of a grassroots-driven, community-based, nationally coordinated mental health network that would provide traumatized children with services closely informed by the best science. That vision ultimately became the National Child Traumatic Stress Network (NCTSN).[1] As it moved beyond this conference room, through the halls of Congress and into reality, many, many people made critical contributions.

The initial legislation was co-sponsored by Senators Edward (Ted) Kennedy (Democrat) and Bill Frist (Republican). The first round of grants was awarded in the immediate aftermath of 9/11. As of this writing, the NCTSN has grown to more than 180 funded sites and about 150 previously funded, now formally affiliated, sites.

What makes the NCTSN exceptionally effective among community-academic-government partnerships is its three-tiered structure that takes advantage of existing working relationships and specialized knowledge unique to each level. A shared sense of mission and a culture of optimistic dedication among NCTSN members, at all levels, play important roles.

Category III (Cat. III) sites are foundational to the NCTSN. As community-based local agencies and child- and family-serving programs, Cat. III sites infuse the NCTSN with grassroots energy and pragmatic goals that are aligned with community needs. Cat. III personnel care deeply for and about the communities they serve and have intimate knowledge about the history and culture of the children and families living there.

The mid-level Category II (Cat. II) sites are usually affiliated with universities or large organizations. They provide Cat. III sites with the tools and know-how to develop new (or adapt existing) evidence-based, trauma-informed interventions that address local needs and glaring deficits (identified by the Cat. IIIs).[2] Cat. II sites have the personnel, expertise, and facilities to train and supervise Cat. III clinicians in NCTSN-approved interventions and to help them evaluate outcomes.

Cat. II and Cat. III sites specialize in specific traumas and/or specific populations. In aggregate, the 100+ Cat. III and scores of Cat. II sites comprise a deep reservoir of expertise and address a wide array of youth and family trauma and adversity. Their specialties range from natural disasters (for example, hurricanes, wildfires, and earthquakes) to medical illnesses (for example, COVID-19) to terrorism and school shootings to grief and bereavement (for example, due to parental separation and loss).

The NCTSN has earned public trust by respectfully working with traumatized children and families. NCTSN sites have long, productive collaborations with critical local child- and family-serving systems such as schools, child welfare, juvenile justice, child mental health, and pediatrics.

The top level, or Category I (Cat. I) site, is the National Center for Child Traumatic Stress (National Center), which tracks and integrates the expertise, products, services, and technical assistance contained within the NCTSN as a whole. The National Center, currently co-located at Duke University, NC, and University of California at Los Angeles (UCLA), link the professionally and geographically diverse Cat. III and Cat. II sites into a dynamic network, sharing knowledge and promoting standardization of services and common measurement of outcomes.

The National Center (Cat. I) has the clinical quality assurance tools to identify successful Cat. II/III programs and innovations and the resources to package them into free (or subsidized) nationally available treatment models, reports, and best practices. Cat. I sites collaborate with national professional organizations – e.g., the American Academy of Pediatrics (AAP), the American Academy of Child and Adolescent Psychiatry (AACAP), and the National Children's Alliance (NCA) – to promote national coordination of trauma services for children and families.

I left the Cape Cod meeting with mixed feelings. I was optimistic that there was a real chance of getting something important started for child mental health. But I was feeling heavy-hearted and cheated; in my now greatly diminished professional situation, I didn't see a way to personally participate.

A Call from Out of the Blue

Early in the spring of 1999, Karen and I were preparing to move to her hometown in the Blue Ridge foothills of Virginia. My NIMH position would end in July. I had done my best to transfer the FGDS lock-stock-and-barrel to Jennie and Penny. Paper records and biological samples had to be abandoned, because we lacked the space and refrigeration to store them. Laboratory equipment purchased with the W.T. Grant funds was donated to a high school science department.

But the bulk of the data was saved to be processed over the next couple of decades. We had completed four evaluations and were funded for Time 5 – although the study would have to move again between Times 5 and 6.

Times 5 and 6 were funded by grants from other NIH institutes and federal agencies, through Penny and Jennie. Ironically, the following year the NIMH touted the FGDS in a press release devoted to its "special" scientific projects. It was abundantly clear it didn't have trouble with the study, only with me.

I was casting about for some way to continue my work in child abuse, but without much success. There were child psychiatry chairs and division director type jobs available and, even marked as I was by Hyman's aggressive efforts to discredit me, I was approached about a few positions. But they were not of interest.

During my year in exile, I had taken long, reflective walks and knew in my heart that I wanted a job that allowed me to focus exclusively on child maltreatment. The epiphany in the parking lot remained my North Star.

Quite unexpectedly, I received a call from Dr. Thomas Boat, MD, chair of the department of pediatrics at the University of Cincinnati School of Medicine. Tom asked me to consider a position as director of a newly authorized child abuse center located at Cincinnati Children's Hospital medical center. In addition, I would be the director of Every Child Succeeds (ECS), a large-scale community-based, child abuse prevention program, soon to be implemented in the greater Cincinnati metro area.

Karen and I visited Cincinnati in April 1999 to see it for ourselves. Afterwards, I discussed the twin directorship positions with my father, the late Frank W. Putnam, Sr., PhD (1917–2006), a distinguished professor of molecular biology. Dad cautioned me against taking a lead position in both a hospital-based clinical program and a community-based prevention program. I would be spreading myself too thin, he said, as both leadership roles required considerable on-site, in-person, presence.

On a follow-up visit, I suggested to Dr. Boat that he consider hiring a local director for Every Child Succeeds, since the position demanded considerable familiarity with Cincinnati's many diverse communities. I would, however, serve as that program's scientific director, guiding the choice of best practices and running an outcome evaluation. And I would gladly accept the position as director of the hospital-based child abuse center, later named the Mayerson Center.

I arrived at Cincinnati Children's Hospital in July 1999, just days after leaving the NIMH, to find the building that would be housing the child abuse center was still under construction. The administrative offices for Every Child Succeeds was to be co-located within the child abuse center. The program's home visitors, who would be providing the child abuse prevention and child development program, would come from social service agencies within their local communities.

While waiting for our dedicated space to be completed, we camped out in a series of temporary offices to plan operations, interview and recruit staff, and become a cohesive team. Eventually, the building was finished and our space, occupying much of the fifth floor of the Albert B. Sabin Center, was ready.

In January of 2001, we hosted an opening ceremony for the center. The giant, gilded scissors traditionally used for ribbon-cuttings had disappeared at the hospital's last event. Consequently, as my nine-year-old son, Will, and the clinical director's young daughter, Mattie, struggled to each work one handle of a pair of razor-sharp pruning clippers (substituted for the purloined golden shears), I worried that the Center for Safe and Healthy Children might be inaugurated with an amputation.

Vanilla, Chocolate, and Strawberry

The Center for Safe and Healthy Children was the vision of the late Patricia (Pat) Myers, MSW, and Dr. Robert (Bob) Shapiro, MD. Pat was head of the hospital social work department, and Bob was an emergency room pediatrician with considerable experience in forensically evaluating allegations of maltreatment. For years, Pat and Bob ran a weekly clinic that evaluated children who were alleged victims of child abuse – mostly sexual abuse. In this capacity, they formed strong alliances with adjacent county child protection systems, local law enforcement, and the county district attorney's office.

Together with representatives from their community partners, Pat and Bob toured child abuse programs around the country seeking a model for the new center. In many respects their vision was a blend of the best programs they visited. I was chosen to run the center, in large measure to add mental health and research components to their forensic evaluations.

At its heart, our child abuse center was a child advocacy center. The CAC model is the brainchild of Robert (Bud) Cramer, a former congressman from Alabama. While prosecuting child abuse cases as a district attorney, Bud had been frustrated by a lack of cooperation and coordination between the doctors, social workers, police officers, and therapists involved in a case.

Prior to the CAC model, an alleged child victim would be subjected to multiple forensic interviews conducted by hospital social workers, county child protection investigators, the police, the district attorney's office, and the defendant's legal team (if it was likely that the case was going to trial). The child might also be medically examined by physicians for the prosecution and defense.

Multiple interviews and repeated examinations are extremely stressful for children for many reasons. In addition to repeatedly probing into painful trauma details and family dynamics, the interviews and exams were conducted by different people from widely divergent backgrounds and perspectives, both professional and adversarial. Most of these interviewers knew little about talking with children in general, much less the nuances of forensically interviewing different ages and genders.

In addition, children – especially young children – if repeatedly asked for specific details of events, will frequently give different (sometimes conflicting) answers to questions posed by different people. Some of the variability is developmental, in that young children have a limited capacity to describe what has happened to them, recall exactly what they said previously, provide accurate anatomical details, or sequence multiple episodes. Young children also tend to assume that whatever they have told one adult is known to all adults. From their perspectives, being asked again and again about the same events may imply their earlier answers were "wrong."

Not surprisingly, there may be discrepancies across the numerous interviews, which complicate a search for the facts. In addition, injuries to mucus membrane tissues, such as the genitalia, anus, and mouth, heal rapidly and are often forensically uninterpretable after a few days.

To reduce the stress on a child as well as the confusion that multiple forensic interviews and examinations could produce, District Attorney Cramer created the first CAC in 1985. He co-located representatives from each of the critical disciplines in an independent program. Later, as a congressman, Bud initiated federal pilot funding for the CAC model, the Chesapeake Institute being one of the first grantees.

When a child is brought to a CAC, the investigation routinely begins with a videotaped interview, conducted by a trained child forensic interviewer. If warranted by history or symptoms, a child abuse-trained pediatrician performs a sexual assault forensic examination and may collect a rape kit and test for sexually transmitted diseases. Injuries are documented and treated.

At full strength, our CAC housed two to four full- and part-time child abuse-trained pediatricians, one or two child abuse fellows in training, two nurses, half-a-dozen hospital social workers, and two Hamilton County Department of Jobs and Family Services child protection teams – one for "in-home" sexual abuse" and the other for "medical" neglect. Each child protection team consisted of four to six home investigators and a supervisor.

We had officers from the Cincinnati police department special victims unit and detectives from the Hamilton County sheriff's office. The police did crime scene investigations (for example, visited homes where injured children were reported to have accidentally fallen down stairs or out of windows, or were scalded by bath water). Two prosecutors (criminal and family court) and a victim's advocate from the district attorney's (DA's) office, rounded out law enforcement.

In addition, there were research assistants, receptionists, and administrative personnel, most notably, my able assistant, Debbie (Deb) Sharp, who looked out for everyone. Deb was expert at getting temporary outside workers, such as rotating police officers, prosecutors, and child protection investigators, through the hospital's ever more complicated temporary worker badging gauntlet.

Our center collaborated with two clinical psychologists, Barbara Boat, PhD, and Erna Olafson, PhD, PsyD, from the Childhood Trust, a trauma treatment program directed by Barbara. They worked closely with us to develop, adapt, and train therapists in child and adolescent trauma treatments, including special populations, such as incarcerated juveniles (Olafson et al., 2016).

I was the outsider, a child psychiatrist and maltreatment researcher brought to Cincinnati from the NIMH. Most of the other members of the center had worked together on legal cases over the years. Indeed, the core group toured the country together, examining key child abuse programs and forming strong friendships. Because practically everyone knew and trusted everyone else, the expectation was that we were all going to mesh easily.

It turns out that simply knowing each other (even well) is not the same as working together, day-in and day-out, on stressful assignments. In the past, collaboration meant reading each other's reports and conducting phone discussions and pretrial briefings. Now, it meant sitting side-by-side, behind the one-way mirror of an interview observation room, listening to children tell their painful stories to a designated forensic interviewer or meeting as a team as a radiologist pointed out fractured ribs and subdural hemorrhages on X-rays and brain scans.

In the beginning, each of us assumed the next person somehow had more authority, autonomy, and resources. We were acutely aware of our own limitations regarding what we knew or could say for certain or could do. It took us about a year of working together before we collectively understood each other's roles and, more importantly, each other's strengths.

Before the center opened, we spent our first day together with a professional facilitator. In the first exercise, we had to classify ourselves into one of three categories: vanilla, chocolate, or strawberry. One's flavor would be based on scores from a questionnaire about our likes, dislikes, habits, need for uniformity, tolerance of ambiguity, and so on.

Although the ice cream exercise was crude stereotyping at one level, it forced us each to talk more openly about who we were, where we were coming from, and how we liked things done. By the end of the day, no one could remember what anyone else's flavor was, but we knew a lot more about each other. For years afterwards, sly, ice cream-flavor-tagged comments would distinguish founding members from newcomers.

The real work of getting to know each other and the larger professional worlds in which we each operated, came with our collaboration on cases. In child abuse forensic evaluations, nothing is routine. There is always enormous pressure to make the right decision with very little solid information, against the ticking of a clock – we were often limited to 24 to 48 hours. There might be several conflicting explanations or possible scenarios that could explain the child's injuries or allegations. Do these need to be checked out further? Do the police need to conduct a crime scene investigation? Do the doctors need to run more tests or scans? Is another forensic interview justified?

We depended on each other to gather the best information and bring it to the conference table, where members of the larger team collectively evaluated it. As we listened to members present their pieces of the case, we learned a lot about each other. We also learned that our greatest strength was our collective wisdom and experience.

Commotion at the Cincinnatus Association

The other half of my new job was to scientifically evaluate the community-based, child development and maltreatment prevention program, Every Child Succeeds. ECS was a regional public-private partnership designed to improve the lives of the region's most at-risk children and families. I was joined by Robert (Bob) Ammerman, PhD, a child psychologist. From our first phone call, Bob and I were on the same page about what was necessary and how to go about it. Bob and I became known throughout ECS as "the science guys." Given our common approach to problems, it was whispered that we shared a brain. In reality, what we shared was a common scientific paradigm.

ECS was very much still gelling when we arrived. The three core community partners, United Way of Greater Cincinnati, the Community Action Agency of Cincinnati, and Cincinnati Children's Hospital, agreed on the program's overall plan, but, as always, the devil was in the details.

There was an understanding that ECS would focus its finite resources on first-time, single (unmarried), lower-income, teenage mothers. Any one of those risk factors would be sufficient to qualify a mother for ECS, which would be delivered by a home visitor trained in one of two national models. On average, the home visitors would spend two to four hours a month in weekly visits with each mother.

One of the first orders of business was to design the evaluation. In addition to collecting ongoing information about the types and amounts of services to be provided to families, the evaluation established a baseline at enrollment with periodic follow-ups of the health and development of the children and mothers. Once we determined the core measures and their administration timepoints, Bob and I worked with computer programmers to implement an internet-based data collection and services management system known as eECS.

The ECS executive committee, largely composed of older, white, male senior business leaders, was highly skeptical that the much younger female home visitors would be willing or able to input data into a computer.[3] When the programmers were finished, home visitors had two weeks to transition from the temporary paper-based data system to eECS. But by the afternoon of the first day of training, they were begging us to let them start using it immediately. The success of eECS, helped to establish the credibility of the research program with the home visitors, who were then tasked with obtaining initial informed consents from the mothers who would be participating in the voluntary research component.

Monthly, we provided feedback to each agency on their workers and families. At first, we respected the confidentiality of each agency's statistics, but we soon learned that agencies immediately shared their "grades" with each other. Shortly thereafter, we made everyone's monthly report cards accessible to qualified users. In turn, agencies doing poorly on certain measures sought advice from agencies doing well, leading to a very positive cycle of improvement across the program. Later, we took advantage of this dynamic to implement a formal quality improvement program adopted from industry (Ammerman et al., 2007).

Recognizing the wisdom of my father's advice, I had declined to be the overall ECS director, and Judith B. Van Ginkel, PhD, was selected to be its president.

The first time I met Judy, we had lunch at the Cactus Pear, a south-western-themed restaurant near the medical center. Dressed in a black pants suit, accented by a dramatic turquoise and silver necklace, her long dark hair pulled tightly back, I felt as if I were sitting with Georgia O'Keeffe.

Judy is an artist – with people. She can make things happen, get diverse people to work effectively together, move stuck things along, and bridge unbridgeable social divides better than anyone I have ever worked with. Every Child Succeeds would never have succeeded without Judy. There were just too many political and social bases that only she could cover. As a result of a lifetime of achievement in public service, Judy is the recipient of many awards (Van Ginkel, 2023).

Judy was the first woman president of the Cincinnatus Association, a local, prestigious, invitational society limited at any given time to 100 members of Cincinnati's civic leadership. Dating to 1920, the Cincinnatus Association weighs in on the political, social, cultural, and educational issues affecting quality of life in Cincinnati. It was important for ECS to get its approval.

At that time, much of what was known about home visiting came from the seminal work of David Olds, PhD, and colleagues in the Nurse Family Partnership (NFP) program. David had done the extremely dif-ficult work of conducting three rigorous randomized clinical trial evalu-ations of NFP. Each evaluation had shown significant improvements in the lives of home-visited families compared to a matched group.

By talking with Dr. Olds, listening to his presentations, and reading his articles, it was clear that, in his view, a major reason for the success of the NFP program – besides the fact that it was delivered by public health nurses – was that it delayed the birth of the second child. By increasing the spacing between the first two children, mothers had more time and energy to devote to their first child, before the next baby required so much of her attention.

This makes sound sense from a child development perspective. We know that the first year of life is critical to the healthy development of the child's personality, increased resilience to stress, good emotional regulation, and appropriate social behavior. Longitudinal research has shown that the quality of the attachment relationship (commonly called "bonding") between mother and infant is powerfully predicative of the child's later mental health and behavior as a young adult.

When we presented ECS to community organizations, like the Cincinnatus Association, one of the essential questions we would rhetorically ask and answer was, "How does the program work?" Implementation science, the discipline guiding dissemination of social service and prevention programs in communities, calls this heuristic device "having an understandable theory of action."

Stakeholders – consumers, funders, providers, the local media, and concerned citizens – need a simple, logical, and feasible theory of action outlining how a proposed social welfare program will achieve its goals. Thus, at the Cincinnatus Association meeting, I was prepared to offer the increased interval between a mother's first and second child as one of the reasons home visiting improved child development.

Having arrived just a few months earlier, Cincinnati's geography was still a blur to me. I believe the meeting was held either at the Cincinnati Club or the Queen City Club. Both are historic institutions decked out in walnut, brass, leather, and marble, where local powerbrokers and influential citizens socialized.

I was aware it was important to convince this audience, but confident we had a strong case to make, which had been well received to date. Besides, I was with Judy, who drew an enthusiastic crowd wherever we went.

Judy presented the rationale and the history of how ECS came to be. Indeed, it was the Cincinnati business community leadership together with the United Way, Community Action Agency, and Children's Hospital that formed a taskforce to investigate ways to improve the lives of infants and their mothers during the critical developmental period from birth to three years of age. The taskforce recommended high quality home visiting as a proven approach. ECS was created to form a consortium of local social service agencies to deliver either of two national models of home visiting, David Old's NFP or Healthy Families America (HFA).

Now, it was my turn to explain why home visiting was the best (most scientifically supported) way to achieve the objectives and goals that had guided the taskforce. About halfway through my 15-minute talk on the science supporting home visiting programs, I mentioned that one of the mechanisms by which home visiting was believed to obtain its positive outcomes was by delaying the birth of the second child.

The audience erupted – not at the brilliance of my explanation, but at its family planning implications! Gentlemen vigorously waved raised hands or shouted questions about exactly what ("the hell") it was we intended to do with these women in their homes. People turned in their chairs and began animated conversations with others around them. Impatient to be recognized, several men in the back rows stood up waving both arms. I didn't know what to do.

In the agitated flurry of noise and commotion that followed, I was hastily seated, and a moderator gave vague assurances that ECS was in no way about family planning, birth control, or abortion. It was about helping every parent become the very best they could be, which is true. Although no rotten vegetables were thrown, we were discreetly hurried out via the backdoor.

Back at the temporary office, we reviewed the political damage, which continued over the coming months. It culminated with the Hamilton County commissioners adding a clause to our contract, specifying that we could not talk to mothers about family planning or birth control – something we never intended to do.

We learned to be careful about which scientific data were emphasized with different audiences, and moved on. But not without disappointment at having to tailor our science-based message to the political and moral sensitivities of our audiences.

"Values trump scientific data!"

Why First-Time Mothers?

Very early in our efforts to build a coalition of Cincinnati metro-area social service agencies to provide ECS services, we convened a meeting at the United Way building. Gathering in the top floor conference room, participants selected seats around a squarish circle of folding tables. Choosing a chair, I looked around the room. Bob Ammerman and I were the only white males. There was one African American man, a minister. All the rest of the participants were women. Many were women of color.

Most seemed to know each other. Listening to a scattering of greetings and conversations, I would catch occasional edged remarks. Sensing an underlying tension, I assumed it was focused on ECS and the profound transformation we were going to impose on the local social services scene.

Waiting to begin, I became uncomfortably aware of how underdressed Bob and I were for what many attendees clearly considered a formal – and potentially adversarial – meeting. Bob and I wore ties and sports jackets, but we were, at best, wrinkled and shabbily tweedy. The Black minister was impeccably dressed in a pale-yellow three-piece suit with a crisp tie and three-pointed breast pocket handkerchief. The women were in business suits and carefully coiffed.

Given the shameful history of research with minorities, as "the science guys," Bob and I wanted to appear as open and approachable as possible. This is what we thought friendly accessibility looked like. But it occurred to me that our failure to dress more formally could be misinterpreted as disrespectful.

The meeting opened with an impassioned prayer by the preacher for the success of our combined effort on behalf of Cincinnati's children. Then, one of the women suggested we go around the circle of tables, introduce ourselves, and state what we hoped ECS would accomplish.

As my turn approached, I wondered exactly what was I going to say? When the spotlight reached me, I gave a two-part answer, which crystallized in the moment.

The first, was that I believed we should work to leave the world a better place – and, for me, helping children was the best way to do that. Second, based on my experiences as a child abuse doctor, I knew that the best way I could help children was to help their mothers.

The critical role mothers play, first came to my attention during FGDS, our longitudinal study of sexually abused girls. Evaluation timepoints 1 through 3 required a non-abusive guardian – usually the mother – to provide information about the child's development and home environment.

But on each visit, we also asked the mothers about their own childhoods (and memories of their parents) and mothering experiences. These extended interviews, conducted by Barbara Everett, PhD, in a comfortable, homey setting over coffee and pastries, were audiotaped and analyzed. Over the following decades, the original FGDS girls grew up and became mothers themselves (some are now even grandmothers). With their permission, we were able to include over 90 percent of their children in our Time 6 evaluation. Thus, we were able to gather information on mothering across three plus generations.

There is a seminal FGDS paper titled "The cumulative burden borne by the offspring of mothers sexually abused as children," that examines the range of impacts of adverse and traumatic experiences over time and across generations (Noll et al., 2009).

My colleagues and I referred to this groundbreaking article as the "rocks" paper, after Bill Harris's metaphor. Bill compared each bad event that happened to these kids to a heavy rock dropping into their backpacks. The rocks would have to be lugged around for the rest of their lives. The more rocks in their backpacks, the harder their lives became.

The paper is notable for a figure (see Figures 4.1a and 4.1b), conceived by Jennie Noll, that graphically represents the lives of the hundreds of women and children in our study as well as the types of rocks (abuse, depression, alcoholism, teen pregnancy, poverty, crime victimization, domestic violence, etc.) that were "dropped into their backpacks" at different points in their lives.

Figure 4.1 consists of two panels, 4.1a (Comparison girls, offspring and mothers) and 4.1b (Sexually abused girls, offspring and mothers), (Noll et al., 2009).

In the two panels of Figure 4.1 above, each horizontal line represents a child (labeled G3) born to one of the original FGDS children (labeled G2). The offspring (G3) of the matched comparison girls are on the first panel (Figure 4.1a). The offspring (G3) of the sexually abused girls are on the second panel (Figure 4.1b).

The X-axis (with the exception of the far left, broken, column on each panel) gives the ages of the original children (G2). Each offspring's (G3) horizontal line begins at the age of their mother (G2) when they were born and ends at the age of their mother when we evaluated the child.

Colored circles and squares representing an array of traumas and adversities (the "rocks"), are placed on the G3 lifelines at the ages that they first occurred. In some instances, they occurred to the mother (G2) before her

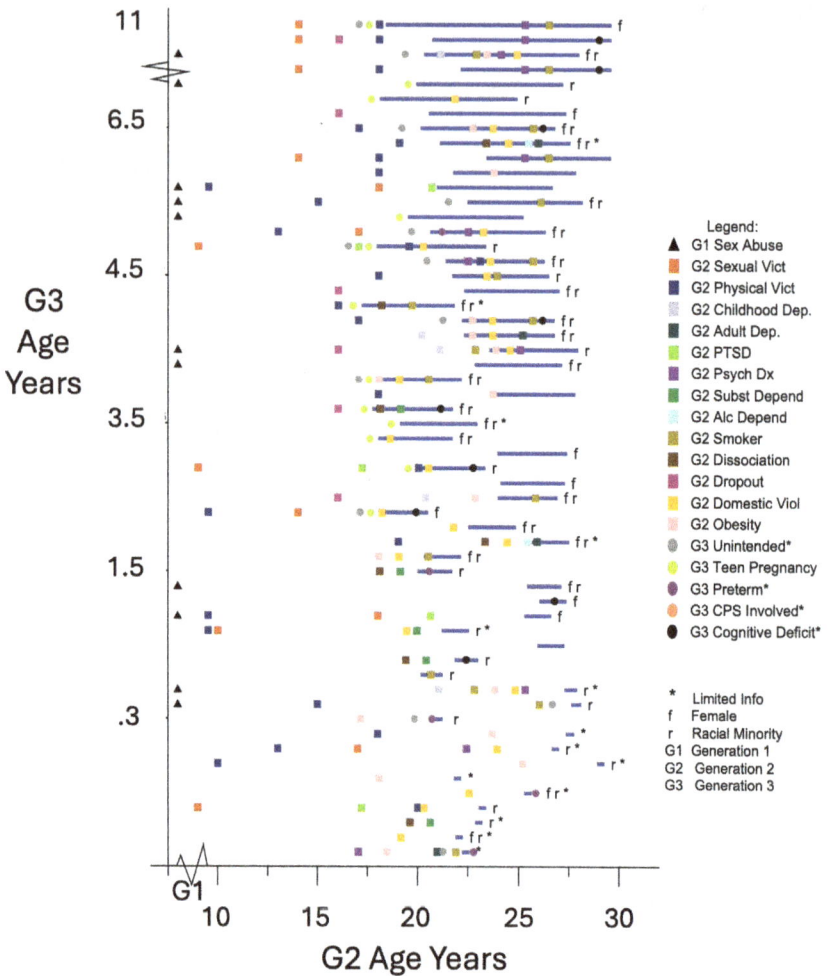

Figure 4.1 Transgenerational risk in (a) comparison and (b) sexual abuse families. (*Continued*)

Source: Noll, J.G., Trickett, P.K., Harris, W.W., & Putnam, F.W. (2009). The cumulative burden borne by offspring whose mothers were sexually abused as children: Descriptive results from a multigenerational study. *Journal of Interpersonal Violence*, 24:424–449.

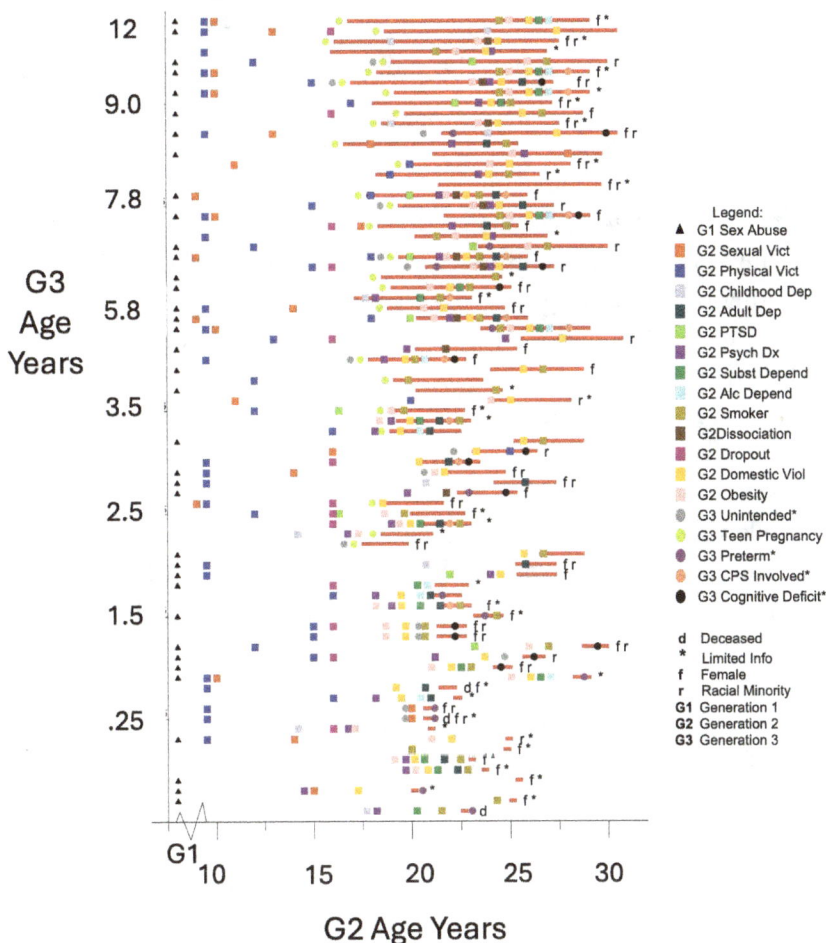

Figure 4.1 (Continued)

offspring (G3) were born. The Y-axis stratifies the G3 offspring by age from youngest to oldest.

The far left (broken column) on the X-axis of each panel contains black triangles for sexual abuse of the mothers (G1) of the original (G2) children (grandmothers of the G3 offspring). Inspection of the left most (broken) column of each panel shows that many of the mothers (G1) of the sexually abused girls (G2) were themselves sexually abused (black triangles). As a group, they also suffered significantly more childhood physical abuse, exposure to domestic violence, and parental loss and separation than mothers of the matched comparison girls.

A comparison of panels 4.1a and 4.1b conveys a powerful global impression of the enormous ongoing trauma and adversity in the lives of children born to mothers who were sexually abused in childhood, compared with the non-abused, matched comparison subjects.

It is clear, that while the matched comparison girls and their offspring (Figure 4.1a) inevitably experienced some trauma and adversity, the offspring of the sexually abused girls (Figure 4.1b) experienced significantly more. A comparison of the far left (broken) columns (labeled G1) demonstrates the high rate of childhood sexual abuse in the mothers of original sexually abused girls (G2), another powerful example of the intergenerational transmission of familial risk for child sexual abuse across generations.

Following the lives of the original (G2) children and their mothers, it became apparent that how well the mothers coped with the circumstances surrounding the disclosure and substantiation of their daughters' sexual abuse, was an extremely important factor in how well their daughters fared.

Disclosure of incest blows families apart. We saw this happen scores of times in the 12 years during which I was director of the Center for Safe and Healthy Children. Perpetrators were frequently the major breadwinners. A separation or divorce – or imprisonment – would often result in serious financial hardship for the mothers and children, food insecurity, and even homelessness. Bitter disagreements among relatives and friends, about the "truth" of the allegations, fractured family bonds and isolated the mothers, limiting their external support.

In the context of these hardships, mothers of abused children often became depressed and experienced guilt, anger, shame, and other powerful emotions, because of what happened.

As for the children, disclosing the abuse changed their worlds. Many had to move, lose close friends, and adjust to new neighborhoods and schools. They had to undergo stressful child protection investigations and, in the case of older children, even court testimony against a parent. Many children ended up spending time in foster or kinship care, until their nuclear families were stabilized. Some had to face tense, court-or-dered visitations with their abusers. And as the children matured and reflected on the abuse, emotions such as fear, anxiety, shame, depression, and self-blame often resurfaced, diminishing their self-esteem, distorting their core beliefs, and impacting their behavior.

If a mother believed and supported her daughter through the diffi-cult investigation and readjustment process, the child generally did well. If the mother doubted her daughter or blamed her for the abuse and breakup of the family – or if she competed with her daughter for the abuser's affections[4] – then the child did poorly.

When we surveyed the treatment that our child sexual abuse subjects received, we found that the focus quickly moved away from their child abuse experiences and feelings about the perpetrator and onto everyday behavior problems with their mothers (Horowitz et al., 1997).

By the mid-1990s, as strong intergenerational patterns of abuse, neglect, and adversity were emerging in the FGDS data, I began includ-ing statements in my presentations about the critical role mothers play in the recovery of their children, following sexual abuse.

As a society, we invest our limited resources to provide for the safety and treatment of abused children and for the rehabilitation of their per-petrators. But we offer little or no support for the mothers, who are fre-quently also the wives and partners of their children's sexual perpetrators. The best that most therapists can do (and still get reimbursed) is see abused children for an hour once a week for a few months. Few men-tal health services are provided for the mothers, even though they will (hopefully) be present and influential in their children's lives for years to come.

If we could help mothers deal with the trauma of their children's mal-treatment (and their own past traumas), they would be able to do more to help their children than any therapist ever could.

By the time I left the NIMH, I knew, unequivocally, that the mothers' mental health and functioning were intrinsically linked to their children's outcomes.

As ECS scientific director, one of our first findings was the high rate, almost 50 percent, of teenage mothers who scored in a clinically depressed range during the first nine months of ECS services (Stevens et al., 2002). In response, Bob Ammerman and I developed and validated an in-home, cognitive behavioral, postpartum depression treatment program[5] for struggling (often home-bound) young mothers (Ammerman et al., 2013).

Perhaps the most valuable insight I gleaned from ECS, was that first-time motherhood was an event like no other in the lives of these adolescent girls and young women. It was *the* moment when all of life's cards were up in the air and could be reshuffled – if only one could catch enough of them on the way down.

During this early period of new motherhood – the first year, really – first-time mothers were open to making enormous and difficult changes in their lives for the sake of their babies. What they were previously unwilling to do to help themselves, they did, because of their babies.

This key first year, then, is when prevention programs should address intergenerational maltreatment risk factors. It is the opportune time to offer education and training to first-time mothers (programs that accommodate the exhausting demands of new, often single, parenthood). This investment in the welfare of teenage mothers, has been proven to reduce mother and child poverty and use of public services over the long run. Of course, prevention and child wellness agendas must never compete with, but rather complement, new mothers' abilities to be the best parents they can possibly be.

I wore a business suit to "power" meetings at United Way and elsewhere, from then on. But irrespective of my casual dress on that day, I received welcome feedback that my answer was well-received.

Saving 40 Children A Year

As the "science guys," Bob Ammerman and I were tasked with putting in place a research infrastructure to determine whether ECS goals were being met. As part of our preparations, we met with representatives of the different domains of Cincinnati civic leadership. Listening to their expectations, it was clear that some of the local ECS promoters were making unrealistic promises about what the program would accomplish. Bob and I were, nonetheless, expected to fulfill them.

New, large-scale social welfare programs such as ECS do not take root and succeed without a great deal of prior political work at the local level.

Cincinnati community leaders were predominantly socially and politically conservative and, justifiably, proud of their city. They were determined to improve the lot of its most at-risk families. The estimated annual budget for a home visiting program sufficient to meet the Cincinnati metro area's needs, was about $25 million at the time. (As the business leaders liked to say, the same amount as annual interest payments on recently sold bonds to build new stadiums for the Reds and Bengals.)

Asking the Cincinnati philanthropic, business, and academic communities for this annual sum required big promises about what ECS was going to deliver.

One of those big promises was that ECS would save the lives of 40 children a year. The origin of the number 40 was a mystery, but, by the time Bob and I arrived in July 1999, it had been widely circulated and accepted as a fact.

At first, we didn't take it seriously. How could you prove you saved the lives of 40 children every year? Further, how do you prove that those 40 children were alive *solely* because of your program and not for other, unrelated reasons? Indeed, one of the major problems faced by scientists who study prevention programs is proving that something that *probably* would have happened did *not* happen because of the intervention. How do you count things that never happened?

When confronted with questions regarding the plausibility of scientifically documenting 40 saved children each year, some stakeholders replied that if ECS saved even one child's life, it would be worth it. Considering the huge amount of effort and money involved, it was in some ways a disconcerting rationale. We were getting ready to embark on a major fundraising effort and spend an enormous amount of time welding together a diverse group of (sometimes competitive) social service agencies into a single, large-scale, high-quality home visiting program. Our intention was to significantly improve the lives of tens of thousands of children and families.

In the lingo of the business community, ECS was going to "move the needle." It was up to Bob and me to determine if the needle "moved".

There was another uncomfortable source of tension around how Bob and I viewed our job versus how the business community viewed it. We believed our mission was to guide programmatic decisions and objectively evaluate their results, using the fledgling discipline of implementation science. But many business community leaders believed our roles were to make sure ECS succeeded (thereby boosting their civic standing) no matter what! A potential conflict of interest.

On one occasion, when we told the ECS executive committee that the data did not support a claim some important backers were making, we heard dark mutterings about "locking Frank and Bob in a room and sending in tap water and stale anchovy pizza, until they get it right." Being of the "*data is what data are*" mindset, Bob and I felt an impartial evaluation was within our capacity.

Crucially, we were ultimately able to prove that we did save many children's lives every year. The precise number of children was difficult to say, but it significantly exceeded "one child."

We matched the birth and death certificates of children served by ECS with the birth and death certificates of children eligible for ECS, but whose mothers either refused an invitation to join (there was about a 50 percent acceptance rate) or were never offered our services (instead of the 25 million dollars promised to us annually, we never received more than about 8 or 9 million in a good year, which severely limited our reach).

We found that children born to mothers eligible for ECS, but who, for some reason, did not receive it, were two-and-a-half times more likely to die in infancy than the babies of mothers who did (Donovan et al., 2007). We statistically controlled for confounding factors that could account for differences in infant fatality rates such as suboptimal prenatal care, maternal smoking, maternal age, previous fetal death, marital status, multi-fetal gestations (twins, triplets, etc.), and low maternal education.

Most significantly, ECS eliminated the enormous racial disparity between Black and White infant death rates. Nationally, the US mortality rate for Black infants at that time was 14.4 deaths per 1,000 live births, while the White infant mortality rate was 5.8 deaths per 1,000 live births. Both Black and White infants receiving ECS services had an infant mortality rate of about 5.0 deaths per 1,000 live births – essentially the same or slightly better than the overall US rate for White infants.

So, we saved the children, moved the community needle, and did much, much more to improve the lives of tens of thousands of families over the years. Think of how many more children's lives could have been saved or improved if we had been given the full measure of promised resources, particularly when the need for ECS increased during the Great Recession (2007–2009).

It comes down to how we, as communities and as a nation, value the lives of our children. Economic analyses show that for every dollar spent on these programs there is a return of between four to seven dollars in savings and taxes over time. Home visiting programs more than pay for themselves, while they reap long-term dividends through improved national medical and mental health. But, for our society, those saved dollars and dividends are somewhere far off in the hazy future.

The babies are here now.

Notes

1. NCTSN.org.
2. "Evidence-based/-informed" – the NCTSN has devoted considerable time and energy to defining and updating the scientific evidence supporting different child and adolescent trauma treatments.
3. Many discussions were held about whether the youthful home visitors (this was before the smartphone era) would (or even could) use computers to input data on home visits. We won the argument by pointing to the growing use of online shopping in that age group. The subsequent success of eECS led the business-oriented executive committee to spend untold hours trying to figure out how to turn eECS into a marketable product.
4. As implausible as it may sound, we have witnessed vicious mother/teenage daughter quarrels over the affections of some scummy perpetrator.
5. MovingBeyondDepression.org.

References

Ammerman, R.T., Putnam, F.W., Altaye, M., Stevens, J., Teeters, A.R., & Van Ginkel, J.B. (2013). A clinical trial of in-home CBT for depressed mothers in home visitation. *Behavior Therapy*, 44:359–372.

Ammerman, R.T., Putnam, F.W., Kopke, J.E., Gannon, T.A., Short, J.A., Van Ginkel, J.B., Clark, M.T., Carrozza, M.A., & Spector, A.R. (2007). Development and implementation of a quality improvement infrastructure in a multisite home visitation program in Ohio and Kentucky. *Journal of Prevention and Intervention in the Community*, 34:89–107.

Donovan, E.D., Ammerman, R., Besl, J., Atherton, H., Khoury, J., Altaye, M., Putnam, F., & VanGinkel, J. (2007). Intensive home visiting is associated with decreased risk of infant death. *Pediatrics*, 119:1145–1151.

Horowitz, L.A., Putnam, F.W., Noll, J.G., & Trickett, P.K. (1997). Factors affecting utilization of treatment services by sexually abused girls. *Child Abuse and Neglect*, 21:137–147.

Noll, J.G., Trickett, P.K., Harris, W.W., & Putnam, F.W. (2009). The cumulative burden borne by offspring whose mothers were sexually abused as children: Descriptive results from a multigenerational study. *Journal of Interpersonal Violence*, 24:424–449.

Olafson, E., Boat, B.W., Putnam, K.T., Thieken, L., Marrow, M.T., & Putnam, F.W. (2016). Implementing trauma and grief component therapy for adolescents and think trauma for traumatized youth in secure juvenile justice settings. *Journal of Interpersonal Violence, 33*:2537–2557. https://doi.org/10.1177/0886260516628287.

Stevens, J., Ammerman, R.T., Putnam, F.W., & Van Ginkel, J.B. (2002). Depression and trauma history in first time mothers receiving home visitation. *Journal of Community Psychology*, 30:551–564.

Van Ginkel, J. (2023). *Chasing Success*. University of Cincinnati Press.

5

INVESTIGATING ALLEGED
CHILD MALTREATMENT

The Mission

The core mission of the Center for Safe and Healthy Children was to conduct state-of-the-art forensic evaluations of allegations of child maltreatment, primarily sexual abuse, severe physical abuse, and medical neglect (failure to give a child the necessary medical care) occurring in the home or inflicted by close family members.[1] For substantiated cases, we provided access to treatment, legal and victim advocacy services, and referrals to community resources. In addition, center staff frequently testified in court.

To fulfill the interconnected elements of our mission, we assembled a core team composed of child protection investigators and their supervisors, special victims police officers, doctors and nurses, mental health providers, and prosecutors, as well as support staff. This core team was augmented by numerous individuals of various disciplines rotating through the center on temporary assignments or for training. We also depended on volunteer specialists in dentistry, ophthalmology, radiology, orthopedics, neurosurgery, and dermatology, who were willing to testify in court.

My challenge was to weld this collection of professions and people into a team, keep it functional, strengthen it, and deliver objective and

DOI: 10.4324/9781003593928-5   111

comprehensive forensic evaluations and appropriate follow-up services. Although the core professions interacted daily, each had its boundaries and domains of expertise that were its sole purview. It was my job to ensure that these diverse people and disciplines meshed optimally, so we could fulfill our mission to deliver safety, succor, and justice to the child and family.

Ensuring that these diverse disciplines shared essential information was critical. Each came at a case from a sharply defined professional perspective with strong, but often unspoken, assumptions. At times, communication was challenging. Developing and maintaining trust in each other was crucial. Processing staff trauma, both acute and cumulative, also proved to be essential.

For me personally, this new job meant a change in venue and values, moving from a research-oriented institution to a strongly service-focused one. I went from studying a select cohort of individuals and consulting on "special cases," to coordinating an array of forensic, treatment, and prevention services to aid children and families in crisis. I would also be influencing programs and policy at the local, state, and national levels. Increasingly, I sought to grasp the larger picture, looking for shared points of leverage among the many systems and agencies involved in child maltreatment and family violence.

Child Protection Investigators

The child protection/child welfare system is complicated and multilayered. It is not well understood, even by some who work in it. Outsiders have difficulty navigating it, and they certainly can't appreciate the stress, strain, and anxieties of CPS workers.

Our center had two teams of child protection investigators, one for sexual abuse and severe physical abuse and the other for medical neglect. Each team consisted of four to six home investigators who worked in cubicles in a central room, while their supervisors shared an office. The vast majority of the child protection investigators were young women, usually just out of college, in their first jobs.

They had tense, high-risk positions, as they frequently visited families with violent perpetrators in the home. At times, they had to remove a child against a family's wishes. They regularly encountered some pretty unnerving stuff. Like a lot of young adults recurrently facing stressful and disturbing situations, they developed a raunchy, in-group, shared sense of humor as part of their esprit de corps. Sometimes, after an especially traumatic case or tense situation, they let off steam back at the office. In general, we tolerated a certain amount of gags and horseplay by these brave women, which was confined to their section of the large, main room.

ECS had recently moved management staff out of several private offices to another building. I quickly endeavored to fill the precious, newly vacant offices with center staff who could use the space and privacy to better do their jobs. That didn't last long. My people were summarily banished back to their cubicles. Instead, two newly hired assistant vice presidents (VPs) and their support staff took possession of the spoils.

The first VP to arrive encountered the CPS workers celebrating a team member's birthday.

They had turned her cubicle into a "crime scene" festooned with yards of yellow police tape impounding a naked male manikin and baby doll posed in a perverted act. Arriving at the height of this bawdy celebration, the assistant VP was horrified. He screamed at them, threatening to fire everyone on the spot. Deb paged me in the clinic, saying that I needed to come immediately.

I arrived to find chastened CPS workers, a few in tears, huddled at the back of the main room by the law enforcement office. Near the front of the room, I could hear the assistant VP loudly ranting that he would not tolerate this kind of behavior in his offices. He met with very important people. He couldn't have them seeing this.

I scanned the crime scene cubical. Truthfully, it went too far in my opinion also, but I was going to defend these women. I'd been there myself. As a trainee rotating through a totally disorganized, crazy-making, county-run general hospital that suddenly went bankrupt leaving the training house staff and a few dedicated hospital personnel to care for scores of largely indigent patients until the university finally assumed management.

It was a desperate time. During those endless days and lonely nights, the house staff resorted to gallows humor to reduce tension. If outsiders could have heard us, they would have been scandalized. Change-over rounds was about the only daily event we looked forward to. Who could give the night on-call team a thumbnail sketch of their patients' probable medical course over the night in the funniest or darkest (usually both) fashion? The crucial medical information was in there, but dressed up in grim hilarity. At least it seemed funny at the time.

I called the blustering assistant VP into my office. Leaving the door open for all to hear, I told him that these weren't his offices, they were mine. That he had no say in how my staff behaved or decorated their cubicles. And what he didn't understand was how incredibly brave these young case workers were. And they sometimes needed to let off steam. I said these things several times in different ways, so staff in the cubicles closest to my office could hear. I trusted they would relay the message.

The assistant vice president was a narcissistic bully and quickly backed down from his sanctimonious rant in the face of my excoriation. He was visibly distressed that his staff could hear his dressing down. As a con-ciliatory gesture, I said that I would speak with the CPS workers about their overly exuberant birthday celebrations (which had been escalating in a tit-for-tat fashion). And I did.

But what was most important to me, was that the CPS case workers knew I had their backs.

Digging into the hospital's organizational chart, I was surprised to learn we had four levels of vice presidency: assistant VPs, associate VPs, VPs, and senior VPs. There were at least 64 people in hospital adminis-tration who were deemed VPs of some persuasion.

The assistant VP who had taken issue with my staff, was fired about eight months later. It seems he had a penchant for holding elaborately catered lunch meetings "with very important people." Typically, he ordered an appetizer from one restaurant, the entree from another, and dessert from a third. He was $50,000 over his entertainment budget. Apparently, the associate VP above him thought that was a bit too much. The other assistant VP hung on a year longer but was eventu-ally fired and replaced, although I don't know the reason. What I did observe, was that he spent hours every day shopping on his computer for neckties.

I concluded that health care systems could do with far fewer VPs and still improve their services – at considerably lower costs.

Cops

One of the greatest leadership challenges and a source of uneasiness for me, as the center director, was collaborating with the police. While at NIMH, I had consulted with the DC metropolitan police department employee support organization and occasionally the FBI. But I wasn't prepared for the tensions and compromises of working daily with police officers.

At any one time, our center was assigned four officers, two from the Cincinnati police department special victims unit and two detectives from the Hamilton County sheriff's office. They conducted our crime scene investigations. In addition, we reserved a desk for officers from other jurisdictions, who worked on occasional cases through our center. The officers rotated over multi-week intervals as they covered other departmental duties, such as night shifts.

Although housed side-by-side in a long, narrow, securely locked office, the two police departments did not always see eye-to-eye. There were also tensions between the center's police and hospital security – although they banded together well whenever we had a perpetrator loose in the building. While Deb discreetly handled many of the minor disagreements, I was the interface between the center's police and the hospital administration.

Shortly after the CAC team was in place, a child psychiatrist threw a tantrum. He vehemently insisted to hospital administration that I lock up the officers' guns when they were on hospital grounds, lest some "psychotic teenager" wrestle one away and commit mayhem. Caught between an annoyed hospital administration and the police and sheriff departments threatening to quit the center, I bought each officer a gun safe and told them that they were free to use it – or not. Shortly thereafter, the objecting child psychiatrist was fired for other reasons, and the issue disappeared.

But this brouhaha established that the police were going to do their own thing. We would have to accommodate – and sometimes cover for – them as best we could. They skirted numerous hospital policies and procedures required of employees and affiliated staff. For example, the officers shared hospital ID badges, parking permits, and other credentials, avoided getting their measles and mumps vaccines, and refused to comply with mandatory trainings and certifications required of affiliated hospital staff.

In what seemed a childish cat-and-mouse game, hospital security attempted to catch them in the act. Whenever security was successful, the hospital administration called me on the carpet and charged me with making the cops obey hospital rules and regulations. For me, it was a no-win situation.

Nurses and Doctors

Doctors trained in child abuse forensics, are required to either conduct or supervise, and sign-off on, forensic medical examinations as well as testify about the findings in court. Trained nurses are equally capable of conducting forensic child sexual assault medical examinations, especially in rural communities.

Under our medical director, Dr. Robert Shapiro, we aggressively supported having Pediatric Sexual Assault Nurse Examiners (PSANE) staff emergency rooms in small, rural hospitals around Ohio. Using "Scotty" phones (encrypted video terminals nicknamed after the communicators on *Star Trek*), the center doctors supervised nurses trained in our PSANE program. This version of telemedicine worked extremely well and demonstrated how a doctor's expensive expertise and authority could be leveraged far beyond local settings.

The doctors really earned their pay when it came to cases of Munchausen's syndrome by proxy and other medical conundrums. Every year, we evaluated half-a-dozen or so alleged cases. These ranged from a parent simply refusing to give up a cherished diagnosis that had been medically ruled out, to horrifying, potentially lethal, criminal acts, such as injecting feces into a child's central venous line.

Typically, we would start investigating an alleged case of Munchausen syndrome by carefully reviewing the child's (usually voluminous) chart, noting every diagnosis, relevant lab value, and radiological report. When there were major discrepancies between the doctors' findings and what the parent said the doctors had told them, we convened a conference (in person and by phone) of relevant prior physicians (who were often out-of-state) to clarify what was actually found, done, and communicated to the parent. Often, this was sufficient to determine whether there was a misunderstanding or deliberate deception.

In cases where we suspected medical fabrications (for example, sur-reptitiously putting blood in a child's diaper), we would hospitalize the child, using a special room with hidden cameras. (We always had a court order, usually for 24-48 hours of surveillance. The bathroom was typically exempt, unless we suspected the parent of flushing evidence down the toilet.)

If we believed the fabrication was potentially life-threatening, staff would watch the video feeds 24/7, at the ready to intervene. I was proud of everyone who stepped up to take these shifts, which were both boring and exceedingly stressful. Usually, nothing untoward happened. But with every parent-child interaction, one anxiously strained to see what was happening on the grainy black and white monitors. Using this method, we stopped several horrendous, life-threatening medical fabrications.

Prosecutors

Prosecutors are the gatekeepers to the courts; they must first accept a case before it can proceed. We worked with two types of prosecutors, civil (family court) and criminal. As CAC team players, prosecutors were a mixed bag. We loved a few of them but felt others shirked their duties, because they were only interested in accepting newsworthy cases that would guarantee them a win.

Most preferred plea bargaining, often to a much lesser charge. In a few tragic instances, child killers and sexual molesters were given short or suspended prison sentences for much lesser crimes. And not long after-wards, they killed or raped another child. This was always hard to take.

Our all-time favorite criminal prosecutor, Jim, was a special forces combat veteran. We knew Jim would do the right thing. And sometimes it cost him. Once, he indicted a popular private school principal for fail-ing to report that one of his teachers was sexually molesting students. Paradoxically, school parents banded together to support the principal. They pilloried Jim with letters to the newspaper and protests outside his office and home. Harassment, however, didn't stop Jim.

At the other extreme, was a county district attorney, who was always accompanied by an assistant, whose sole role seemed to be to stand behind the DA holding his overcoat. This DA refused to accept even the most egregious cases. Apparently, he was fearful that if he was seen as curtailing parents' rights to brutally abuse their children, it would cost him votes.

My experiences with prosecutors left me a tad cynical. I do recognize that child abuse criminal trials are an all-or-nothing, "beyond a reasonable doubt," win-or-lose proposition. And that, like a football coach, a prosecutor's win/loss record is a determinative factor in their career. Plea bargaining down to lesser charges allows them to enact a degree of punishment (and a scrap of justice) and claim a "win." But, sadly, plea bargains often undervalue victims' rights and fail to block dangerous perpetrators' future access to children.

Judges

Judges. What can one say about judges?

I have testified before judges. The center has held annual child maltreatment forensic workshops for judges (and prosecutors and defense attorneys). I have participated in child abuse trainings and panels at judicial conferences, including two state supreme courts. I've co-authored articles with judges. I've conducted discussion groups with judges on a topics ranging from forensic assessment to child mental health to secondary traumatic stress symptoms experienced by judges.

But I don't know judges. Nor do I understand all their decisions.

Judges, like a lot of complicated professionals, keep to themselves. They mostly interact with other judges.

Judges sit at a critical decision point in the child maltreatment legal journey – often the end-of-the-line. With children in front of them, they must make timely rulings that will profoundly affect the rest of those children's lives. Most judges feel a strong sense of responsibility to get it right. They want specific, detailed guidance, which, honestly, is impossible to provide. They are frustrated with academic types who can only offer probabilities and percentages. More than once, I've heard a judge describe lying awake at night agonizing over whether their decision was in the child's best interest.

Judges have high caseloads and a lot of paperwork. Their decisions are subject to critical scrutiny and reversal on appeal. They are expected to remain impartial, even in the face of personal threats or disruptive courtroom behavior. It is a lonely world in that they cannot share cases or decision making. They can't discuss their work with their spouses, partners, or best friends. Typically, they feel that they can't talk openly about their own problems and emotions or ask for help. As they witness similar tragedies over and over, they experience anger, frustration, and often a sense of helplessness and hopelessness about making a difference.

Judges are neither omnipotent nor omniscient. Nonetheless, they are expected to definitively "fix" the problem. They must weigh the expertise of the various "expert witnesses" who testify before them. They are required to communicate effectively with children and with people from other cultures in a courtroom setting. They must have the know-how to assess how their limited options will impact a child's psychological development or family dynamics.

Because child maltreatment and family violence are so often intergenerational and multigenerational, judges do sometimes encounter longer-term outcomes that they set in motion years earlier. Unfortunately, by definition, they rarely get to see rulings that turned out well.

So in my experience, most judges are very real human beings (with all the usual baggage) who work in demanding, lonely jobs, and are trying to do the right thing. And it takes its toll.

Coroners and Medical Examiners

One of the essential links in the medico-legal chain investigating potential child abuse fatalities is the local coroner or medical examiner. In general, coroners and medical examiners investigate violent deaths, unexplained or unnatural deaths, suicides, and the deaths of all infants and children under a certain age (typically two-years-old). Medical examiners are physicians, ideally board-certified in forensic pathology. In contrast, most coroners do not have to be physicians or to have any medical training at all. The vast majority (around 80 percent) are elected. In rural counties, the coroner is often a local undertaker or the sheriff.

In Cincinnati, the Hamilton County coroner was usually an MD, although rarely a forensic pathologist. Since its inception, our child abuse center had maintained an excellent working relationship with the coroner's office. The coroner allowed our trainees to attend autopsies of suspected victims of maltreatment. This gave us the added bonus of rapid feedback on preliminary results, which was important given time pressures related to protecting siblings or other children potentially at risk.

An autopsy is not an easy thing to watch. Even more so when it involves an infant or child. The coroner's staff was supportive of our trainees. On occasion, staff from the coroner's office came to our team meetings to present findings on complicated or ambiguous cases.

In 2000–2001, a local photographer, Thomas Condon, with the aid of a member of the coroner's staff, took hundreds of photographs of corpses posed with props as part of a "personal" art project. When eventually discovered, this repugnant scandal naturally received sensational local news coverage. Although the coroner, Dr. Carl Parrott, MD, had been cleared of knowing about his staff member's involvement, he was ensnared in the consequences. As election time rolled around, the previously well-regarded Dr. Parrott was far behind in the polls. O'Dell Owens, MD, a reproductive endocrinologist, was running against him.

Given the center's strong working relationship with Dr. Parrott, our medical director, Bob Shapiro, sought to personally support his re-election bid and held a fundraiser or two. Unsurprisingly, Parrot lost.

The next time our residents and fellows showed up to observe an autopsy of one of our child fatality cases, they were denied access by the newly elected Dr. Owens. He had taken Bob's interest in the election very personally. He also misinterpreted Bob's support of Dr. Parrott as reflective of Cincinnati Children's Hospital's official position, which was not the case.

Suddenly, we had a serious hole in our training program and were no longer privy to timely feedback on autopsy results. Bob met with Dr. Owens in the hope of making amends, but Dr. Owens' anger remained unwavering. Several difficult years followed, until another coroner was elected.

In 2007, Thomas Condon was convicted of corpse abuse and sentenced to two-and-a-half years in prison. He apologized to the 532 families affected (they won an 8 million dollar lawsuit).

Local Media

During the late summer and early fall of 2006, the tragic story of the abusive death of Marcus Fiesel, a three-year-old foster child, played out in daily headlines in local papers and TV news. The perpetrators were a married couple, Liz and David Carrol, who worked for Lifeway, a commercial foster-care agency.

According to the initial reports, Liz, a contract foster mother, took her brood, including Marcus, to play at a local park in Clermont County, Ohio. While at the park she suffered a very public fainting spell that attracted a crowd as well as emergency responders. When she was "revived," Liz became hysterical because Marcus was missing. Initially Marcus, an autistic child, was believed to have wandered off or to have been abducted while Liz was unconscious.

Marcus's disappearance triggered a massive search with police, dogs, helicopters, and hundreds of volunteers. Closely followed by local media, the fruitless search went on for days. About a week into it, Liz held an emotional press conference, tearfully begging whoever had taken her loving and beloved Marcus to return him.

Finding absolutely no trace of Marcus or any evidence that he had been in the park on that day, the police zeroed in on the Carrols. (Unfortunately, this wasn't the first time caretakers staged an abduction to hide a child's death.) Marcus's charred remains were eventually uncovered on an estate in Brown County, Ohio.

The horrifying story that emerged was that the Carrols were going to an out-of-state family reunion and didn't want to be bothered with Marcus. So they did what they had apparently done on previous occasions. They rolled Marcus up in a heavy blanket, wrapped it tightly with packing tape, and stuffed him in a small closet while they went away for two days.

When they returned, Marcus was dead. While deprived of food and water for at least two days, it was believed Marcus died from hyperthermia. In the August heat, temperatures in the small closet were estimated to have reached 110° F. The county social worker who monitored Marcus's case, twice attempted to see him, but was stymied by Liz's various excuses. Seeing the social worker's growing concern, Liz knew she had to create an explanation for Marcus's disappearance.

The belated discovery that Marcus had been dead for some time angered some in the media who, by focusing on the arduous but futile search and broadcasting Liz's emotional appeals, had unwittingly helped to perpetuate her deceit.

The president of the local chapter of Prevent Child Abuse America (PCAA), the oldest, largest, and best ranked non-profit devoted to preventing child abuse, alerted me to a behind-the-scenes situation developing at the local newspaper. She learned that the newspaper was planning to publish the names and addresses of all the foster parents in Hamilton County.

A reporter who had by-lined articles on Marcus's "kidnapping" felt deceived (as did everyone else) and was looking for a way to rectify her errors. She believed that printing the names and addresses of foster parents would increase public awareness and somehow avert another tragic foster-care death.

I knew that pedophiles would eagerly seize upon this information to identify and stalk children in foster care, who, as a group, are extremely vulnerable to victimization. A public meeting was arranged, where upon I debated with the reporter about the inadvisability of publishing the locations of children in foster care.

She righteously defended the public's need to know about foster children living near them, so they could be vigilant for possible abusing foster parents. The Fiesel case notwithstanding, I argued that pedophiles were a much greater threat than foster parents, who were regularly screened and monitored by county social workers.

Our debate became heated and ended without a resolution. So, I called the newspaper's editor, arguing that if they published the information, they would be printing "a roadmap for perpetrators." For whatever reason, the newspaper did not publish the names and addresses.

Multiple trials, appeals, and plea deals followed, as Ohio and Kentucky counties charged the Carrols (and the husband's girlfriend, Amy Baker) with Marcus's death and other related crimes. The barbeque pit used to incinerate Marcus's remains was demolished and replaced with a memorial. Lifeway lost its license. Over 50 changes were made to the Ohio foster-care system as a consequence of this heartbreaking case.

Unexpected, quasi-political situations, such as the vindictive coroner and the righteous reporter, occurred from time to time, revealing just how interdependent the mission to protect children is with local players and community institutions. Despite the refreshing informality of working in a children's hospital, I learned to come to work dressed ready to appear on local television news at a moment's notice.

Cases

There are innumerable personal accounts of severe child abuse in the media. These stories are augmented by numerous fictional dramas that include child maltreatment as a plot device or backstory. While the vast majority of stories are told from a victim's point of view, they are, in reality, highly filtered and shaped by the reporter, the co-author/ghost writer, the novelist, the editor or director, etc. who prepares the media version. These secondary, tertiary (and beyond) interpreters, usually have little deep knowledge of the complexities of child maltreatment, relying instead on making the first-hand accounts conform to the worn clichés and simplistic stereotypes that have been imprinted on us all by the media. These misguided editorial influences are instrumental, in my opinion, in perpetuating misleading and erroneous, but widely shared, mistaken beliefs about child maltreatment.

One of the goals of this book is to challenge some of the myths and misunderstandings based on misleading, media-promoted stereotypes that seriously impede progress in recognizing and understanding the long-term effects of severe child maltreatment.

In the evenings before I went home, I opened our electronic medical record and reviewed the completed cases waiting for me to countersign. I focused on the history, medical findings, mental status examination, and disposition of each. I typically reviewed about five to eight charts a day. Thus, over the dozen years in which I was center director, I reviewed many thousands of cases.

After reading a couple thousand charts, a strong sense of déjà vu sets in. Most cases followed a basic scenario: a father, live-in boyfriend, uncle, cousin, or older brother molested a very young girl, often for years. The largest age grouping we saw was 3- to 5-year-old girls. The next most common was 13- to 15-year-old girls. Boys, as we had first discovered while doing preliminary investigations for a male version of the FGDS, are relatively rarely seen in the CPS system after ages 9 or 10.

In all-too-many cases, the mother had moved back home to her family of origin where the perpetrator, who had abused her when she was a child, still lived. When I've asked mothers why they would expose their children to the same person who molested them, I was typically met with a defiant denial along the lines of: "He knew that if he did that to my daughter, I would kill him."

But he did do that to her daughter (often his grandchild). And, somehow, she didn't notice until it became glaringly apparent.

Also, too often, we had to live with the knowledge that a very young, essentially non-verbal, child was clearly abused, but we were unable to pinpoint the perpetrator. The child might have an STD (sexually transmitted disease) or seizures from abusive head trauma, but we couldn't be certain who the offender was. The reason for the uncertainty might be that several family members had the same STD or that a prime suspect had recently visited a doctor, but we weren't allowed access to his medical records. There were also instances in which young children showed clear evidence of abuse but, because they passed through the hands of multiple caretakers (all of whom swore the child was just fine when they handed him on to the next caretaker), we couldn't be sure of the culprits.

Admittedly, there are disheartening similarities across cases that can mislead one to think they are all the same. But upon deeper investigation, each is unique, distinct from the other.

Here are some examples.

Three Sisters

We were close to the end of the child abuse team meeting devoted to a family with three daughters. Gathered around the table in the large conference room, were the CPS case worker, her supervisor, a county social worker, the county civil prosecutor, the principal and a teacher from the girls' school, our clinical director, Heidi, and me. Just scheduling this meeting had taken considerable effort. The prosecutor was glancing at his watch.

The sisters were diagnosed with a rare gastrointestinal inflammatory autoimmune disorder that severely limited their diet and activity. The family was receiving a host of medical, educational, and social services. Still, the girls continued to deteriorate. Their school behavior swung erratically from uncontrollable disruption to spaced out lethargy. The two oldest were being treated for an eating disorder. Although their intelligence testing was in the normal range, they lagged far behind academically.

"Have you seen the girls break their diet? Have you seen them eat foods that are on the prohibited list?" The prosecutor was testing the teacher to see if she would make a good witness.

"Oh, yes. They either buy or trade for forbidden foods – especially cookies and candy – from other kids," the teacher confirmed.

"Can you give me some 'for instances' when you've seen this?" the prosecutor pressed.

"I caught S. eating a chocolate bar last week."

"What happened?"

"Nothing. She was fine. I didn't see anything out of the ordinary. Kids aren't permitted to bring candy bars to school. Parents know this. But some mothers put candy in their lunches or send a snack bag anyway. There isn't a lot we can do about it."

Finally, after multiple team meetings, we seemed on the verge of convincing a family court prosecutor that the sisters needed an out-of-home trial with a foster parent to see if their mother was somehow responsible for the girls' striking behavior changes and continued deterioration.

The conference room door abruptly opened. Standing in the doorway in a white coat and scrubs was Dr. P., a pediatric gastroenterologist. Dr. P. was considered a world authority on the girls' rare immune condition.

"How do you feel about placing the sisters with their aunt for about a month," the prosecutor asked Dr. P.?

"I can't support it," he replied. "I've scoped these kids many times. They have a real illness."

I experienced a familiar sinking feeling.

"Well, that's it," the prosecutor said, gathering his notes. "I can't petition the court for temporary custody if there is a doctor who says that their illness is real." The meeting broke up.

The most stressful thing about child maltreatment evaluations is that you can't afford to be wrong. You don't want to miss even one child who is being abused or neglected. Conversely, you don't want to mistakenly find maltreatment when none has occurred. There is a lot at stake for the child, the family, and society.

The majority of allegations that come to the attention of a child protection system are not substantiated on the first investigation.

In most jurisdictions the overall rate of CPS substantiations is about 25–30 percent. This does not mean that the maltreatment didn't occur. In many instances, the allegations reported to authorities are just not legally provable. In some cases, no clear perpetrator can be identified. And then there is an unknown (but probably substantial) percentage of actual cases that are never brought to the attention of authorities at all.

Sometimes it takes multiple reports and repeated investigations, perhaps spread over years, before the child protection system can substantiate an allegation. In which case the child has suffered cumulative injury.

This was the situation involving the three sisters, whom we evaluated and re-evaluated, off and on, over three years. Their mother claimed the girls suffered from a rare allergic condition that required special diets and educational arrangements. To outside observers, however, the draconian home remedies and severe dietary restrictions she imposed on the girls seemed to be contributing to their serious behavioral problems, educational deficits, and bulimic eating disorder.

Teachers and the school nurse reported that at lunch, the girls were observed eating forbidden foods with no ill effects. Their mother, however, reported that the same foods induced violent vomiting, bloody stools, excruciating abdominal cramps, and life-threatening allergic reactions.

We held multiple special meetings, initiated by county child welfare workers and school administrators, to address what observers considered pathological fabrications of the daughters' symptoms by the mother. The Damoclean sword hanging over our deliberations was the esteemed physician, Dr. P., who was ever willing to testify on behalf of the mother that her children suffered from a rare syndrome. Inevitably, Dr. P. – who was always invited to these special team meetings – dropped by toward the very end, stood in the doorway, and forcefully delivered his unwavering opinion that the girls suffered from a very rare, but nonetheless, very real medical condition.

On hearing that there was a doctor who would testify that there was a medical cause, the prosecutor would refuse to accept the case. This stark difference of medical opinions also made the hospital administration nervous. The last thing they wanted was a sensational child abuse court case in which the hospital's doctors publicly disagreed with each other. It wasn't good for anyone's credibility.

Our team was tormented by the belief that we were failing these children.

The parents were estranged but lived together. The father refused to meet with us or otherwise become involved in his daughters' care. CPS investigators felt the parents' mutual hostility contributed to the mother's need for outside attention.

The breakthrough came suddenly and unexpectedly. We had recently concluded yet another futile investigation into this case and were more convinced than ever that the girls were being harmed. Suddenly, their mother was hospitalized for a suicide attempt. Her husband had left her and returned to their country of origin. She overdosed on medications that had been prescribed for the girls.

Suicidally depressed, she admitted to fabricating the girls' symptoms and to giving them homebrewed emetic potions and hot pepper enemas to make them ill before medical examinations. Although she was not prosecuted, her confession was sufficient to justify greater child welfare involvement and mandated supervision.

During an out-of-home stay with an aunt, the sisters thrived and were able to tolerate normal diets. Despite protestations from Dr. P., their medications were stopped, without a problem. (I think the doctor was simply too in love with his rare disorder and, perhaps, saw himself as the embattled mother's medical advocate.)

Our ability to act on the results of our evaluations was sometimes constrained by the opinions of other professionals unfamiliar with the existence and dynamics of uncommon forms of child maltreatment. In this case, Munchausen syndrome by proxy.

Parental Trauma

In general, deliberately making false allegations of sexual abuse is rare – especially, relative to the number of actual cases. Although it is difficult to be certain, the few careful studies conducted found that this occurs in only a tiny percentage (typically 0.5–2 percent) of cases.

"She insists on talking with you," H., our front desk receptionist, said over the phone.

I knew that this mother must have exceeded a high threshold for H. to call me. H. manned the front desk of our walk-in reception and waiting area, registering families and scheduling interviews and examinations. She was extremely good at working with distraught parents and disturbed children. H. was also sensitive to the many demands on staff and only asked for help when she felt the issues were beyond her.

"Okay. Give me ten minutes. Can you bring her back or do I need to come out there?"

"I'll bring her back. Call, when you're ready." H. used her ID badge to buzz the upset mother through two locked doors meant to protect center staff from vengeful perpetrators.

I recognized the mother. Although I did not know her name, I had previously noted her in the waiting room.

"My daughter is being sexually abused. And *you* …," she said, pointing an accusing finger at me, "*you* aren't doing anything about it!"

I pulled up her daughter's chart from our electronic medical record and scrolled through the two recent visit summaries, which I had countersigned. Now, I remembered the case.

The mother had brought her ten-year-old daughter to us twice in recent months, claiming that her ex-husband was sexually abusing her. From the chart, I could see that the mother had also visited child advocacy centers in Northern Kentucky, Dayton, and Columbus looking for somebody to take the case. On both visits to us, the child's interviews were negative. In fact, the girl indicated that her mother had coached her to say that she was abused. On the first visit, no medical examination had been performed. On the second visit, she had a normal colposcopy.[2]

The parents had long been divorced. There were no court actions pending that might prompt false allegations. In fact, the ex-husband lived over a thousand miles away. He had previously denied seeing his daughter or being in the Cincinnati area in many years. The girl said that she had not seen her father since she was about seven.

Reviewing these facts with the mother didn't alter her convictions. During our discussion, I inquired if she had ever been a victim of the sort of thing she believed was happening to her daughter.

Bursting into choking sobs, she described her sexual abuse by a stepfather, which started at about the same age as her daughter. I did not question her further, but did provide her with local therapy resources. She never returned to our center.

Over the years, we saw a few similar examples in which a parent, who was a survivor of childhood sexual abuse, repeatedly alleged the (improbable) sexual abuse of their children by their spouse, often starting around the age that their abuse began. I think this transgenerational "anniversary" reaction is akin to the fear of dying some people experience when they approach the age at which a parent, with whom they strongly identified, dies.

What About Boys?

My pager went off about halfway through my morning commute. I stopped, waiting for a slow line of grimy black tank cars to clear the railroad crossing at the Ivory soap factory, and called the unfamiliar number. It was a hospital division chief.

"I didn't want to leave a voice message," she said. "It's about my son. I found out he was sexually assaulted at a wrestling tournament. Can I see you today?" The distress in her quavering voice was palpable.

"Of course. I'm about 15 minutes from the hospital. Give me a few minutes with my clinical director to see what the day holds. I'll call you."

Arriving at my office, I found the visibly upset division chief waiting impatiently. She described finding blood in her son's underwear while doing the laundry. After repeated emotional questioning, he admitted that he had been "broomed" by older boys on his team. He refused to name the offending teammates and begged her not to tell the coaches or anyone else. He was worried he would be blamed for sabotaging the team and made to pay for it.

"Brooming" involves anal penetration by a phallic object, such as a length of broom handle. But lots of bizarre objects have been used. I've seen a stick with notches carved for each victim. Brooming can become part of the initiation rites of sports teams, clubs, or gangs, inflicted by older members on initiates.

Victims are told not to tell their parents or other adults. And the victims who, in time, become the next generation of perpetrators stay silent for obvious reasons.

While the conventional stereotype of a child molester is an adult male, survey research finds that, statistically, the most common sexual molesters of children, both male and female, are other children, typically, males

(Gewirtz-Meydan and Finkelhor, 2020). The majority (approximately 60 percent) of these sexual assaults involve acquaintances or friends. Despite knowing the identity of their perpetrators, most youth-on-youth sexual assaults are never reported and therefore not counted in official cases.

Many male victims tend not to regard these assaults as "sexual" in nature but, rather, as acts of intimidation and dominance. Instead of classic PTSD symptoms, male victims report feeling ashamed, humiliated, and guilty. They worry most about being ostracized by peers.

In this instance, we examined the division chief's son. Fortunately, his anal injuries were healing well. The forensic investigation was referred to the downtown CPS unit, which handled out-of-home sexual assault cases. We provided his mother with referrals to experienced child trauma therapists.

About a year later, I asked her how her son was doing.

At first, she said "okay." Then she bitterly added that he had felt forced to change schools because of the CPS investigation. Ultimately, charges were never filed against the perpetrators, who were allowed to graduate. The coaches denied knowing that brooming or other types of hazing were going on among their teams.

The greatest disappointment of my career, is that we were unable to conduct a parallel, longitudinal study of the growth and development of sexually abused boys. For years, Penny and I attempted to interest federal and foundation funders in a male study similar to the FGDS. As we learned more about the profound biological and psychosocial impacts on girls, we submitted pilot grant proposals to test the methodology and demonstrate the feasibility of an "MGDS." But sadly, there was never any serious interest in boy victims on the part of funders.

As we wrote these proposals, we investigated referral sources for sexually abused boys aged 6 to 15 years. The same child protective services agencies from which we recruited the sexually abused girls rarely saw boys after about age 9.

This was before the shocking revelations about the Catholic Church, the Southern Baptist Convention, the over 80,000 Boy Scout victims, the elite prep school scandals, and the outing of athletic and youth organizations harboring serial sexual molesters of boys. Now we know the male child sexual abuse victims were always there – and still are. The safeguards currently in place to protect children are likely missing the majority of sexually abused boys.

We also know that young boys are extremely vulnerable to early trauma and adversity. This was first (and best) documented by research on the effects of maternal depression on offspring. Boys, especially early in life, are highly vulnerable and far more negatively affected by maternal depression than their sisters.

In part, the increased sensitivity of males to early life stress is thought to be related to the fact that male brains are less developed at birth and mature more slowly than female brains. Which is why, in general, girls outperform boys socially and academically during the preschool and elementary school years.

Given the profound examples of psychobiological dysregulation that we were finding in sexually abused girls, there is every reason to hypothesize that analogous biological, developmental, and behavioral effects occur in sexually abused boys.

Many years later, we were able to compare a large sample of traumatized youth, aged 1.5 to 18 years, almost evenly divided by gender, from the NCTSN's core data set (Putnam et al., 2020). We found notable differences regarding which combinations of trauma and adversity significantly contributed to severe behavior problems in boys and girls at different ages. As a scientific field, we have yet to analyze enough large, representative samples using well-accepted measures to make definitive statements about which combinations of trauma and adversity are universally negative for males and females of all ages and which trauma-related outcomes are unique functions of gender, age, or circumstances.

Based on current data, sexual abuse, especially in combination with physical abuse, neglect, or exposure to domestic violence, is the most pernicious form of childhood maltreatment for both males and females (Putnam et al., 2020). However, sexual abuse impacts males and females differently depending on the age at which it occurs, the relationship to the perpetrator(s), how long it persists, and other contextual variables.

We have a lot to learn about male victims.[3] Especially now that we know there are large numbers of boys who have been sexually abused across a range of contexts. As clinicians, researchers, and, most importantly, as a society, we have seriously failed male sexual abuse victims.

The volatile – and sometimes violent – male MPD cases I encountered early in my career, are only one of many devastating outcomes of severe childhood abuse and adversity in males.

Disclosures of Sexual Abuse

Waiting for a child abuse team meeting to begin, I leaned over and asked the detective seated next to me, "What percentage of child sexual abuse cases do you solve with trace evidence?"[4]

On crime shows, trace evidence figures prominently in solving rapes and murders.

He thought for a moment, "I don't remember a case."

Sexual abuse, unlike physical abuse and neglect, rarely leaves clearly discernable signs that an outside observer is likely to recognize. Hypersexual behaviors offer a clue but are difficult to document, unless someone (such as a teacher or daycare worker) repeatedly sees the child interact with other children or adults.

Casual observers unfamiliar with the sexuality of children (yes, it does exist) of various ages, genders, and identities, have difficulty distinguishing normal from not-so-normal behavior. Plus, so much of what a given observer considers "normal" is a function of that observer's age and personal history. (Consider generational differences in the acceptance of explicit sexual lyrics in pop songs or in the public expression of nonbinary sexual identities.) Therefore, facilitating a child's or adolescent's disclosure of abuse takes on extra importance and scrutiny. But disclosures, when they happen, are often complicated processes that can play out in ways that obscure the underlying message.

Retrospective studies of adults who report histories of childhood sexual abuse find that one-half to two-thirds never told anyone about the abuse while it was occurring. Of the third or so who did disclose to an adult, many of them say the adult did not report it or, if it was reported, no action was taken. Studies of adults who, as children, did disclose their CSA to an adult, found that the interval between the onset of the abuse and their disclosure is typically three to five years. (This parallels the delays in #MeToo-type disclosures that often occur years after the incidents and may be encouraged by disclosures of others or by recent events.)

There can be a variety of explanations for these delays. First and foremost, children do not always recognize or understand that what is occurring is abuse, they think it happens in every family. Or abused children may see themselves as "co-conspirators" or "willing" participants. They may be afraid no one will believe them and may have already met with denials and shaming. They may be concerned about the devastating effects of a disclosure on their family or that the perpetrator/caretaker will go to jail.

Some children describe the relationship with their perpetrator as "positive." In one study, over half of children said that they "loved" their perpetrator. In general, the closer the familial relationship with the perpetrator, the more reluctant the child is to disclose abuse.

Perpetrators often enforce victim secrecy in a couple of ways. The first, is as a "special secret" that must only be shared between perpetrator and child or something terrible will happen. This works with younger children. With older children and teens, perpetrators enforce silence through physical coercion and threats of harm or death to the victim, family members, friends, or pets.

The misleading stereotype that an incest disclosure happens as a single, discrete event, is a bit like the mistaken "shattered mirror" myth. The CSA is rarely revealed as a single, emotionally explosive, but chronologically linear, detailed narrative – like a crime report. In fact, many disclosures play out as protracted processes with a gradual unfolding of details, confounded by hesitations, avoidance, and even retractions that fragment and cloud the narrative.

Disclosures are often triggered by events, most commonly exposure to or proximity of the perpetrator. In younger children, inappropriate comments or sexualized behaviors may lead to investigation. In adolescents, conflicts with adults may trigger disclosures made to justify their angry or oppositional behavior, which, unfortunately, may mistakenly discredit their disclosure. For teens, educational programs, television dramas, and disclosures by peers and celebrities may also influence them to disclose their own abuse.

Most often the disclosure is to a non-abusing parent, followed by a close friend. The quality of the relationship is critical. Children with a supportive parent (usually the mother) are about three times more likely to disclose than a child with a non-supportive parent. The severity of the abuse is not clearly related to a child's likelihood to disclose. In fact, studies have found that children with genital contact sexual abuses are less likely to disclose than those who experience non-contact CSA. Boys are significantly less likely to disclose than girls.

Recantations of disclosures, while not common, complicate the search for the facts. Common motivations for taking back accusations include threats from perpetrators, pressure from family members, and negative consequences, such as removal from their homes. Retractions are highest in the six- to ten-year-old range, particularly among boys. However, a large percentage (more than 90 percent, according to one study) later reaffirm their disclosure.

Sexually abused children often have severe behavioral problems and psychiatric symptoms such as depression, anxiety, PTSD, dissociation, suicidality, self-harm, sexual offending, aggression, and eating disorders. These symptoms and behaviors may lead to referrals for mental health treatment, during which the child or teen discloses CSA.

Standard therapeutic techniques used with younger children may promote disclosure – these include play therapy, drawing, story stems, role-play, and naming feelings. Journaling, trauma narratives, and group therapy may evoke disclosures by adolescents. Disclosures made in therapy are to be expected, because it's where children usually feel safe and listened to. (Contrary to what some people might insist, such disclosures are not "false memories" implanted by malevolent therapists.)

It is clear that, unlike fictional crime shows, we can't depend on trace evidence to solve cases.

However, today's social media-savvy, techno-adept younger generations have a powerful tool to document their abuse – smartphones.

"Confessions"

There are very few clear-cut "wins" in child abuse forensic evaluations. Great saves are rare and far between. Our cases came to us after – sometimes long after – a child's maltreatment had started. You cannot prevent or undo what's already happened.

The best we could do was to try to protect the child in the future and provide (time-limited) services. In the real world, most of our options were less than satisfactory, prone to their own problems, and far, far less than what was really needed. There are limited choices and scant resources.

In the trenches, staff desperately needed something that symbolized victory, so we grasped at proxies. Unfortunately, alleged perpetrator "confessions" all too frequently were viewed as winning touchdowns. This was especially true for the most egregious cases – those whose victims were shaken-babies with brain damage (dead or living), starved and beaten children raised in closets or dog cages, and tortured children pockmarked with cigarette burns or branded by BIC lighters.

In addition to ensuring safety, part of a child advocacy center's mission is to support restorative justice for the child. But justice is, at best, a long and complicated process that must slowly wend its way through a byzantine legal system. It took at least a year before cases we evaluated made their way to trial. Frequently, we were subpoenaed for records of cases that we had seen three, four, or more years prior. The doctors, social workers, and CPS investigators involved, especially our trainees and fellows, might well have taken new jobs out of state and not be available for testimony.

Whatever the legal outcome, at best only a handful of staff might remember the case. If there was a conviction, it was often for a much lesser charge – for example, "child endangering" – rather than the murder or sexual assault charges that would be applied to an equivalent adult victimization. We might hear about a conviction incidentally or never – capriciously depending on word of mouth. There is little feedback from the distant justice system to the child protection front lines.

Confessions filled the bill as proxies for victory. They usually happened within a couple of days after a child was admitted to the hospital or died. They were closely linked, in time and emotion, to events. When the cops got a confession, the news quickly spread through the center. Passed from one staff member to another through in-house social networks, it would reach me repeatedly over the course of a day, usually in the form of an emotional question.

"Did you know that alleged perpetrator X confessed to the killing/burning/starving/beating/sexual abuse of child Y?" Often there was a breathless, excited quality – as if this were news to be shouted from the rooftops.

As center director, I was pleased whenever anything happened that improved staff morale, especially when it reflected well on the largely thankless work we were doing. So, in the first few years, I was as gratified as everyone else whenever the cops obtained a confession. But somewhere along the line I began to have doubts.

The cops who worked with us, especially the special victims officers and detectives detailed to our center, were among the finest law enforcement professionals I have ever known. "John and Jane Q. Citizen" will never understand nor appreciate what they owe these women and men.

A few however, found child abuse too disturbing a beat and went back to other police units that promised clearer-cut victories. My all-time favorite police officer, J., abruptly returned to the homicide division after a sexual abuse sting went horribly wrong. A 17-year-old girl with a full athletic scholarship to a top university ran away to live on the streets after disclosing to J. years of incest by her socially prominent father. Following her disclosure, the father died by suicide. For years afterward, J. spent her free time searching for that girl – without luck.

When I left Cincinnati Children's Hospital, the cops gave me a ceremonial nightstick (truncheon) as an honorary partner of the Cincinnati police department. I knew many of them professionally and socially for years and liked and respected them. They are good people, albeit sarcastic and cynical professionals.

But, as a group, cops are also a highly competitive bunch. For them, confessions are notches on a gun – a coup, a score, the finish line. Case closed!

At first, the confessions occurred downtown at the police station. All we knew was what we were told. Much of the time the details fitted the injuries we saw. Occasionally, the details didn't seem to fit a child's injury, but there is sufficient ambiguity in child abuse forensics that we weren't especially troubled.

A confession is the "gold standard" – right?

I first became concerned about confessions when a couple of cops – one of our regulars and his superior from downtown – approached me. They had detained a father who was visiting his severely brain-injured baby daughter in the intensive care unit.

"Doc, we're sure he did it. Can you go in and tell him that you have run a test on the baby that one hundred percent proves that he did it?"

I was incredulous and naively explained that there wasn't any such test.

"Oh, we know there's no test – but he doesn't. Just tell him that you have a test that one hundred percent proves that he did it. That's all."

"But that would be lying."

"It's okay to lie to a suspect. The Supreme Court decided that ages ago."[5]

Of course, I didn't oblige. But that was only the first of several occasions where the police asked me to lie to a suspect in the same way. As far as I know, none of the other physicians at our center ever went along with such requests. But it got me concerned about confessions.

In the beginning, our center had two interview rooms with state-of-the-art video recording. One had adult-sized furniture for older children, the other a small table and chairs for younger children. Painted a tranquil blue or soothing green, with only a large analog clock on the back wall, the interview rooms were meant to be as non-stimulating and calming as possible. We offered the children paper and colored pencils so they could draw during the interview. This would enable them to avert their gaze while telling their story. The drawings were not forensically or psychologically analyzed, unless the child specifically flagged something as being relevant to the allegation. They could keep their pictures if they wished.

Two cameras recorded each interview. One was in the team observation room and recorded through the one-way mirror. An observer behind the mirror could pan and zoom a high-quality image. We usually left it focused on the child's face, rarely fiddling with it unless the child moved around a lot.

The second, a wide-angle camera, was mounted high up in a far corner of the interview room and aimed at the one-way mirror, behind which the CAC team sat watching the forensic interview. The reflection of the entire room in the mirror showed that there was no one off-camera influencing the interview. The image was digitally inset in a corner of the first camera's recording. A date stamp, with a digital clock, was embedded in another corner of the video. The children and their parents were told about the cameras and the people behind the mirror, before the interview.

After seeing our interview set-up in action, the police began to ask if they could use it for cases in which parents and family were visiting an allegedly maltreated child in the hospital. We declined, because we had a policy never to knowingly allow a recognized or suspected perpetrator into our center – it would endanger the children with whom we worked.

Eventually we compromised. Because many family visits occurred in the evening when our center was closed, the police could use the interview rooms after hours. This required at least one staff member (usually Deb) to remain and run the recording equipment. As law enforcement (including FBI and Department of State) requests to use our center interview rooms became more frequent, I was determined to move this activity out of the clinical area.

Fortunately, we were awarded a grant that allowed us to wire up a third room that would serve many functions. Privately accessed from a side hallway, we used it for therapist training, therapy sessions, research, and police and FBI interviews. As part of the project, a dedicated monitor and headphones were installed in my office, allowing me to observe the room remotely. This was especially useful for monitoring training and supervising treatments. It also allowed me to watch law enforcement interviews of suspects and special victims. Most of the time I did not tune into these, but over the years I watched enough to form an opinion.

I'll share what I've told others. If the police arrest you and take you to the station for anything – and I do mean anything – no matter how innocent you truly are, do not talk to them without your lawyer present. Deception, in the interest of interrogation, is an integral part of police training and culture.

I've heard officers gleefully swap stories about the dumb things they were able to convince suspects of (for example, that if the room telephone rings while the suspect is answering a question, it means he is lying). The police also strongly believe in the validity of polygraphs and voice stress analysis, although scientific studies show that such "lie detectors" are no better at determining guilt than flipping a coin.

This mentality around suspect interviewing, is the legacy of the "Reid technique," a police training method developed in the 1950s. Even during an interview with a known child abuse victim, police tended to quickly slip into the Reid interrogational approach, treating the victim as if s/he was the victimizer.

The Reid technique interprets all non-verbal signs of anxiety and discomfort as definitive evidence that the person is lying. Regrettably, it does not account for the ways in which anxious children and traumatized adolescents fidget and verbally stumble when they feel intimidated.

We owe both victims and alleged perpetrators the most objective and the highest quality forensic evaluations we can deliver. We have only begun to examine day-to-day operations in the messy, real world of child protection investigations. Since it is estimated that by age 18 years, one-third of US children are in some way touched by CPS (which addresses child abuse, neglect, and exploitation), it is critical that we fund research to improve it. Doing so will impact the lives of literally millions of children and their families every year.

Stings

Stings make for good theater. They appeal to a sense of poetic justice, turning a sexual predator's self-blinding depravity against himself.

As director, I regularly witnessed or heard details of the stings police had conducted from our center. These usually involved older children and teenage victims who would, on a taped phone call, confront their perpetrators about long-existing patterns of sexual abuse. The victims were coached to bring up specific, verifiable incidents that the abuser had to acknowledge and respond to.

A surprising number of perpetrators apologized to their victims, asked for forgiveness or talked about their own guilty feelings. Some expressed surprise that their victims didn't view the sexual abuse as acts of "love." Only a few realized, too late, that they were being ensnared by their own words. At least one committed suicide after the phone call.

I was not involved in the authorizing, planning, or executing of these stings; I was a mere observer. They were set up by the center's cops, using a phone line in the small conference room that was rigged for audiotaping. So, I routinely encountered stings in progress or heard about them at team meetings. In general, they were effective at extracting from perpetrators incriminating acknowledgement of the abuse.

As a participant in various internet child abuse prevention task forces and training, I attended presentations on state-of-the-art (at that time) internet stings. They involved text messaging and exchanging of photos; it was before video chats became common. An officer would impersonate a confused, underage girl in a chat room or on a message board. The "girl" was looking for love or to have her first sexual experience.

Presenters loved to show side-by-side the photo that the perpetrators sent the "girl" – usually of an older "heartthrob" teenage boy – next to the perpetrators' mug shot. The perpetrators were some of the most disgusting "dirty old men" that you have ever seen.

For the sting, a face-to-face meeting would be set up at a public place in another city (so the predator had to travel out of his way). One fast food restaurant parking lot hosted more than a score of stings, until word spread among pedophiles. One of the first things cops would do during an arrest, was to seize the printed Google Maps directions from the perpetrator's front passenger seat (today, their phones are confiscated). This would establish that he acted on information sent by the "victim."

I don't know what the prosecutorial success rate is for this type of sting. But, for the officers, they were more sanctimoniously satisfying than processing the huge backlog of rape kits, which would probably take more perpetrators off the internet and the streets.

One major network carried a multi-season program, *Dateline: To Catch A Predator*, that used similar methods to generate dramatic content. The series had been canceled, following a lawsuit by the family of an alleged perpetrator who killed himself as the police and camera crew stormed in. Today, livestreaming enables individuals to post homemade versions of *To Catch a Predator*. This is lunacy masquerading as righteous revenge. But it generates millions of followers, likes, views, re-tweets, and other cyber tokens of influence.

Like other forms of vigilantism, homemade stings virtually guarantee that alleged perpetrators, no matter how guilty, will evade justice. Stings should be left to professionals, rather than self-appointed citizen enforcers.

The criminal justice system must continuously pursue and adapt to the latest social media technology, not only because it changes the nature of predator-victim interactions (and therefore the types of legal evidence), but it spreads fraudulent child abuse conspiracy stories (like "Pizzagate") that incite true believers to violence.

Revictimization

My awareness of revictimization (a pattern whereby first-time child abuse victims later have a high rate of repeat victimizations by non-family members) began early in my research with dissociative adults. Later-life victimizations by non-family members were part of most of the histories of the adult MPD subjects in my NIMH studies. However, I really tuned into adult revictimization as a common post-childhood abuse outcome when I volunteered as a consultant to the Prince Georges County Rape Crisis Center (Maryland). Over two years, I evaluated more than a dozen victims who were seen by the rape crisis center three, four, or more times for alleged sexual assaults.

Common sense would suggest that these previously victimized women should have been the wariest of people, with a "once burned, twice shy" mindset. Instead, many of them were on an escalating trajectory in which the intervals between "stranger" rapes (as opposed to acquaintance rapes) decreased, as the number of incidents increased. In fact, more than 20 cross-sectional, retrospective studies have found that adults with histories of childhood sexual abuse are at significantly higher risk for stranger rape than are non-abused comparison adults.

After having heard me present on dissociative disorders to the Prince Georges County Rape Crisis Center staff, the director, Lynn, asked me to consult on a woman who kept "finding" herself tied up and sexually abused in makeshift basement "torture chambers" and "dungeons." Her accounts of the different episodes were startling, but they shared a common thread of suddenly "coming to," bound, gagged, and blindfolded, with various fetish devices being painfully thrust into or clamped onto her. Even in public settings, such as a restaurant, she might suddenly become aware of a man's hand in her bra or underpants. She was unable to recall how she had gotten into these situations (and, therefore, how she might have avoided them).

As a consequence of this woman's narrative, and similar extraordinary accounts, when Penny and I conceptualized the FGDS, revictimization was one of the outcomes I wanted to track forward in time.

We looked at revictimization twice over the course of the FGDS and found essentially the same results both times (Noll et al., 2003; Barnes et al., 2009). The sexually abused girls were more than twice as likely to be sexually and/or physically assaulted by a strange male, at least one or more times, than the comparison girls. Their rapes and assaults were also more likely to result in serious injuries. For subjects who had experienced multiple rapes and assaults by strangers, the interval between episodes decreased as the number of events increased.

Psychoanalysts conceptualize this repetition of trauma as a compulsion or identification with the aggressor or an attempt at mastery. I'm not sure any of those explanations work. I believe the pattern of revictimization is due to the following two contributing factors: "coy" ("sexual" mixed messages), non-verbal behaviors, which we documented in the very first minutes of the FGDS with the Strange Man protocol; and, perhaps most powerfully, increased levels of dissociation in incest victims.

When pimps describe the signs and behaviors they look for to identify their prey, dissociative behaviors, especially dazed or trancelike mental states, are critical "tells." Often, they approach potential victims and attempt to evoke an even stronger dissociative reaction by casually mentioning the girls' fathers, uncles, or other male relatives. They know exactly what they are doing. They are that calculating, that evil.

Trauma is cumulative. Understanding the special vulnerabilities that child sexual abuse victims have for revictimization in adulthood, is essential for effective treatment – and necessary for multigenerational prevention. As disconcerting as it may be to acknowledge that child sexual abuse victims are at greater risk for sexual assault when they are adults, it is necessary to remember, *data is what they are*.

Secondary Traumatization

Our child advocacy center evaluated well over a thousand children and their families every year. In most instances, the parents were stressed and frightened, and sometimes angry, shocked, and horrified. The children were equally distressed – in part, in reaction to their parents. They regressed to using basic coping mechanisms, ranging from semi-catatonic muteness to off-the-wall hyperactivity. This intense family upset impacted the staff in ways large and small. Without question, the Center for Safe and Healthy Children was a challenging place to work.

Pausing outside the closed door to the "sorority," as we called the office shared by the center's social workers, I hesitated a long moment before knocking.

A young boy had just died from horribly abusive injuries. The closed door was a sign that the social workers, who shared the half-dozen desks lining the walls, were processing his death.

"What!" came an angry response to my restrained knocks.

"It's me, Frank."

"OK. You can come in."

I felt privileged to enter. Pulling up a chair, I sat quietly, listening to the outpouring of grief and anger about the unspeakable horrors the child suffered. Most of our social workers were mothers. These brutal deaths always hit hard. The first time I encountered a young child's abusive death, as a child psychiatry fellow, I tried to tell Karen that evening. I couldn't get the words out. I just cried.

Like a cold, the flu, or Covid-19, you can catch post-traumatic stress from someone else. That is, if you have been in the company of a severely traumatized person who has shared the details of their trauma – and especially if you've listened to stories of people's trauma on a regular basis – you may become traumatized, without ever being directly exposed to the source of trauma yourself. This is referred to as secondary traumatic stress or vicarious traumatization. Either way, your post-traumatic stress comes from being around people who were traumatized.

I first became aware of secondary traumatic stress while we were working on the Time 2 and Time 3 evaluations of the sexually abused girls in the FGDS. Leaving one staff meeting, I recall thinking that we spent at least a third of the time talking about how distressing it was for the research assistants to hear the details our subjects spontaneously shared about their abuse.

After tracking this over several more staff meetings, it became evident that we were spending a substantial percentage of time processing what had happened to the sexually abused girls and how it was affecting the research assistants. I began leaving time for this in staff meetings.

At Times 2 and 3 we were getting our information about the abuse histories from two basic sources – the child protection investigation records (all were CPS-substantiated cases) and interviews with the non-abusive guardians, usually their mothers. The girls, however, knowing that they were in a study of the effects of sexual abuse, sometimes volunteered details during their psychological testing or medical examinations. The explicit details were disturbing. Many of the abused girls were deeply troubled.

None of the research assistants or graduate students working on the FGDS developed fully fledged PTSD from what they had learned about our subjects. They were, however, visibly distressed by it. At least, we all believed, the horror was past. The crime had been reported and safety measures were in place. In most cases the perpetrators were in jail or out of the picture. So as far as we knew, the terrible abuse was over – or so we thought at the time.

We did not know then that past trauma begets future trauma. How, once victimized, many sexually abused girls go on to be re-victimized in the future – often repeatedly.

The next time I confronted secondary traumatic stress, it was taking an enormous toll on my staff and colleagues.

The abused children's stories evoke intense emotional and protective responses in those who interview and examine them and are responsible for ensuring their safety. When you sit with these children, as they describe what was done to them – it affects you powerfully. And when you see hundreds of these children every year, the cumulative weight of their tragic stories and pain-filled lives bears down in ways that defy words.

Deaths evoked the strongest reactions. At the same time, they helped to momentarily release the rage and profound sadness we felt. Often, we would gather in the large conference room, share food – sweet, sugary food – and just be together. Someone would start talking about how wrong, how unfair, how horrible the case was. And the discussion would begin. There was never a solution, but we felt better.

My office door was usually open. Sometimes after those sessions or a difficult case, people would drop in and we would talk. I don't think I had much to offer beyond reassuring them that what they were experiencing was to be expected. I encouraged them to try to balance their pain with the satisfaction they felt whenever we saved a child's life or rescued one from an awful situation.

By this time, two decades or more after my encounter with the secondary traumatization of the FGDS research assistants, a great deal more was known about the effects of secondary traumatic stress on those in the caring professions. To support my staff, I periodically gave an informational talk on the subject – a short, educational PowerPoint followed by a general group discussion. My intention was to help destigmatize secondary trauma and provide a language with which to talk about it.

Soon I received invitations from other hospital divisions to give this talk to their staff. Those working in intense services, such as the transplant unit, ICUs (intensive care units), the burn unit, oncology, and emergency department were experiencing their own versions of secondary traumatic stress. Eventually, I was invited to give the talk to all kinds of groups, including police departments. Perhaps my most memorable talk was for an association of police chaplains.

It was a lunchtime talk at their monthly meeting. I observed them as they unpacked their brown bag (homemade) and white bag (fast food) lunches. As a group they were heavyset, older men with hearty appetites. They appeared worn by life. Religious affiliations were evident in a few by their dress, but the denominations of most were not obvious. Only one or two wore a police uniform.

In many respects they were similar to other police groups I had worked with. They had a "no bull" directness but were also much funnier than you might expect. As they settled in to eat, the chaplains were making religious jokes and taking friendly gibes at each other's faiths. With all the semi-sacrilegious banter flying back and forth, I wondered why they were interested in hearing about secondary traumatic stress.

As soon as my talk was over and the general discussion began, the reason became clear. Police chaplains were responsible for notifying family members of deaths from automobile accidents or shootings, anything that had involved the police. The chaplains had to find family members and tell them that their husband, child, sister, or brother was dead – sometimes even killed by the police.

You can imagine their emotions as unsuspecting family members struggled to understand who the chaplains were and what had just happened to their loved one. Police chaplains were the bearers of the worst news a family member could hear. They experienced – indeed, in a way they inflicted – the immediate trauma. There would be shock, grief, anger, bewildered denial – a gauntlet of emotions and anguish at having learned about the sudden, unexpected, incomprehensible death of a loved one.

When I was acting chair of the bioethics consultation service at Cincinnati Children's Hospital for several years, I had occasionally been called upon to give families similar terrible news in support of what their primary doctors had already told them.

"There is nothing more that can be done for your child. The doctors have tried everything."

It is a supremely difficult message to deliver.

You never forget the pain and grief your words trigger. So I understood something about what those chaplains experienced.

We now know much more about secondary traumatization. It is very real and it affects a lot more people than is generally realized. Certain front-line professions are known to have higher rates – nurses, child protection workers, police, firefighters, emergency medical technicians (EMTs) – but everyone is vulnerable.

Recommendations to front-line workers for self-protection and care mostly fall into the "get a life outside of work" category (Osofsky et al., 2008). Although they're helpful, I believe institutions and agencies that routinely expose employees to traumatizing experiences should take the initiative to provide mental health support. Unfortunately, the administrators who make the important financial and policy decisions are too far removed from the hazards of front-line work. They fail to grasp the toll secondary traumatic stress can take on the health, morale, and productivity of their staff and, ultimately, their organizations.

The Perpetrator Helping Hand Award

Most professionals who work at or near the front lines of child protection, receive death threats. They come with the territory and are something that we usually don't take sufficiently seriously because the majority are empty bluster coming from cowardly men. Every once and in a while though, we can be mistaken.

The heroes – really the heroines – are the child protective services workers. Their jobs are to make home visits to assess and ensure the safety of children who are the focus of maltreatment allegations. The typical front-line CPS workers are just out of college, with less than two years' experience.

Often, they had to make several visits to the same home, sometimes arriving unannounced, to determine if the "safety plans" were being followed. If they weren't, those entrusted with the child's care and safety would have to be confronted.

Visiting homes as a CPS worker is similar to a cop making a traffic stop. One never knows what awaits. You may walk in on domestic violence or a drug deal or a vicious dog. Family members are inclined to be hostile, assuming the worst about your intentions. In housing projects, there are neighbors who hate CPS workers or see them as potential prey. Your possessions risk being stolen; your car vandalized.

The most dangerous situations are those in which a mother has left her abusively controlling partner after discovering that he sexually molested her children. He would be out hunting for her and vowing to kill anyone associated with her leaving him. Sometimes he would have the name of the CPS worker or a doctor and would be looking for them specifically.

On this occasion, the enraged perpetrator was vowing to kill me.

Arriving at Cincinnati Children's Hospital medical center, the perpetrator was confused by the many multistory buildings and sprawling campus. Lost, he stopped the center's business director, Mark, in the hospital main lobby by sheer chance, and asked for directions to my office. Recognizing that Cincinnati Children's Hospital was a confusing place, the administration encouraged employees to go out of their way to escort lost parents to the clinic or center they were seeking.

In this spirit, Mark courteously brought the would-be assassin to my office. On the way, he buzzed him through several locked doors that were meant to provide a modicum of protection for center staff.

Luckily (the perpetrator had brought a gun), I was not in when they arrived.

Even better, the police, who had been searching for this man, arrested him as he and Mark crossed the hall to look for me in the clinic. The "takedown" occurred in our waiting room, in front of children and families.

At the next staff meeting, the social workers ceremoniously presented Mark with "The Perpetrator Helping Hand Award," complete with an inflated examination glove and framed certificate, which he hung in his office. Once again dark humor helped us deal with a disturbing situation.

Given increasing societal violence and availability of firearms, we shared an ever-present concern for our personal and collective safety. While social media seems to have increased the ubiquity of death threats in general, child protection workers at all levels live with a heightened risk of coming face-to-face with their reality.

Micro Healing

I had a brief, but deeply healing experience one day. It had been an especially bad start to the week. Three young brothers with fading belt-buckle-shaped bruises on their bodies and more recent angry red welts on their backs and buttocks. A battered, brain-dead baby with tubes, leads, and lifeless eyes in the ICU. A toddler run over by a backing garbage truck in front of her horrified mother. Not to mention more than the usual administrative hassles that come with directing a money-losing community service like our child advocacy center.

Deb, my assistant-for-all-seasons, came in and sat down in the chair directly in front of my desk – a sign that she wanted my undivided attention.

"CPS just brought in a little boy. He doesn't talk. He bit one worker and kicked another. Can you see him?"

I expected to find a feral child in our playroom, but instead I found a quietly sleeping boy of about three. The worker holding him looked uncomfortable in his winter attire, so I took the sleeping child while he shed his heavy coat, hat, and gloves. When he was ready to take the child back, I knew that I didn't want to let the little boy go. It felt so right to hold this child in my arms, to feel him snuggle up against my chest and go trustingly limp. I held the sleeping child for about an hour.

As I held him, we gently examined the toddler for injuries and neglect. Although he was underdressed for the blizzard raging outside, we could see he had been well cared for. We guessed that he wandered away from a daycare somewhere in the neighborhood where he was found.

The cops were great. They got his picture aired on local TV channels and posted on the station websites. Off-duty officers went door-to-door in the neighborhood where he was found. Eventually, the in-home daycare provider (who claimed she didn't know the toddler was missing) was located and he was returned to his mother. The deep, healing, peaceful connection I felt when I held that sleeping child for that hour remained with me for the rest of the day.

Notes

1. Out-of-home maltreatment was evaluated by CPS teams based in downtown Cincinnati.
2. This colposcopy examination involved only visualizing and photographing the external genitalia. If an internal examination was required, the child was offered sedation and the examination was performed in the operating room by a pediatric gynecologist.
3. The fact that so many deadly school and mass shootings are carried out by adolescent males – who often have histories indicative of serious psychiatric problems and family dysfunction – should be sufficient reason to get a better handle on the nature and prevalence of mental health issues among US youth.
4. Trace evidence is physical evidence left at a crime scene, usually in minute quantities (e.g., hair, textile fibers, body fluids, paint chips, gunshot residue) that ties a perpetrator to that crime scene.
5. People lie to cops all the time. So it isn't surprising that cops regard lying as simply part of equalizing their adversarial relationships with suspects. *Frazier v. Cupp*, 394 US 731 (1969), was a US Supreme Court decision that confirmed the legality of deceptive interrogation by law enforcement.

References

Barnes, J.E., Noll, J.G., Putnam, F.W., & Trickett, P.K. (2009). Sexual and physical revictimization among victims of severe childhood sexual abuse. *Child Abuse & Neglect*, 33:412–420.

Gewirtz-Meydan, A., & Finkelhor, D. (2020). Sexual abuse and assault in a large national sample of children and adolescents. *Child Maltreatment*, 25:203–214.

Noll, J.C., Horowitz, L.A., Bonanno, G., Trickett, P.K., & Putnam, F.W. (2003). Revictimization and self-harm in adolescent and young adult females who experience childhood sexual abuse. *Journal of Interpersonal Violence*, 18:1452–1471.

Osofsky, J.D., Putnam, F.W., and Judge Cindy S. Lederman (2008). How to maintain emotional health when working with trauma. *Juvenile and Family Court Journal*, 59:91–102.

Putnam, F.W., Amaya-Jackson, L.M., Putnam, K.T., & Briggs, E.C. (2020). Synergistic adversities and behavioral problems in traumatized children and adolescents. *Child Abuse & Neglect*, 106:1–10.

6

THE "POLITICS" OF
CHILD MALTREATMENT

Practicing "Politics"

A friend and dedicated advocate for children and families once observed: *"You can write* [academic] *papers or you can write laws."* The clear implication was that laws were far more powerful (for better or for worse) in terms of their impact on the lives of children and families.

Although I've testified before the US Congress twice and several times before state legislatures, I had no idea how to begin to enact legislation. So I looked for ways to influence those who did. I would seek out those who debate, draft, and decide state and national laws, regulations, and policies and advocate for what was needed to help reduce child maltreatment and family violence.

One way to have input was to serve on local, state, and national level committees and workgroups making recommendations to the legislative, executive, and judicial branches. Another way was to collect data and develop investigative tools, and interventional and capacity-building models, that would inform and improve child welfare treatment, policy, and service delivery. A last way was to participate in state and national training, promoting programs, policies, and best practices.

DOI: 10.4324/9781003593928-6

Local Politics: The Trauma Treatment Replication Center (TTRC)

Given the volume of traumatized children forensically evaluated by the Center for Safe and Healthy Children, it was clear that we did not have the in-house resources (trained personnel and space) to provide adequate trauma treatment for most of them, not to mention the costly administrative burden of convincing reluctant health insurance companies to reimburse our services.

On the other hand, after a series of meetings with local mental health providers, it was also evident that there were very few therapists trained in proven child trauma treatment models who were available to accept referrals. So connecting our children to community services wasn't a sustainable option.

Indeed, my documentation of this unmet, largely unacknowledged, community need led to vociferous behind-the-scenes complaints that I, in particular, and our recently established child abuse center in general, were "case finding," and in danger of overwhelming already overburdened local mental health systems with a tsunami of newly identified, complicated cases.[1]

Given the magnitude of the unmet need, the obvious long-term answer was to build community capacity by providing high quality training to therapists at a price that their agencies couldn't refuse – free. This was further sweetened by the additional incentive that some health insurance companies were actually willing to pay extra for the proven treatment models that we trained. My problem was that providing free training is expensive and not something that my hospital administration could see itself funding.

My vision was to create a trauma treatment training center that would grow through a series of "self-augmenting replication cycles" for want of a better description. This program would train batches of therapists, some of whom would go on to become certified trainers themselves, further increasing capacity. Instead of money, trainees would owe us data (their first five, later reduced to three, cases) so we could evaluate the success of a given treatment model and the effectiveness of our training program in real-world settings (Pearl et al., 2012).

Fortunately, I had key collaborators in Drs. Barbara Boat, PhD, and Erna Olafson, PsyD, PhD, both clinical psychologists with the Childhood

Trust, an existing trauma treatment program. In addition, Lisa Connelly, project manager extraordinaire, provided the gentle, but firm, structure necessary to keep the program on track.

Together, we implemented the Trauma Treatment Replication Center (TTRC), which trained local and regional therapists in a number of well-proven treatment models, especially Trauma-Focused Cognitive Behavior Therapy (TF-CBT) and Parent Child Interaction Therapy (PCIT). In addition, the TTRC adapted and evaluated special versions of proven treatment models for unique settings or underserved populations such as incarcerated adolescents, foster parents, daycare providers, and schools.

Selling the vision of the TTRC to potential funders proved difficult initially. Fortunately, the NCTSN awarded us a grant to enact the program. Over the ensuing decade, the TTRC proved extremely successful at increasing community capacity, ultimately training hundreds of therapists and scores of certified trainers from all over the US as well as international trainees from Europe, Asia, and the Middle East. Offshoots of the TTRC continue to exist, although many of the original contributors have retired or gone their separate ways.

In most instances, the TTRC focused on training already well-proven trauma treatment models, saving us the time, effort, and resources required to conduct the clinical trials necessary to validate a given model. Our trainers were always officially certified in the models that they trained.

The selected models, however, were continuously undergoing change themselves, as more people and organizations adopted them. Sometimes, they even split into competing national camps that refused to accept each other's versions. These internal spats could become problematic when we were caught between warring factions disagreeing about who was qualified to be trained or to train a given model.

An anonymous colleague coined the term "developeritis" to characterize the tendency of some treatment model developers – originators and later tinkerers – to zealously micromanage the use of their models, usually for the sanctimonious reason of "fidelity." In an effort to call attention to the negative impacts of this excessively controlling dynamic on the dissemination of child trauma therapies, a loose ring of co-conspirators elaborated "developeritis" into a parody of the DSM-IV PTSD diagnosis, as follows.

Diagnostic Criteria for "*Developeritis* – 308.77"

Criterion A. The person has developed, created, adapted, or otherwise believes he/she has an exclusive claim to specific intellectual property such as a clinical scale (measure) or a therapeutic intervention (model).

- At least one other person (usually an academic colleague/ competitor) has expressed interest in, or has actually used, the first person's measure/model eliciting intense feelings of anxiety and paranoid ideation that this colleague/ competitor will steal or take credit for the developer's intellectual property and become fabulously wealthy by doing so.
- Or, that the colleague/competitor will deliberately misuse the measure/model in some fashion, so as to discredit it and thereby cast aspersions on the developer and undercut the credibility of the measure/model.

Criterion B. Persistent intrusive concerns regarding ownership of the model/measure (two or more of the following responses).

- Insists that all related measures/models (even when they pre-date the developer's own work) are plagiarized versions of his/her creation.
- Will not speak with colleagues whom he/she believes have "stolen" his/her measure/model.
- Copyrights the measure/model and aggressively demands payment from users.
- Insists on personally training, supervising, and certifying all users, despite lack of time, resources, and infrastructure, leading to shortages and bottlenecks in capacity.
- Vehemently objects to measure/model users publishing research and outcome results without consultation with and/or credit to the developer.

Criterion C. Avoidance or denial of reminders of the contributions of others (two or more of the following responses).

- Minimizes all prior or related measure/models as flawed, inadequate, or plagiarized.
- Insists that his/her measure/model should be used even when other measures/models have a stronger evidence base or are more appropriate.
- Banishment from the developer's inner circle of any user who adapts the measure or trains the model without the developer's express permission.
- Unconcerned about potential conflicts of interest when reviewing scientific articles and grant applications using competitive measures/models.

Criterion D. Persistent increased arousal (two or more of the following responses).

- Hyperalert to signs (real or imagined) that the measure/model is being used in ways "not intended" by the developer.
- Pervasive need to be overcontrolling, micromanaging of users – usually citing "fidelity to the model" as the rationale.
- Obsessively requires users to adhere to inane or idiosyncratic elements of the measure/model as "critical" to its success, e.g., restriction to highly unique subjects or expensive settings, or absolute allegiance to the developer's every passing whim.
- Intense desire to cast aspersions on others believed to have contaminated or denigrated the measure/model in word or deed.
- Hypervigilance and intense need to know what competitors are doing in order to continually spotlight supposed slights or "misuse" of their measure/model.

Criterion E. Duration of the disturbance (symptoms in Criteria B, C, and D) is more than one month.

- Onset can often be traced to the publication or presentation of the developer's measure/model by another party.
- Developer can recite author and source of all perceived slights and insults toward their measure/model.

Criterion F. The disturbances cause significant distress or impairment to others including: organizational, collegial, collaborational, interventional, financial, or other important mental health system functions.

My plan was to circulate these pseudo-DSM criteria via social media platforms shared by therapists and developers as a (hopefully) viral intervention calling attention to some of the jealous, paranoid, and excessively controlling behaviors satirized above. Cooler heads prevailed, however. I was warned that too many people would recognize themselves and I would make more than my usual share of enraged critics and internet trolls.

There should be a fair way to license treatment models, including royalty agreements if necessary, although most training programs are lucky to break even. Model developers do need to plan for the future of their programs and to arrange continued quality oversight to manage the inevitable evolution of their models, especially when they are no longer available. Nothing stands still.

Given its modest financial support, the TTRC was extremely cost effective in building community capacity to treat child trauma. We found that the most effective trainees were master's-level therapists with a couple of years in the trenches. Having encountered the complexities of trauma cases and how few sessions the health insurance companies would cover, trainees eagerly embraced our more session-structured and outcome measurement-based, treatment models. Certification in a clinically proven model often simplified their reimbursement process and enhanced their résumés, frequently leading to promotions and better jobs.

Building and sustaining local and regional training capacity is essential to meeting the huge, largely unmet, need for proven child and family trauma treatments. While there were always bureaucratic obstacles and the model developers' narcissistic sensitivities to negotiate or finesse, after a couple of replication cycles, the TTRC ran remarkably smoothly under the day-to-day management of Lisa Connelly, assisted by Lacey Thieken.

State Politics: Committees and Workgroups

The reputation of our child trauma programs led to my appointment by Ohio governors of both parties to several state committees and task forces, including the Ohio Children's Trust Fund advisory board and an Ohio Supreme Court taskforce.

Virtually every state has a Children's Trust Fund. While not required by federal law, a state would be foolish to refuse the dollars that come with complying with the Child Abuse Prevention and Treatment Act, widely known as CAPTA. Those federal dollars, the amount of which is determined by the number of children in the state, are for spending on state-level programs and services that reduce and prevent child abuse. Decisions about which programs receive CAPTA dollars are usually made by an advisory board for the state's Children's Trust Fund.

The governor appoints some of the Children's Trust Fund board members to fixed terms, usually with term limits. In addition, state legislatures may control board seats apportioned by a party's control of the legislature. I was first appointed to the Ohio Children's Trust Fund (OCTF) advisory board by Governor Robert Taft (Republican) in 2003. Re-appointed by successive governors, I served three consecutive terms, the most allowed by Ohio law.

During my terms, I had a fly-on-the-wall perspective, learning as much as I could about a tiny patch of state politics. With each election cycle, new Ohio legislators and cabinet officers passed through the board, although, after making one or two appearances, most sent a junior staffer to attend the monthly meetings in Columbus.

Always eager to vote, the junior staffers brought the larger partisan issues dividing Ohio (at the time, a notorious "battleground" state) into the board's deliberative processes. The rest of us – the non-elected, gubernatorial appointees – had little in common with each other and probably varied as much in our politics. Thus, we were not unified enough to carry the day, at least at the beginning.

My strongest first impression of the OCTF was arriving for a meeting early in my first term and finding that the director had been fired. By whom and for what reason was deliberately made unclear. In her place, were two members of the Ohio National Guard, a major and his personally attentive female sergeant. The sergeant was described as an expert in "organizational strategic planning." It was explained that the major and sergeant were there to help us – as a board – create a strategic plan now that the director was gone.

We were taken aback. None of the pre-meeting emails hinted at this. Remarkably, all the elected members and their representatives were absent. Only we governor-appointed folks showed up for this meeting. No one would answer our questions about how and why the director was fired. The sergeant repeatedly let us know she was ready to start her presentation. In fact, we were already seriously behind schedule, and she needed every remaining minute to do her thing.

The lights went off, and the sergeant began her PowerPoint. For a while, we sat in confused silence as she clicked her way through slide after bulleted slide. Then someone started passing a note from member to member suggesting that we stop her presentation and call a meeting among ourselves. When the note circled by me again, I saw that there was unanimity.

As the doctor on the board, I stood up and asked the sergeant to stop. The board was going to hold a meeting (although we didn't have a quorum). She and the major were welcome to stay – our meetings were open to the public under Ohio's sunshine laws – but the board needed to discuss the implications of these changes before drafting a strategic plan. The sergeant and her major were incensed at the interruption and unwilling to remain, as there would be too little time afterward to draft a strategic plan. Gathering their things, they left with an ominous warning that we would be sorry for missing this opportunity.

Over the next several years, the board went through several acting directors and was administratively batted around within the huge Ohio Department of Jobs and Family Services (ODJFS) bureaucracy, which provides or regulates most of the state's social services. The Ohio Children's Trust Fund was sitting on a budget surplus (about $5–7 million unspent CAPTA dollars – the actual sum was never clear). Washington sends CAPTA dollars annually, but states have several years to decide how to spend them. Our leaderless board could not spend the CAPTA funds at a sufficient rate to draw down a growing surplus.

Meanwhile, the fiscally strapped state legislature eyed our accounts. Some warned us that unless they were committed soon the CAPTA funds would be raided, and they were right. Ohio faced an increasingly desperate fiscal situation. The OCTF lost the accumulated CAPTA dollars overnight. But there was still that annual check from Washington, 2 million dollars and change. How should those dollars be best spent? That became an internal struggle between child abuse prevention policy and state politics that played out in board meeting after meeting, year after year.

The two positions can be summarized as follows: The prevention policy folks (my side) argued that we needed to invest the funds in a centralized training and support center that would serve all Ohio counties. It would provide first-rate training in best practices to county workers and their replacements (county child protection agencies experienced high rates of front-line worker turnover). The center would also provide consultation to county CPS agencies.

High-quality training – prosaic as it may seem – is essential to the implementation of high-quality government services. As a rule, county-level child protection agencies experience high rates of front-line worker turnover. Thus some cost-effective form of high-quality training of replacements is essential. This is best centralized as opposed to each county trying to independently manage its training needs.

The political argument was that these dollars belonged to the local people and they, and only they, could best determine how they should be spent. (This position is known as "home rule.") Thus, the annual CAPTA funds should be divvied up among 88 counties, based on the number of children in each. This was the way it had been done in Ohio since the beginning of CAPTA, and this is how it should continue.

A small nucleus of the board, primarily the governor-appointed front-line folks (later joined by Governor Ted Strickland's (Democrat) cabinet officers) favored investing CAPTA dollars in centralized training and support of evidence-based, statewide prevention programs. For a considerable (depressingly long) time we failed to make headway against the home rule political interests. The state legislature did pretty much as it wished with the OCTF funds during our largely leaderless years.

Fortunately, we finally got an executive director, Candace, who understood the dual political and prevention roles of the OCTF. At first there was disbelief and anger by counties, when their long-funded, but unproven, prevention programs (one was "scrapbooking," which involved creating family albums with photos, clippings, and mementoes) were turned down. These counties eventually did move from "feel-good," but unproven, programs, to more evidence-based prevention. (Predictably, Candace was forced out with the next change in political control.)

At this time, I was also a member of a workgroup convened by the Ohio Supreme Court. One of the Supreme Court committee's tasks was to reconcile contradictions and discrepancies in definitions of child maltreatment between the Ohio criminal and civil codes. Another was to investigate a new, potentially destigmatizing approach to child protection evaluations called alternative response (also known as differential response).

Destigmatizing Child Protection Investigations

When we began Every Child Succeeds, we were given an in-kind donation of three professionally run consumer focus groups. A year or so after we started services, we chose to use this gift to learn what participating mothers thought of ECS, specifically their concerns and criticisms.

Members of the first focus group were chosen from mothers who regularly participated in home visits and were doing well on our measures of success. The second focus group consisted of mothers who were doing poorly, in terms of involvement or improvement. We were especially interested in what they thought wasn't working for them. The third group was selected from the home visitors (all female) who provided ECS services to the mothers.

We thought that we were going to hear three very different takes on ECS from these contrasting groups. Instead, they all told us essentially the same thing. By far the biggest shared concern was that the home visitors were going to report them to child protective services for messy homes, dirty dishes, holes in their kids' clothes, head lice, dirty hands and faces – and their children would be taken away from them.

The most successful mothers (by our measures) were just as frightened of this possibility as the ones who were really struggling. The home visitors, in turn, felt that the mothers' suspicion and distrust seriously impacted their ability to form strong relationships with them. A truism across all home visiting programs is that a mother must first trust her home visitor before she will accept and follow the home visitor's advice.

Unfortunately, the seriously mistaken belief that children are routinely taken away from their parents for minor messiness or dirty faces is widespread and underlies public fear and reluctance to participate in public health programs of many stripes. In fact, only a relatively small percentage (about 10–15 percent) of *substantiated* child maltreatment cases involve removal of a child from the home. Child protection services much prefer keeping children in their homes or at least with other family members (kinship care) and removing the alleged perpetrator.

Irrespective of whether an allegation of child maltreatment is ultimately substantiated, the mandated investigation can be arduous, intrusive, confusing, and distressing for the family and the child. The child advocacy center (CAC) movement is one effort to coordinate and reduce the stresses of CPS investigations. Another, more recent, effort is alternate response (AR).

In the AR model, once a child is determined to be at low risk for further harm, appropriate services for the family can be started immediately. Child protection workers in the AR model are given greater flexibility in what they are allowed to provide for the family (for example, paying for car repairs so a breadwinner can resume working). The motivating reason for this model is that in many cases of alleged maltreatment the situation does not demand a prolonged, intrusive, and sometimes humiliating investigation.

In 2004, the Ohio Supreme Court established the Subcommittee on Responding to Child Abuse, Neglect, and Dependency to which the governor appointed me. Meeting monthly in the beautifully restored Art Deco Judicial Center in Columbus, Ohio, the subcommittee worked with the National Center for Adoption Law and Policy and the American Bar Association Committee on Children and the Law for about a year and a half.

This taskforce ultimately recommended that Ohio conduct a pilot project to assess the AR model. This recommendation made its way up channels. In June 2006, Ohio Senate Bill 238 was signed authorizing an 18-month pilot trial of AR in up to 10 counties. Serving on both the Supreme Court committee and the OCTF advisory board, I played a role in getting 1 million CAPTA dollars allocated to the AR pilot study.

The AR trial was a success (Loman & Siegel, 2015). Based on an equal risk assessment, families were randomly assigned either to the AR (n = 2,382) or the standard investigational (n = 2,247) condition and tracked for between 45 and 60 months from the date of assignment. Extended outcomes included reduced child maltreatment recidivism, decreased the number of subsequent child removals, decreased new threats to child safety, and reduced parenting problems in AR families.

Both the families and the child protection workers strongly preferred AR to the standard investigation protocol. It destigmatized the process and resulted in greater willing participation by families. The child protection workers – most of whom have a social work orientation – loved it. AR gave them the discretion and resources to help solve problems rather than imposing a rigid investigational protocol that delayed needed services, often complicating a family's problems.

As a result of this success, a second wave of counties was accepted into the AR implementation program (Ohio has 88 counties). This time, Hamilton County (home to our center) was included.

I asked a long-time, trusted colleague, Sue Moore, for an example illustrating how AR works in the real world. The cool million bucks we found to facilitate the original Supreme Court pilot study was long gone. But at least worker flexibility remained. Sue's story (lightly edited) illustrates AR in action.

Hamilton County Children's Services started an alternate response unit in Oct. of 2010. The concept is that child abuse is investigated using a different approach, there is no disposition and there are no labels used, such as alleged victim or alleged perpetrator. The idea being, if you take the labels out then the family is less threatened and more likely to work to solve the issue. The goal of the alternate response (AR) workers is to engage the family so they can identify the issue and work to resolve it. The approach is meant to be very family friendly and problem solving, versus the blaming and shaming approach that sometimes goes along with traditional child abuse investigations. Typically, the AR response is used on cases that are at lower risk.

Most AR cases are not seen in child advocacy centers. However, Hamilton County Jobs and Family Services (JFS), the departmental home of Children's Services [child protection] was in a unique position given that our child advocacy center was co-located at the children's hospital. It was decided that one worker stationed at the Center for Safe and Healthy Children at Cincinnati Children's Hospital would be trained in the AR approach.

The thought was that this AR worker would work with families who had been reported to child protection for alleged medical neglect. These are children, for example, who are "neglected" because they were not getting their insulin for diabetes or who were not getting their asthma medication. Not surprisingly, most reports of alleged medical neglect come from doctors and clinics. So in practice, this worked well, because the AR worker located at the hospital could build and maintain cooperative relationships with the relevant doctors and clinics.

Sandi was assigned to a case where a grandmother had guardianship of her grandchildren. The allegation was medical neglect of one child. The grandmother was extremely resistant when Sandi started working on the case. She would not cooperate with home visits. She would not return phone calls. She continued to miss the child's medical appointments. In a traditional child maltreatment investigation, the worker would file a legal complaint to obtain a court order to gain access to the child and home.

As an AR worker, Sandi was able to take a different approach. She worked extremely hard to get the grandmother to just agree to a home visit so they could talk. In the home, Sandi discovered that the grandmother only had a dorm size refrigerator. The grandmother said that it was a struggle to keep groceries as well as fit the medicines she needed into the small refrigerator.

Returning to the office, Sandi told co-workers about her desire to find the grandmother a full-size refrigerator. Coincidentally, one co-worker said that her father owned a business located in a large warehouse. There was a full-size refrigerator in the warehouse that was not being used. The co-worker called her dad. He was happy to donate the appliance. A second co-worker called her family who had a truck. Plans were made to move the refrigerator. A strong male caseworker was recruited to help. Within a few days of Sandi's visit, the grandmother was surprised to receive a full-sized refrigerator.

Immediately, Sandi's rapport with the grandmother improved. She returned Sandi's phone calls, talking about her struggles getting to medical appointments. Sandi was able to help her problem solve, and navigate the complex medical system. Soon the child was receiving the necessary care.

Now Sandi had full access to the home and the children. She was able to find secondhand clothing for all the children. The grandmother was overjoyed. Allowing Sandi the flexibility to gain the grandmother's trust, enabled her to achieve AR's ultimate goal – for the child to receive the necessary medical treatment. Sandi was able to successfully close the case. For weeks afterward, the grandmother called to update Sandi on her progress.

Sue added that, unfortunately, because of budget cuts, the lone AR worker stationed in our center was eventually let go. The larger AR unit, located downtown, was understandably unable to maintain the same strong partnership with medical clinics as a hospital-based AR worker.

The AR approach to child protective services is spreading across the US, based on the success of the Minnesota and Missouri pilot studies and bolstered by the positive Ohio and Nevada randomized clinical trials. My concern is that these promising pilot studies and clinical trials all occurred under special circumstances (for example the extra million dollars that the OCTF was able to give to the first round of the Ohio AR clinical trial). Without this extra fiscal and administrative support, the AR model will not be able to achieve the same positive outcomes.

Although many AR workers, like Sandi, use a great deal of ingenuity, few can count on the good luck of finding a co-worker with the solution back at the office. For AR to achieve its considerable promise of destigmatizing and improving child protection services, workers need discretionary funds and administrative flexibility to be able to address the needs of the children and families in front of them swiftly.

Illuminating the Bigger Picture

The success of the Dissociative Experiences Scale (DES) has shaped my philosophy that creating and disseminating quality "tools" is a powerful way to influence scientific and clinical landscapes. There are now thousands of peer-reviewed publications that include the DES among their battery of psychological measures. It's been translated into scores of languages. But more important than the journal citations, are the thousands of patients whose pathological dissociation has been identified by clinicians using routine DES screening.

Early in my time at Cincinnati Children's Hospital, I attended a demonstration on geocoding (sponsored by a software company) that made me aware of just how much of the county where our center was located was geocoded. Every telephone pole, manhole cover, bus stop, mailbox, storm drain, traffic light, and fireplug is in a GPS dataset. The speaker presented a range of sophisticated applications made possible by geocoding. He included a dramatic demonstration that mapped the best highway routes from different fire stations to various sites around Cincinnati, according to time-of-day and day-of-the-week traffic patterns.

For the finale, the presenter showed a video clip of the mapping of gunshots fired in Los Angeles on New Year's Eve. Recorded by a network of microphones arrayed throughout the city that triangulated the gunshot locations (in essentially the same way that your cellphone tracks your location), the map sparkled as the population cut loose in celebration.

For several minutes around the midnight hour, gunshots crackled like popcorn, as flashes lit up all over the map of LA. It became obvious to me that the gunshots were primarily concentrated in certain neighborhoods where staying indoors and parking your car under cover would be prudent. I was struck by how powerful a new tool GPS was. If you had good data, which we didn't at that time, it could reveal the all-important big picture.

About five years later, I was reasonably well established in Cincinnati, at least for an outsider. Between working with Every Child Succeeds in the community and our Center for Safe and Healthy Children at the children's hospital, I had a general sense of the city, had met many of the local power players, and learned a bit about Ohio state politics. I also had ideas about what needed to change if life was going to improve for local children.

But we needed a community level "DES" to see the big picture.

A critical first step was finding a comprehensible way to show local and state decision makers (especially legislators and public service adminis-trators) the overlapping, interactive, and synergistic relationships among poverty, infant mortality, child abuse, domestic violence, substance abuse, and children's mental and physical health. That is, to enable them to see clearly how, and to what extent, child and family trauma and adversity negatively impacted child health and development in our communities.

By now we had the data. Within months of opening the center, we had a sophisticated electronic medical record (EMR) system in opera-tion, years ahead of the EMR fad. Much of the credit goes to our medical director, Bob Shapiro, and to a talented programmer, Jim.

We were evaluating 1,200 to 1,500 children a year and, by now, had half-a-dozen years' worth of metro area data in the bank. We could geocode these data and "map" child abuse, primarily in-home sexual abuse and serious physical abuse, in Cincinnati and surrounding coun-ties. Theoretically, geocoding and mapping our data sounds easy, but it required time and effort for us to climb a steep software learning curve. After my research assistant, Jackie, and I tried a few simple examples to get a sense of the issues, I searched for a skilled geocoding programmer who could do it right.

Fortunately, I knew Mark Carrozza from our eECS programming pro-ject, when we developed a sophisticated, web-based data collection and client services tracking system supporting Every Child Succeeds. Mark's design for eECS was brilliant. With him on board, I was off and running. Using some of the center's OhioCANDo funding, donated by an anonymous benefactor, I set about creating a child risk mapping service.

The basic idea was that we would develop a tool to help people display geocodable data from their communities. Ideally, they would have their local data, such as locations of child abuse cases or infant fatalities, which we would map together with public domain data on local resources, like federally accredited health care centers or failing schools (an important indicator of community problems). The maps would be interactive – with a few mouse clicks, one could overlay different datasets and see how problems and resources lined up, or didn't.

The child risk mapping service focused on two major agendas. Neither were published, although results from both were presented or displayed as posters at professional meetings.

The first agenda was to create a mapping tool for communities to identify high risk "hot spots" for children (Figure 6.1). In brief, hotspot analysis is a statistical approach that looks for clusters of incidents (child abuse, vehicle theft, reports of domestic violence, cancer cases, etc.) that are occurring closer together and at a higher rate than would be expected by chance.

There are several ways to go about computing hot spots. We chose software developed by the National Institute of Justice for police departments. Hot spots can be defined in several ways: by specific types of crime, like drug trafficking, vehicle theft, and pickpocketing; by local land use, such as bars, adult bookstores, and itinerant hotels; and by interactions between the two (for example, purse snatching around bus stops). We were interested in all these levels of analysis.

We had data for Cincinnati, but most communities do not keep records that lend themselves to hot spot risk analyses for children. So our task was two-fold. We had to first determine if there were child risk hot spots in Cincinnati, then independently predict where they existed, using US Census tract data (which are available for the entire US).

If we could use variables from the public domain US Census tract data set exclusively to predict neighborhoods that held significantly greater risks for children, literally every city and town in the US could also use these data.

Of course, we didn't think it would be simple, but the preliminary results were promising. In addition to the Cincinnati data, we had data for Cleveland and Columbus, Ohio. Indeed, we found multiple, sharply delineated hot spots for child abuse, infant mortality, and domestic violence in each city. Remarkably (or perhaps not), in each city these three types of hot spots closely overlapped each other (Figure 6.1).

Dividing the Cincinnati data set in two, we used the first half to derive a regression equation (used in statistics to find the relationship between sets of data) from the census tract data that predicted risk for child abuse based on our center's data. The equation was able to correctly predict over 90 percent of the hot spots identified by hot spot analysis in the second half of the data set. When the equation was applied to Cleveland, it performed equally well. It was not quite as good a predictor for Columbus, although it did identify the majority of hot spots.

Thus, we had a tool that potentially could be of general use. It would need to be sharpened and tested against data from diverse cities across the US, but there was real merit in the idea.

The second agenda for our Child Risk Mapping Service was to create interactive maps that policy makers, investigative journalists, and citizen advocates could use to discover for themselves the co-locations of clusters of risks to children. We wanted to create powerful documentary tools that geographically illustrated big picture narratives related to the wellbeing of children and families in their communities.

Politicians know maps. They may trance out when plied with the bar charts, scatterplots, and line graphs favored by academics, but show them a map of their district and they are on it. We figured that interactive maps allowing politicians and their staff to explore their districts from a child risk perspective would be the best way to capture and hold their attention.

We created maps of selected Ohio legislative districts and put them on CD-ROMs. In deference to concerns that our information might reflect poorly on some, we personalized each CD, so it contained only those data relevant to the legislator's district. Only one copy was made of each. It was given to either the legislator or a staff member. Once the CD booted up, the user would see a map of his or her district. By clicking on a menu, various data sets were overlaid, geographically illustrating how risks to children related to other measures of community health or dysfunction.

This was so cool!

Blessed with friends who had influential Ohio political connections, I carried a handful of personalized CDs to the state capitol in Columbus to meet with selected legislators. I expected a positive reaction; surely they and their staff would welcome the opportunity to look at interactive maps of child and family risks and resources in their districts!

Instead, while I was received with polite attention, no one embraced this fancy new tool. Comments ranged from, "I don't need a map to tell me where the poor people in my district live" to "Don't give this to the news" (from an assistant to a legislator under scrutiny for his lavish lifestyle).

Party affiliations didn't seem to matter. They either felt they already knew the information I was offering or believed this information was politically harmful. Either way, they didn't want to look at the data – and they didn't want anyone else to see it.

Values trump scientific data!

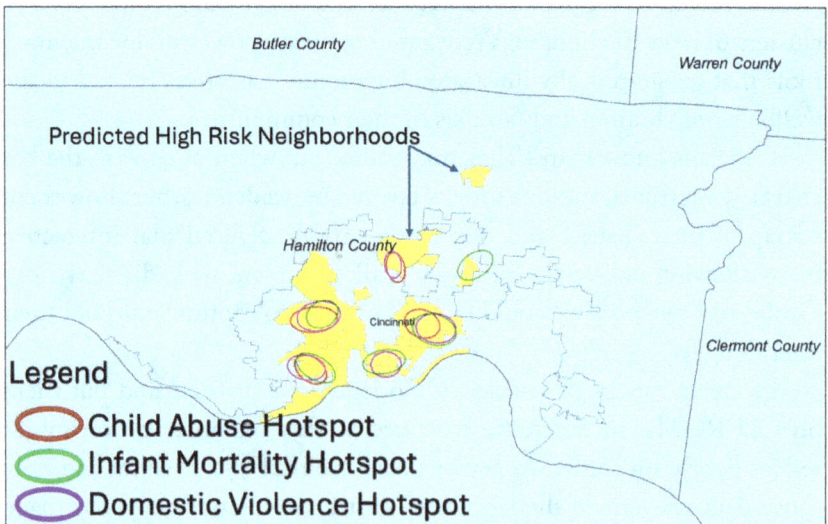

Figure 6.1 Comparison of Cincinnati child trauma hot spots with predicted high risk child trauma areas.[2]

Source: Author.

National Politics: The Great Recession

In late 2007 and early 2008, as the Great Recession began to grip Cincinnati, we had been operating the Center for Safe and Healthy Children for about seven years. In many respects, we were at our best.

We had worked a lot of tough cases together. We knew and trusted each other. Our clinical and forensic protocols were tested in practice and in court. Our complex video system for recording and archiving forensic interviews and medical examinations was humming along smoothly. The center's electronic medical record system, with thousands of cases, remained well ahead of its time. We were on top of our game – and nationally recognized for it.

But the world around us was collapsing. We were in the midst of a recession and unemployment was quickly rising. Hamilton County social services were overwhelmed. In downtown Cincinnati, the line to sign up for food stamps stretched out of the door of the Jobs and Family Services building and curled around the block.

The child protective services were especially hard hit by budget cuts and layoffs. On Fridays, selected workers were called into the supervisor's office and laid off. Given just 15 minutes to clear out their desks, co-workers in the adjacent cubicles witnessed their colleagues' tearful exits and wondered what next Friday might hold for them. The morale at CPS was at an all-time low.

Despite what was happening, county officials assured the public that no essential services were being affected. Children's lives were not being jeopardized. Indeed, although the county's child welfare statistician was among the very first to be let go, "official" statistics indicated that the local rate of child abuse was falling.

We started noticing something that didn't compute; not so much a huge increase in numbers of abused children, but that they were far more seriously injured. Fatalities were up. The relatively rare, closed head, abusive brain injuries, commonly known as "shaken baby syndrome," were becoming increasingly frequent.

Comments on email listservs (electronic mailing lists) used by a national network of child abuse physicians, primarily pediatricians working at hospital-based programs like ours, indicated that many others were seeing essentially the same thing at about the same time.

Yet not everyone observed this change. A few programs reported steep declines in their numbers. Within our professional networks, questioning, debate, and a troubling uncertainty arose about whether we were missing something major happening to the rate of child maltreatment.

Several national authorities, notably David Finkelhor, PhD, at the University of New Hampshire, Crimes Against Children Research Center (CCRC), using data from the National Child Abuse and Neglect Data System (NCANDS), claimed child abuse was actually decreasing during the recession. However, Dr. Finkelhor could not explain why there was a rise in childhood fatalities over the same period.[3]

Although the NCANDS is the US government's child abuse and neglect data system (hastily appended to a reauthorization of the Child Abuse Prevention and Treatment Act), most child maltreatment researchers regard it highly unfavorably. It is handicapped by serious limitations in its mandate to collect national statistics on child maltreatment, lacking the federal incentives and regulatory teeth necessary to enforce standardization and compliance across states and US territories.

To gather data, states are asked – but not required – to send annual statistics to Westat, a private firm in Maryland, where they are compiled. Each state, as well as DC and several US territories, is allowed to define child abuse and neglect however they wish; there are literally scores of different definitions for each of the maltreatment types. The result is a mélange of apples, oranges, elephants, and Chevrolets – largely meaningless data. To top it all off, NCANDS annual reports are released at least two years after the fact, making them utterly useless for timely interventions.

Simply inspecting the summary tables in any of the NCANDS annual reports reveals enormous discrepancies in the rates and types of child abuse and neglect reported across different states. For example, in 2022 (the last year data are available at this draft), Pennsylvania reported that 42.9 percent of all its child abuse cases were classified as "only sexual abuse." That same year, only 4.3 percent of CPS-substantiated cases in neighboring New York State were classified as "only sexual abuse." (In 2018 the difference was 80-fold: PA 41.7 percent, NY, 0.5 percent.)

Who knew that crossing the Delaware River at Port Jervis, NY, makes a ten-fold or greater difference in the rate of "only sexual abuse" cases?

Annual NCANDS reports are rife with such implausible discrepancies, often exceeding an order of magnitude. This glaring difference immediately calls into question the validity of the data which many of us on the front lines have.

Several of us carried on private conversations with Dr. Finkelhor about the legitimacy of his findings that the rate of child maltreatment was improved or unaffected by the unemployment and economic stress gripping American families. From our perspective, we were seeing the wholesale destruction of child protective services in our cities and counties.

Instead, we were hearing from pediatricians, family practitioners, emergency room (ER) doctors, police officers, and teachers who described having reported egregious cases of child maltreatment – broken bones, serious burns, multiple bruising – that their local CPS refused to accept for investigation. We heard about repeated calls to child protection hotlines with overflowing, but unanswered, voicemail boxes.

We were seeing the caseloads of CPS workers skyrocket as their co-workers were laid off around them. To make matters worse, the most competent and dedicated CPS workers, especially veteran supervisors, were fleeing the child protection system in droves, because they saw it as a disaster in the making. Privately, they described feeling as though they were stepping off the deck of the *Titanic*.

Dr. Finkelhor always had an answer whenever we questioned his data. It usually boiled down to "I don't know what is going on in Ohio, but that's not what we're seeing." He was unfailingly polite and collegial, but remarkably unconcerned about our collective concern. He wanted us to show him data, but at the beginning of the Great Recession, we didn't have it.

Eventually, we collaborated with CACs around the country that had kept accurate records dating to before the start of the recession and were able to accrue sufficiently large samples of abusive head injuries by combining our cases (Berger et al., 2011).

Overall, these studies showed an approximate doubling of the number and rate of abusive head injuries during the recession, although there was some variation across the US, with the Midwest showing the largest increases. At the same time, accidental child head injuries were declining in the same places where there were large increases in abusive ones.

Other studies, using databases that included hundreds of thousands of admissions to more than 100 children's hospitals, found significant increases in the numbers of children hospitalized for child abuse-related injuries. Thus, research utilizing readily countable "hard" measures (numbers of dead and injured children seen at children's hospitals), found that severe child maltreatment increased significantly.

While Dr. Finkelhor was made aware of these contradictory studies as they became available, he and his supporters continued to tout enormous decreases – over 50 percent for physical and sexual abuse – in child maltreatment.

And here is where this increasingly contentious disagreement remained stuck. Until I was alerted to a *New York Times* guest editorial (July 13, 2013), "How Googling unmasks child abuse," by Seth Stephens-Davidowitz, PhD, that brought an entirely new lens to focus on the question of whether child maltreatment had increased during the recession. Stephens-Davidowitz's answer was an unequivocal "yes."

Child maltreatment had gone up dramatically. In addition, Stephens-Davidowitz found that the child protection system, put in place to safeguard our children, was simultaneously being devastated. Furthermore, the people whom we relied upon to make referrals of suspected maltreatment to the CPS – teachers, police, social workers, and daycare workers – were suffering massive layoffs as a consequence of the recession, and therefore were less available to report suspected cases.

It was a triple whammy. More and more children were being maltreated, but the people and systems that were supposed to report and protect them were less and less there for them.

While a post-doctoral fellow at Google, Stephens-Davidowitz, a Harvard-educated data scientist, used its eponymous search engine to investigate the effects of the Great Recession on rates of child maltreatment reporting (Stephens-Davidowitz, 2013). Using multiple proxies for child maltreatment and a set of Google search terms, he found that incidents of maltreatment increased by 10–24 percent over an average of the 2 years prior and 2 years post-recession. Reports of maltreatment, however, decreased by 12 percent compared with an average of two years before the recession and two years after.

The increase in child maltreatment was closely tied to local increases in unemployment. For every one percent increase in the local unemployment rate there was a 2.5 percent increase in maltreatment and a 3.3 percent decrease in reporting to the CPS.

The strong relationship between unemployment and maltreatment in the Google study explained many of the regional differences that had created painful uncertainty among child abuse doctors. States most affected economically by the recession showed the largest increases in maltreatment. Ohio and Kentucky were both well above the national unemployment curve, so our center was seeing a real effect.

Overall, child maltreatment increased significantly during the recession but, because of its economic impact on the systems and people who work with children, only the very worst cases were being reported or accepted for CPS investigation. The forensic evidence in more serious cases is often undeniably obvious. As a result, the percentage of legally substantiated cases was much higher than before the recession.

There are, of course, legitimate criticisms that can be made about this study (more recent research continues to support Stephens-Davidowitz's findings). Every research study has its weaknesses and limitations. Because of his large sample and unique methodology, Stephens-Davidowitz had been able to control for numerous confounding factors. He also used combinations of search strategies that were relatively independent, but which nonetheless yielded similar results.

When one views the convergence of many independent sources of data, they all point to an increase in child maltreatment during the recession (as well as increases in domestic violence, parental substance abuse, and parental mental illness). It is now tragically evident that we (as a society and as professionals) missed some of the atrocities that were happening to children – at a time when they needed our protection the most.

The one clue we should have seized on was that the fatality rate was rising, while everything else appeared to be going down.

The National Academy of Sciences and the National Academy of Medicine – two of the most prestigious scientific institutions in the US – jointly recommended that NCANDS be junked and replaced with a scientific child maltreatment surveillance system like those deployed for cancers, flu, and mosquito-borne viral infections, among other threats to public health (IOM & NRC, 2014).

Hopefully we can learn and will remember this lesson when the next economic downturn hits – as it will. The strong relationship between child maltreatment and local economic indicators of family stress, such as weekly unemployment and 90-day delinquency on rent or mortgage payments, allows us to identify regional child abuse hot spots. Families affected should be eligible for increased preventive services, such as respite breaks for overwhelmed parents. In times of economic hardship, we should be augmenting social services for hard-pressed families, not cutting them.

The National Children's Study

In the year 2000, Congress appropriated funding for the National Children's Study (NCS), a study of children's health and development. Signing the bill, President Clinton predicted that the NCS would provide critical information to help prevent and cure disease. In December 2014, Francis Collins, director of the National Institutes of Health, issued an order terminating the NCS. Based on outside reviews, Collins concluded that although "… the overall goals of examining how environmental factors influence child health and development are meritorious …," the 1.2 billion dollar NCS had been a failure.[4]

The NCS was in trouble long before it was terminated. In June of 2012 moving vans rolled up to the 40 university-affiliated sites, and wheeled away freezers, computers, and records. I'll skip further details, except to note that from its earliest conceptualization, numerous authorities predicted that the NCS was a disaster in the making.

I had little to do with the NCS beyond serving on a Cincinnati Children's Hospital workgroup charged with drafting a grant application. Fortunately, we were not chosen.

I did, however, privately lobby NCS leadership to include measures of child maltreatment, adversity, and family dysfunction. I was not alone, as influential colleagues, independently and collectively, urgently pressed the designers of the NCS to add standard measures of maltreatment and childhood adversity to the list of factors thought to be critical in shaping children's health and development.

We believed these childhood experiences played a larger role in the negative mental and physical health outcomes the NCS was seeking to understand than did the lead paint and diesel fumes they were narrowly focused on. But the NCS designers pointedly ignored our appeals.

Their resounding silence was reminiscent of an earlier debacle in which I participated more directly.

In the late 1990s the NIMH geared up to conduct a national, longitudinal study of the mental health of America's youth, as little epidemiological mental health data existed. I was a member of a multi-agency government committee whose role was to facilitate communication about child and adolescent mental health research and policy across diverse federal agencies, institutes, and bureaus. Although we did not control decision making, our committee, chaired by child psychiatrist Peter Jensen, MD, was a major advocate for a study that would determine the extent, contexts, and evolution of mental health problems in American children.

We often referred to the proposed research as a "Framingham for children's mental health," after the landmark study of heart disease conducted in Framingham, Massachusetts. Many of the diet and exercise recommendations for the prevention of heart disease originate from the Framingham heart health study, which is currently following its third generation of subjects.

The proposed study was designed to evaluate a large, representative sample of children and adolescents and their environments, and extrapolate the prevalence and types of child and adolescent mental health and addictive problems for the country as a whole. To test the scientific methods, a pilot study, known as the MECA study (Methodology for Epidemiology of Mental Disorders in Children and Adolescents), was funded. It called for recruiting about 1,300 children aged 9 to 17 years and their parents at four different sites. The MECA study would test recruitment strategies and refine a research interview (the NIMH Diagnostic Interview Schedule for Children (DISC)). The improved DISC would then become the gold standard for assessing the mental health of children across the US.

And therein lies the rub. When you take into consideration the many factors – age, gender, race, socioeconomic situation, family composition, and cultural background to name just a few – that influence how parents and children present, and then add a stranger asking all sorts of weird questions to the mix, it becomes difficult for experts to agree on what "normal" responses are. What is the gold standard against which to calibrate the next gold standard?

At its essence the scholarly debate boiled down to whether to diagnose youth mental disorders in a dichotomous manner, as we do with adults. That is, to see if children meet criteria for one or more mental disorders as defined by the DSM's "Chinese restaurant menu" of symptoms. Or if we should assess them along a set of developmental, cognitive, and behavioral continuums to determine how similar or deviant that child is from their peers.

With the former, the outcome is binary – the child either has or does not have a given mental disorder. With the latter, mental health is measured on a set of continuums. How well does the child resemble other children? Is the child having trouble conforming to and functioning within the larger expectations of the real world they live in? The clinical absolutists versus the developmental relativists!

Our interagency committee was largely composed of developmental relativists. We believed that normal behavior was, to a large degree, a matter of how well the children were adapting to the reality-imposed circumstances of their lives.

Studies find that psychiatric diagnoses are unstable in children. The same child evaluated a couple of years apart may meet criteria for a whole new set of disorders and no longer qualify for the previous diagnoses. Therefore, we rejected research designs that simply counted the number of DSM disorders in a child at a single point in time.

We criticized our opponents, calling them "bean counters," because they were only interested in how many children met criteria for what were essentially adult mental illnesses.

Penny, Jennie, and I witnessed this long-term diagnostic instability in our FGDS subjects (primarily the sexually abused girls). It is not as if the girls with serious mental health problems got better. They simply met DSM criteria for new sets of diagnoses as they grew older, and they no longer qualified for the earlier ones.

This change in their mental health was especially evident as the girls passed through puberty, when, all of a sudden, in the words of many mothers, they became "a different child." When I've asked adult sexual abuse survivors about such changes, among the first reasons offered was that they had become aware of sex in a new way and were reacting to the understanding about what had been done to them.

As the two camps (bean counters and developmental relativists) sniped at each other, the MECA data became available. On average, the degree of agreement between two parents about their child's symptoms and behaviors was deemed "acceptable" (a low bar). The DISC child interview, however, proved "less satisfactory" in terms of a blinded second interviewer independently reaching the same diagnoses only one to three weeks later (Shaffer et al., 1996).

More telling was the fact that just using the DISC diagnostic criteria alone, without accounting for how well the child was actually functioning, resulted in more than 50 percent of the 1,300 children meeting DSM criteria for one or more mental disorders. However, if you took into consideration how seriously symptomatically impaired a given child was, then only 5.4 percent of US children had a diagnosable mental disorder. That's a ten-fold difference in the prevalence of mental health problems in youth.

Congress, which had appropriated funds for a national study of child mental health (about 40 million dollars if I recall correctly), was most unhappy to learn that half of America's youth were mentally ill – at least by one definition. There was pushback about the MECA results from other quarters as well, notably prominent foundations that funded youth programs.

In the wake of the discrepant results from the MECA pilot study, disagreement about how to proceed with the proposed national study was reaching fever pitch. It was decided (well above my level) to hold a national meeting that would bring together prominent spokespersons for the two sides to make their cases in front of an audience of stakeholders.

A panel of renowned experts on child mental health was selected to represent contrasting viewpoints. Much to my surprise, I was asked to be the panel chair and moderator.

Following each presenter there was a short question and answer period, which I moderated. It is a gross understatement to characterize these Q&A sessions as contentious. As we fell further and further behind schedule, I struggled to maintain order as members of the audience (most of whom were senior to me) engaged in heated debate with the eminent presenters and other audience members.

Sitting next to the lectern at the speakers' table, my attention was fixed on the schedule, as the next to the last speaker was winding up his presentation. We were already seriously behind. I wasn't listening as I tried to figure out how to handle the next Q&A session, while expeditiously allowing the final speaker a decent opportunity to present his case.

Suddenly the audience was yelling at me. People were frantically waving and screaming things that I couldn't quite understand. What had I done to offend so many people? Mystified, I turned toward the speaker just in time to catch him as he collapsed onto me, dragging us both to the floor.

An ambulance was called, while a milling circle of MDs, primarily child psychiatrists and pediatricians, attended to the speaker until he was evacuated. (His ailment was reported not to be serious.)

The meeting broke up without resolution (I doubt that one would have been possible in any circumstance). A few weeks later a decision was made to go forward with the bean counters' methods – a decision made by NIMH director Hyman.

The private foundations had the final word, however, abruptly withdrawing their approval and financial support, based on concerns about the bean counter approach. The proposed national study collapsed and we, as a nation, were again left in the dark about the nature and prevalence of serious mental illness among US children and adolescents.

Why can't we conduct large-scale, representative mental health studies of children and adolescents in the US?

Many modern nations collect population-wide data that provide important insights into their youth's current and future health needs. On the surface, neither of the planned US national studies were conducted, because the pilot studies revealed "insurmountable" problems with the proposed methodology. Despite measuring many things, they could not account for enough outcome variance to make it worthwhile.

What both studies lacked were good measures of family psychological health and functioning – the emotional world in which children live. It is my contention that much of the missing variance that the pilot studies could not account for was hidden within the unasked questions about trauma and family dysfunction.

But US researchers who are typically selected to conduct epidemiological studies of children's health, will not, as a rule, investigate the possibility of maltreatment and related familial traumatic exposures in the children they study.

They offer many reasons for their refusals to include measures of child trauma and family dysfunction in their battery of tests.

Chief among them is one I have encountered many times: fear that asking about child maltreatment will insult parents and/or traumatize children and lead families to withdraw from the study. Epidemiologists, who are focused on size and representativeness of their samples, fear this the most.

If they were to ask, and someone indicated there is or had been child maltreatment, what would researchers be expected to do about it? Most states (but not all) require researchers to make a report to local child protection services, which would then independently decide whether to investigate or not.

For most child health epidemiologists, asking questions about child abuse, neglect, and parental dysfunction is too much trouble. It involves too great a risk of losing valuable subjects, and it is legally intimidating. It is easier not to ask, so as not to have to tell.[5]

Then there is the mistaken fear among investigators and Investigational Review Board (IRB) personnel (who independently scrutinize human subjects protections), that asking about sexual abuse or other painful traumas will cause research subjects "to go crazy."

In general, child maltreatment researchers report that the vast majority of survivors, although sometimes emotional during this type of questioning, are relieved to be asked about their abuse experiences. Statements to the effect of "Thank you – nobody ever asked me about that before" are common. No one goes crazy.

We can measure all the chemical pollutant and diesel fume levels we want or ask about all manner of psychiatric symptoms and behaviors, but without collecting information on children's traumatic and adverse life experiences, we will miss the largest share of the variance. Given the recent rapid increase in depression, anxiety, self-mutilation, and suicide in the current generation of adolescents, national epidemiological studies of youth mental health are needed more than ever. Not to mention studies on the effects of the extensive use of social media on the development of self and socialization.

Improving the Child Protection System(s)

Over the years, I have been asked what I would do if I had a chance to change the Child Protection System.

In August 2018, the newly created National Foundation to End Child Abuse and Neglect (EndCAN), sponsored an essay contest challenging contributors to propose a "disruptive" model to end child abuse in a lifetime. The winning and second-place essays would be published in a special journal issue. Essays could focus on disruptive innovation in one of several domains: forensics, treatment, prevention, and research. Presumably the foundation would use the essays to guide funding decisions.

The notion of "disruptive innovation" was especially hot at the time (maybe it still is?). In particular, the novel application of emerging technologies such as video streaming, augmented reality, GPS mapping, block-chain, 3-D printing, and generative AI were upending established practices, undercutting monopolies, and transforming services and industries.

I was excited by The EndCAN Foundation's challenge. Here was an opportunity to gather my thoughts about CPS and put them down in a constructive manner. I set aside a project developing methodologies to improve the scientific evaluation of child trauma treatments in messy, real world clinical settings, and got to work on my essay.

I didn't win or even make the podium. In fact, I received no feedback on my submission. But the important thing was that I spent a lot of time reading critiques and thinking about the strengths and weaknesses of the child protection system as I had observed it, interacted with it, and participated in it for more than three decades.

Reviewing the winning and runner-up articles, I didn't see anything I considered truly disruptive. Winners and runners-up called for better integration of research and practice, increasing cross-disciplinary and graduate level training, and even adopting strategies that were similar to protocols that had increased survival rates for childhood acute lymphoblastic leukemia, or that improved compliance with handwashing in hospitals.

No one suggested an innovative practice or new technology that wasn't already being tried somewhere on something.

That's because it is hard to imagine any single thing that could positively change the US (and global) responses to child maltreatment in that short of a span of time. Child maltreatment is an extraordinarily complex problem. It is deeply embedded in all the issues, problems, and pathologies that afflict humanity.

Short of implanting a GPS trackable "child maltreatment sensor" in every child, backed by local quick reaction teams to follow up on alarms, it is difficult to imagine a truly disruptive technological approach to intervention and prevention. Even if a solution as impossibly radical as that were possible, it would still be hackable.

My proposal called for a fundamental reorganization of CPS at a federal level, something far beyond the capacity or authority of even the wealthiest foundation. In my opinion, the core impediment to improving CPS is that there are literally thousands of different CPS providers, essentially one for every county in the US. Many major urban areas are served by several, and each is essentially a world unto itself.

Much has been written about the issues and problems faced by the child protection movement. The primary problem I addressed in my essay was that CPS providers vary enormously in the quality of their investigations and interventions. There is no national authority to monitor cases and advance best practices. Lessons learned in one context are rarely transferred to others. Successes achieved at state and local levels are seldom sustained following changes in political and administrative leadership. Tragic failures at one agency are often misleadingly portrayed by critics as representative of CPS as a whole.

Although our CAC primarily served Hamilton County, Ohio, we regularly consulted on difficult cases from 20 to 25 counties in three states (Ohio, Kentucky, and Indiana). Through a heavily encrypted network that peer-reviewed video recordings of each other's forensic interviews, we interacted weekly with about a dozen regional CACs. This gave us numerous opportunities to see how different counties, cities, and states handled similar cases.

For any given type of allegation, there is an enormous variability in how investigations and dispositions are handled across CPS jurisdictions. The only practical way to get a handle on this disparity is to impose evidence-based standards and practices, incentivized as much as possible, but also firmly enforced. Given the "home rule" disposition of many states, the federal government is going to have to find a carrot-and-stick balance to bring states along.

The most "disruptive" aspect of my essay was calling for the creation of a three-tier national Child Abuse and Neglect Network (CANNet) much along the lines of the highly successful National Child Traumatic Stress Network. The overall goal of CANNet would be to reduce/eliminate child maltreatment through widespread adoption of evidence-based prevention programs, with a strong focus on reducing the intergenerational transmission of risk.

National leadership would be provided by a federal level agency (Level 1), responsible to Congress, that sets, supports, and enforces national priorities in child maltreatment prevention, treatment, training, research, and policy. Level 1 would also provide the secure communications infrastructure and technical support essential to networking and coordinating clinical, research, and prevention programs across Level 2 and 3 centers.

Primarily located at universities and not-for-profits, Level 2 centers would be the research, development, training, and program implementation engines of CANNet. They would work with Level 3 sites, which are primarily the currently existing county and community CPS agencies and CACs that man the front line of child protection. Partnering with Level 2s, the Level 3s would be trained in best practices and would collaborate in research on prevention and treatment.

The Level 3 sites, which evaluate allegations daily and provide the bulk of the forensic evaluations, treatment, and prevention services to their communities, would contribute their cases to a national database maintained by the Level 1 center. To ensure a steady stream of independent evaluations of national and local programs and practices, appropriately anonymized data would be made available to qualified investigators. These data would also provide rapid feedback to Level 2s and 3s and timely reports to Congress and the public.

The federal government provides funding for Level 1 operations and grant-making. Level 2s are funded in part by research and training grants from Level 1 as well as state and foundation sources. Level 3s bill Medicaid and (when available) health insurance for their services.[6]

I outlined a sequence of steps to progressively implement CANNet nationally. Voluntary adoption by states would be motivated by a combination of financial incentives and federal regulations. These inducements and requirements would facilitate an ongoing national transition from the current hodgepodge of CPS programs into a unified CANNet. The remainder of my proposal provided examples of how the three levels could collaborate to address fundamental problems (training and staff retention, standardizing data collection, implementing evidence-based interventions) plaguing current child protection systems.

The Covid-19 pandemic has amply demonstrated the public and professional confusion, social inequities, lack of comprehensive and reliable data, conflicting policies, partisan politics, and glaring leadership deficits inherent in letting each state (county or community) go its own way. It has also demonstrated the importance of states as "laboratories" to innovate and implement successful strategies. We need to take advantage of the standardization inherent in implementing scientifically documented best practices, while allowing communities and states sufficient flexibility to innovate when faced with unique circumstances or dysfunctional (or exceptional) infrastructure or partners.

There is no magic bullet or single disruptive innovation that is going to result in meaningful reductions in child maltreatment and family violence. National change will require sustained federal leadership and may take more than one generation to accomplish. Change this profound, takes time, but the rewards, in terms of national wellbeing, will be enormous.

The Next Great Thing?

"I spent 13 years at NIMH really pushing on the neuroscience and genetics of mental disorders, and when I look back on that I realize that while I think I succeeded at getting lots of really cool papers published by cool scientists at fairly large costs – I think $20 billion – I don't think we moved the needle in reducing suicide, reducing hospitalizations, improving recovery for the tens of millions of people who have mental illness," Insel says. "I hold myself accountable for that." (Rodgers, 2017).

Thomas R. Insel, MD, was director of the National Institute of Mental Health in Rockville, Maryland, for 13 years (2002 to 2015), substantially longer than any of his predecessors, except the founder, Robert Felix, MD. Tom took hold of the NIMH reins at a propitious moment. Neuroimaging and the genomic sciences were exploding, promising to reveal the neural circuitry and genetic foundation of the mind – and its disorders.

Over the dozen plus years that Tom held tightly to the NIMH reins, he profoundly changed the focus and course of mental health research in the US. He took it from a broad-based bet on an eclectic mix of normal and abnormal behavior, neurobiology, brain imaging, cognitive psychology, child development, animal models, and psychopharmacology to an almost exclusive emphasis on neurogenetics and brain circuitry.

Very late in his tenure as NIMH director, Tom began doubting his limited vision[7]. He attributes the change in his thinking to a challenge from an audience member, following one of his stock presentations touting the wonders of brain research.

"You don't get it," the man said (Friberg, 2017).

"Excuse me. I don't get what?" Tom responded.

"Our house is on fire and you're telling us about the chemistry of the paint. We need someone to focus on the fire."

"I heard that," Tom said.

His response was to resign as NIMH director five months later, move to California, and accept a position with Google. As of this writing, Tom has since changed companies twice and is at the Silicon Valley startup, Mindstrong.

As NIMH director, Tom largely killed funding for research on human behavior, annually redirecting hundreds of millions of those dollars toward his fixation on neurogenetics. Scores of promising research programs on depression, anxiety, PTSD, eating disorders, substance abuse, and other pressing national mental health needs were defunded – and disappeared.

Psychology was particularly hard hit by Tom's narrow focus and his erroneous assumption that once the underlying neurogenetic mechanisms were identified, drug and biotech companies would quickly produce antidotes.

As part of his war on existing psychiatric research paradigms, Tom imposed a new diagnostic system – the Research Domain Criteria (RDoC) – to classify mental conditions (Insel, 2014). Although Tom now admits that the RDoC cannot diagnose mental disorders, during his tenure scientists wishing to submit competitive NIMH research grants were wise to frame their proposals in RDoC speak.

This often led to absurdly reductionistic "scientific" rationalizations – for example, the escape response of a tiny, wormlike, nematode, *C. elegans*, to aversive chemicals in its environment is a model for the human brain circuitry responsible for the phobic avoidance of traumatic reminders in post-traumatic stress disorder.[8]

Predictably, Tom's narrow, reductionist focus was not well received by the mental health community at large, although recipients of the redirected funding were supportive. During the second half of his term, vehement calls for Tom's departure were increasingly heard at professional meetings.

Many of these criticisms were, no doubt, dismissed as sour grapes, until Tom's startling admission that despite spending tens of billions of tax dollars, he had failed to improve the life of even a single mental health patient demonstrably. As news of Tom's confession spread, shouts of outrage and blistering emails circulated among the mental research health community. The mental health field now ignores the RDoC.

One of Tom's most vocal critics, Allen Frances, MD, a nationally prominent psychiatrist, said, "I think very highly of Tom Insel. But what he did at NIMH was disastrous" (Friberg, 2017, p. 83). Others wryly suggested that if his Silicon Valley startup proved successful, Tom should be required to pay back taxpayers.

The mental health world, individually and collectively, had been telling Tom for at least a decade that he was on the wrong track. At very best, he was wildly overemphasizing the role of neurogenetics and brain biology, while virtually ignoring the well-documented contribution of environmental and behavioral stressors to mental illness.

My own experiences talking with Tom about childhood trauma as the single greatest source of preventable and remediable risk for adult mental illness were similar. Richard Loewenstein and I once met with him to discuss the enormous contributions child maltreatment and family violence make to a range of common and costly psychiatric illnesses.

Scientists understand more about the psychological, social, and biological pathways by which childhood maltreatment, trauma, and family dysfunction affect adult mental health than all the putative neurogenetic risk factors combined. We have proven treatments and prevention programs for them, which we can continue to systematically improve.

At the end of our private presentation to Tom on how child maltreatment contributes to national mental health problems, his only notable remark was, "I don't need another study to tell me that child abuse is bad for kids."

It was enough to make us scream with frustration. But Richard and I kept it together, shaking our heads in disbelief as we left the director's conference room.

I have known Tom since July 1979, when we were first year clinical research fellows at NIMH. Slight of build, bespectacled, and soft-spoken, Tom usually wears a look of boredom while listening to other people. He can become mildly excited, however, when plugging his favorite subjects.

Using his own words, one could paint Tom as an idiot or a villain. But in fact, Tom is an intelligent man and compassionate physician, who is genuinely interested in improving the lives of mental patients.

In his profile of Tom in *The Atlantic*, Michael Friberg says he noticed, during Tom's TED Talk, a subconscious tension brewing between Tom's obstinate belief in neurogenetic brain science as the one and only answer and his growing realization that he wasted enormous amounts of time and money on what has proven a bad bet. Not to mention condemned "tens of millions" of Americans to suffer mental disorders that could have been prevented or, at least, better treated.

Tom's moment of epiphany is the breaking through into conscious awareness of the dissonance between his dogmatic belief in neurogenetics and the glaring lack of clinical progress over the dozen plus years that he guided our nation's mental health research agenda.

"You'll think that I probably ought to be fired," Tom would tell audiences, acknowledging the paltry progress in treating mental illness on his watch. "And I can certainly understand that" (Friberg, 2017, p. 80).

So, when Tom finally left NIMH, what source of data did he substitute for his previously cherished neurogenetics?

Ironically, behavior. More specifically, the potential of smartphones and devices to collect vast streams of personal and behavioral data that can be parsed by deep learning algorithms to detect pathological mental states such as depression, anxiety, or suicidal thoughts.

Not an especially original idea, given the large number of apps that already collect mood, cognitive, activity, exercise, sleep, dietary, and biological data on hundreds of millions of us.

We can't afford to make this mistake again. So much good could have been done with 20 billion mental health research dollars – that didn't happen. We can't wait until the mysteries of the human brain – the most complicated object in our immediate universe – are solved to improve public mental health[9].

If we were to adequately fund current evidence-based child abuse and family violence prevention and treatment programs, we would make an enormous improvement in the global health of our society and the quality of all our lives. Obviously much more can be learned and applied in the future. But we already know enough to make a huge difference today if we choose to deliver these services at levels commensurate with their prevalence and multigenerational impact on our society.

The White House is on the Phone

I didn't realize how close I came to being an unwitting player in a national drama, until many years later.

When I read an interview with Anita Hill, JD, about her latest book, *Believing: Our Thirty-Year Journey to End Gender Violence* (2022), a long-standing question of mine was finally answered. The question resurfaced for me each time Professor Hill was mentioned in the media.

The interviewer, Jessica Bennett, observed, "For those who didn't live through the testimony, can we just take a moment to note how bizarre the whole thing was? There was a senator suggesting you'd taken inspiration for your charges from *The Exorcist*" (Bennett, 2021).

Hill responded, "It was so bizarre that it was hard to be even seeing it as real. You question, like, – Is this really happening?"

Finally, I understood! And I shuddered to think of the consequences, had I gone along with what was being demanded of me at the time.

I was aware of Clarence Thomas's Supreme Court confirmation hearings, but paid little attention. In addition to my usual workload, I was cleaning up and repairing damage after a small tornado travelled down my street in Kensington, MD.

Driving home after the storm, I found my usual route blocked by downed trees. When I finally arrived, I was surprised to see a fire engine in the driveway and a firefighter standing guard over a hissing, sparking electric wire dangling over our side yard. Large tree limbs and twisted branches were strewn all over.

Houses on either side of ours had taken direct hits. Our house seemed unscathed, but the tornado had wreaked havoc with our trees. The top 15 feet of the huge tulip poplar in the back was deeply impaled, spear-like, in the front lawn. The side yard was covered with branches. The backyard was impassible, a dense tangle of trunks and limbs.

Hightailing it to the rental store, I scored their last chainsaw. The next day I began the task of clearing the mess, starting at the curb along the side yard and slowly working toward the kitchen backdoor. It took pretty much the entire day. Exhausted, my arms covered in bloody scratches and numbed by hours of chainsaw vibration, noxious fumes, and deafening racket, I opened the garage door to put the rental saw away.

I was dumbfounded. The garage was filled with tree limbs and branches. Uncomprehendingly, I stared at the mess for a minute until I thought to look up. There was a gaping hole in the garage roof. We hadn't escaped unscathed after all.

A few days later, as the Thomas hearings continued, my father-in-law and I were standing on the garage roof replacing a tarp with a plywood patch when Karen leaned out of the kitchen door and shouted something about "… house … phone."

I waved Karen off. Given all the downed wires, it wasn't surprising we were having phone trouble.

Karen walked out and stood, hands on hips, in front of her dad and me.

"The White House is on the phone. There's a woman who says the White House urgently needs to talk with you."

Climbing down from the garage roof, I wondered what the White House wanted with me. I had come to the attention of some national security agencies (Putnam, 2016, pp. 118–120), so it was possible someone got my name from one of them.

A secretary was holding the line. The man who picked up introduced himself as a lawyer in the Office of the White House Counsel. Early in the conversation I had the sense he was trying to entrap me.

He kept asking if I thought Anita Hill suffered from MPD. He continually expressed (pseudo) astonishment at her rapidly changing demeanor. He pushed me to explain what I thought could possibly be happening to her. He even implied that I could examine Ms. Hill.

He was creepy, and the call became increasingly uncomfortable.

I played dumb, repeatedly begging off on his demand that "as a government psychiatrist it was my duty" to render a professional opinion about her mental health.

After that call, every time I encountered Anita Hill's name in the media, I wondered why the White House had tried so hard to get me to "diagnose" her with MPD. Bennett's observation in that interview gave me my answer. It had been suggested that Professor Hill was suffering from demonic possession à la *The Exorcist*. So, of course, a diagnosis of MPD would have been a tad more credible – especially if they could have gotten me to make it.

What if I had allowed myself to be cajoled or coerced into going along with their demands? Not only would I have done a grave injustice to Professor Hill, but it would have been a violation of professional ethics and forever stained my career. And the diagnosis of MPD/DID would have been tainted by its politicization.

Although intimidated by his White House connection, I was never tempted to agree with the lawyer. While I could not foresee the future prominence of Professor Hill's case in the national discourse on the sexual harassment of working women, I just knew on a fundamental level that what I was being asked to do was very wrong.

Notes

1. In response to my critics, I volunteered on the advisory boards of several county government and local non-profit mental health providers to work within their systems.

2. PowerPoint slide taken from a poster: Putnam, F.W., Carrossa, M., & Harris, W. (2008). Mapping trauma: Tools for intervention and advocacy. (Abstract #179790) presented at the 2008 ISTSS meeting, Chicago, IL.
3. For example, a CBS news story (April 1, 2010), linked to David's CCRC website, was headlined "National child abuse rates drop: Figures dip to lowest rate since 1990, but child-abuse fatalities continue to rise." Media coverage, as measured by the sheer number of news stories linked to CCRC reports or quotes from CCRC researchers, made it the US media's most influential source of information about child victimization.
4. http://www.nih.gov/about/director/12122014_statement_ACD.htm.
5. In the FGDS, we uncovered more than a dozen unreported maltreatment cases. We supported families while they self-reported to CPS. If they were unable to self-report, we reported the case. I am not aware of losing a single family from the study for that reason. In fact, most thanked us for helping them do this.
6. In retrospect, it would simplify the administrative load of Level 3 sites by having them submit completed cases through the data system to Level 1 for reimbursement. Level 1 would then bill Medicaid or health insurers as appropriate.
7. In a March 1, 2024 interview with National Public Radio's (NPR), Rhitu Chatterjee, Dr. Thomas Insel discusses the shortcomings of the research policy he guided. Chatterjee observes, "…in the very first pages of his new book, *Healing: Our Path from Mental Illness to Mental Health*, he [Insel] admits that the results of that research have largely failed to help Americans struggling with mental illnesses. https://www.npr.org/sections/health-shots/2022/03/01/1082993901/in-healing-a-doctor-calls-for-an-overhaul-of-the-mental-health-care-system
8. *C. elegans* is one the most primitive animals to have a recognizable nervous system, which primarily stimulates contractions in four muscles allowing the tiny (~1 mm long) worm to wriggle about in search of bacteria to eat. Many scientists question whether *C. elegans* has a "brain."
9. It is not all Tom's fault. A major erosion of the child and adolescent mental health research base in general and trauma research in particular occurred under a prior NIMH Institute Director, Steven Hyman.

References

Bennett, J. (September 25, 2021). Anita Hill has some perspective to offer. *New York Times*.

Berger, R.P., Fromkin, J.B., Stutz, H., Makoroff, K., Scribano, P.V., Feldman, K., Tu, L.C., & Fabio, A. (2011). Abuse head trauma during a time of increased unemployment: A multicenter analysis. *Pediatrics*, 128:637–643.

Friberg, M. (July/August, 2017). The smartphone psychiatrist. *The Atlantic*, pp. 78–86.

Hill, A. (2022). *Believing: Our Thirty-Year Journey to End Gender Violence*. Penguin.

Insel, T.R. (2014). The NIMH Research Domain Criteria (RDoC) project: Precision medicine for psychiatry. *American Journal of Psychiatry*, 171:395–397.

IOM (Institute of Medicine) & NRC (National Research Council). (2014). *New Directions in Child Abuse and Neglect Research*. The National Academies Press.

Loman, L.A., & Siegel, G.L. (2015). Effects of approach and services under differential response on long term child safety and welfare. *Child Abuse & Neglect*, 39:86–97.

Pearl, E., Thieken, L., Olafson, E., Boat, B., Connelly, L., Barnes, J., & Putnam, F. (2012). Effectiveness of community dissemination of parent–child interaction therapy. *Psychological Trauma: Theory, Research, Practice, and Policy*, 4:204–213. DOI: 10.1037/a0022948.

Putnam, F.W. (2016). *The Way We Are: How States of Mind Influence Our Identities, Personality and Potential for Change*. IPBooks.

Putnam, F.W., Carrossa, M., & Harris, W. (2008) *Mapping Trauma: Tools for Intervention and Advocacy.* (Abstract #179790) Poster presented at the 2008 ISTSS meeting, Chicago, IL.

Rodgers, A. (11 May, 2017). Star neuroscientist Tom Insel leaves the Google-spawned Verily for ... a startup? *Wired.* Website Science and Health Column.

Shaffer, D., Fisher, P., Dulcan, M.K., Davies, M., Piacentini, J., Schwab-Stone, M.E., Lahey, B.B., Bourdon, K., Jensen, P.S., Bird, H.R., Canino, G., & Regier, D.A. (1996). The NIMH Diagnostic Interview Schedule for Children Version 2.3 (DISC-2.3): Description, acceptability, prevalence rates, and performance in the MECA study. Methods for the epidemiology of child and adolescent mental disorders study. *Journal of the American Academy of Child and Adolescent Psychiatry,* 35:865–877.

Stephens-Davidowitz, S. (2013). Unreported victims of an economic downturn. Retrieved from Seth Stephens-Davidowitz website, https://static.Squarespace.

7
LESSONS LEARNED

What Did We Learn from the FGDS?

My initial motivation for evaluating behaviorally disturbed children for possible dissociative disorders was to see if I could prospectively trace how adults with MPD/DID became psychologically organized as an "us" rather than as an "I." My 2016 book, *The Way We Are*, is devoted to this question (Putnam, 2016).

By the time Penny and I started the Female Growth and Development Study, my aims had crystalized around three large questions: the nature of the maltreated children's behavior problems; the mechanisms underlying their apparent biological dysregulation; and the reasons for the enormous individual variability in their symptoms and behavior for what was, supposedly, the same trauma.

I suspected that the answers to these questions were interconnected in a complex way, but I was, at best, limited to demonstrating they were correlated. And, as we all know, correlation does not prove causation. The cross-sequential FGDS, however, adds the developmental elements of timing and sequential order, so we know what came first, what followed, and what paralleled what.

While there are undoubtedly differences in the developmental and biological pathways and outcomes of different forms of childhood trauma and adversity, the FGDS findings are sufficiently generalizable

DOI: 10.4324/9781003593928-7

to be representative of how all childhood traumatic experiences embed themselves in individuals' minds and bodies and then are expressed throughout those individuals' lifetimes – and across generations.

As Bessel van der Kolk has famously observed (2014), "The body keeps the score." The FGDS reveals the many ways in which this truism plays out.

In 2007, around the 20th anniversary of seeing our first FGDS subject, Penny, Jennie, and I came together to write a comprehensive review of what we had learned. To organize the copious findings, we divided the major outcomes into seven general categories (Trickett et al., 2011).

Another decade-plus on, these categories still hold: (1) subject variability, (2) mental health problems and seriously disturbed behavior, (3) sexual identity alterations and risky sexual behaviors, (4) revictimization and domestic violence, (5) cognitive development and educational outcomes, (6) biological development and medical health, and (7) multigenerational effects and intergenerational transmission of risk.

First and foremost was the enormous variability in the sexually abused girls' symptoms and performances on tests and measures that we encountered at each evaluation timepoint.

Despite seeking to study a homogeneous sexual abuse group (compared to prior CSA research), we found considerable individual differences within the incest group. For virtually every comparison, standard deviations (a quantitative measure of variability) were larger for the abuse group than the comparison group. Important contributors to this variability included differences in ages of onset, types, frequencies, and durations of the abuse as well as victims' relationships with the perpetrators (e.g., Figures 2.1, 2.2, 4.1).

This empirical measure of variability reinforces my clinical experience in that every case, every victim, every survivor is unique in important ways.

One manifestation of this variability was the wide range of mental health problems exhibited by the abused girls. Using the Diagnostic Interview for Children and Adolescents (DICA) at Times 1, 2, and 3, we found that the abused girls met DSM criteria for significantly more mental disorders than the matched comparison girls. As children and adolescents, the abused girls qualified for a wide range of psychiatric disorders, averaging about three-and-a-half DSM diagnoses per child, compared with an average of less than one for the comparison girls.

From a continuum perspective, the sexually abused group scored much higher on measures of depression, anxiety, dissociation, PTSD, somatic symptoms, and delinquent behavior at many timepoints. By adulthood, the largest group differences were for depression and for drug and alcohol abuse.

This enormous variability is why the child trauma field continues to struggle to define and appropriately diagnose traumatized children in general. More inclusive diagnostic categories, such as developmental trauma disorder (DTD) and complex post-traumatic stress disorder (CPTSD), have been proposed. They have not, as yet, been adopted by mainstream psychiatry or psychology, much less by pediatrics or child welfare.

In addition to a plethora of DSM-defined mental disorders, we found numerous examples of unusual or risky antisocial and sexual behaviors among the abused girls. Overall, there were two main groups.

One group exhibited precocious and risky sexual behavior, while the other group was ambivalent with highly constricted sexuality. When averaged together, the two groups nullified each other, which is why prior studies failed to identify the profound impacts of childhood sexual abuse on adolescent and adult sexual identities, attitudes, and behavior.

Degree of dissociation, both concurrent and as first measured at Time 1, proved highly predictive of multiple mental health problems and unusual or risky behaviors across the lifespan. At Time 4, for example, Time 1 and Time 4 dissociation scores prospectively and retrospectively predicted significantly more physical and sexual revictimization, domestic violence, self-harm (especially self-mutilation), and risky sexual behaviors. As adults, high levels of dissociation predicted harsh parenting practices that are correlated in other studies with attachment disorders and behavior problems in offspring.

High levels of dissociation, in turn, correlated with earlier onset and longer durations of childhood sexual abuse, most common in biological father-daughter incest (e.g., Figure 2.2). Far more than either depression or anxiety, pathological dissociation was associated with severe, early-onset childhood sexual abuse perpetrated by biological fathers. As adults, three of the abused girls were independently diagnosed with dissociative identity disorder.

Dissociation can be understood as the psychological escape from trauma when there is no physical escape. Children and teenagers are relatively powerless against determined adult perpetrators. Especially when perpetrators are family members. To survive being sexually molested hundreds of times – as was true for many of the FGDS girls – they had to find a way out, if only psychologically.

Dissociation allows the incest victim to "go away," to "not be there," to feel that "this isn't happening to me." The victim may go "out of body" or "black out" or "switch into another identity state" to mentally disappear. After surviving dozens to hundreds of sexual assaults, children (who naturally dissociate more than adults) become good at "not being there."

The long-term cost of these recurrent gaps in memory and altered experiences of self, however, is that they disrupt a child's developmental task of consolidating their different life experiences, identities, and behaviors into a more continuous and unified sense of self.

As the sexually abused girls passed through adolescence into early adulthood, they continued to experience significantly more traumatic life experiences than the comparison girls (Figure 4.1). They were more than twice as likely to be raped by a stranger (as opposed to date/partner rape, which was about equal across groups). They were more self-destructive, practicing self-mutilation and attempting suicide. They were more likely to be in abusive relationships.

They were also prone to violence towards their domestic partners. While they tended to commit mild to moderate violence (for example, verbal abuse or throwing objects), they were more likely to be victims of severe domestic violence that resulted in serious injury. They also got into more physical fights with female peers and tended to carry weapons.

We found that by early adolescence the abused girls had significantly lower IQ scores as well as other cognitive deficits that increased in severity with age (Noll et al., 2010; Felt et al., 2022). They were far less likely to finish high school, had lower verbal IQs, and poor ability to problem solve or use what they "know" (to identify and apply cause-and-effect lessons from life experiences). They had higher rates of school avoidance and more unexcused absences.

In terms of social and academic skills, their teachers, who were unaware of the girls' abuse histories, ranked them at the bottom of the class. As a rule, they did not like the abused girls, because they had behavior problems (Trickett et al., 1994). None of the sexually abused girls earned a four-year college degree.

These cognitive deficits and social and behavioral problems, in turn, limited the abused girls' opportunities for friendships with healthy peers and nurturing adults outside of their abusive homes. Their social networks comprised more older males than peers and older females.

From a medical perspective, we found that the sexually abused girls, as young adults, utilized more kinds of health care at greater frequencies. They had higher rates of somatic symptoms, gynecological problems, and sleep disorders. They were more than twice as likely to give birth to premature infants (Noll et al., 2007a).

In the FGDS, the abused girls who suffered the worst outcomes had experienced sexual abuse at younger ages, for longer durations, with more threats or use of violence, and at the hands of a biological father or father figure perpetrator. Over their lifespans, the influence of these factors diminished somewhat, although sexual molestation by a biological father remained remarkably powerful.

Again, it is important to stress the individual variability in outcomes. Not every sexually abused girl did poorly, although tragically, the vast majority did. This lifelong accumulation of traumatic experiences has led therapists to sarcastically refer to childhood abuse as "the gift that keeps on giving."

Dr. Haggerty's Question

We found evidence of dysregulation and disruptions in multiple biological systems, especially related to the body's ability to manage stress and insult. These included increased obesity, heightened autoimmune activity, dysregulation of the hypothalamic-pituitary-adrenal (HPA) axis and acceleration of epigenetic aging. We also answered the question that had worried Dr. Haggerty for 20 years: Does sexual abuse accelerate puberty in girls?

Our controversial hypothesis that incest biologically and behaviorally accelerates female puberty both helped and hurt us over the course of the

FGDS. It prompted the W.T. Grant Foundation to invest in our study. But it also led to Dr. Udry's repeated attacks during the grant renewal site visit. It drew derision again during my final NIMH scientific review, when the panel called our hypothesis "improbable" and cited it as part of their justification for shutting down the FGDS.

It took about 30 years before we were able to publish proof of our hypothesis (Noll et al., 2016).

More than anything, we required time to be able to systematically measure and analyze the timing of numerous pubertal Tanner-stage transitions in the sexually abused and comparison girls. Tanner-staging involves comparing children's (male or female) secondary sex characteristics with a set of standard photographs or drawings that depict stages of pubertal development. This method is far from perfect, because everyone's body is unique, but it is precise enough to be able to compare rates of pubertal maturation between groups of sexually abused and matched comparison girls.

To test our theory that incest accelerates puberty, a nurse, blinded to whether a subject was in the sexual abuse or comparison group, Tanner-staged the girls. She also measured their height and weight and drew blood to analyze their stress and sex hormones.

There are five Tanner-stages of female breast and pubic hair development. A statistical model was used to estimate the probability that (after controlling for confounds) girls in the sex abuse group would transition to a more mature Tanner-stage at a significantly younger age than girls in the matched, non-abused, comparison group.

We compared rates of transitions across all five Tanner-stages (from Stage 1 to 2, 2 to 3, 3 to 4, and 4 to 5). The sexually abused girls were about three-and-a-half times more likely to transition to a higher pubic hair Tanner-stage and three times more likely to advance in breast stage than non-abused comparison girls of the same age. On average, sexually abused girls transitioned to a higher (older) pubic hair Tanner-stage about one year ahead of the comparison girls and eight months ahead in breast development. These group timing differences held through all four Tanner-stage transitions.

While the timing of these differences in sexual development may not sound like a lot, they are important. For more than 50 years, research on child development has found that early pubertal maturation in girls is linked to earlier sexual activity, alcohol, tobacco and drug use, depression, and delinquency. Early puberty also contributes to menstrual and fertility problems and reproductive cancers later in life.

Their earlier, more extensive consensual sex, substance use, and delinquency are generally attributed to the sexually abused girls' association with predatory older males, who seem to be able to spot them from blocks away.

To test this older male connection, in addition to the "Strange Man" protocol, we asked all of the girls to complete measures, ranking who they could count on to help them with the various issues and social situations they, as young women, often encounter (Noll et al., 2000). When we compared the "who" that comprised their social support networks, a large subset of the early maturing abused girls included many more males, specifically "boyfriends," who were typically about three to four years older (think 17- to 18-year-old guys "dating" 13- to 14-year-old girls).

The sexually abused girls also had fewer peer-aged and older female friends. Indeed, the most positive protective factor we found in the social networks analyses, for both abused and comparison girls, was the number of quality relationships they had with older females. Throughout my career, I have been impressed by how important it is for at-risk girls and young women to have healthy relationships with older women. The grandmothers, aunts, teachers, coaches, and "big sisters," who are role models for these girls, providing protection, understanding, and support, are especially important during adolescence.

Sadly, yet also affirmingly, the FGDS was highly ranked as a social resource by many of the sexually abused girls. Throughout the years, many have privately shared their successes and setbacks with Jennie, who is an important person in their lives.

Cortisol and the HPA Axis

The stress hormone cortisol and the larger HPA axis have proven a scientific Rosetta Stone, a key to unlocking an understanding of how childhood trauma biologically embeds itself within victims and then is expressed over the lifespan. This is a prime example of how the body keeps the score.

Although there were few cortisol data for children when we began the FGDS, we chose to study cortisol for several reasons. First, we could get accurate measures from blood. Second, we knew that cortisol secretion reacted quickly to both physical and social stressors, enabling us to investigate stress responses rather than just single values at a point in time. Finally, the maturation of the HPA axis (known as adrenarche) was a critical precursor for the onset of puberty.

Based on our (and now others') research, it became clear that sexual abuse profoundly changes many children's HPA axes and, thus, their stress responses. It took time, however, to see how these changes interacted with other biological systems to change their bodies – and even their genes.

Our next insight came a few years later when we found that the sexually abused girls, as a group, went from having higher baseline levels of cortisol at rest than the comparison girls, to having lower baseline, resting levels. This "attenuation curve" was characterized by high (relative to comparison subjects) resting levels of cortisol in childhood and early adolescence and, later, lower (relative to comparison subjects) resting levels of cortisol in late adolescence and early adulthood. Now the abused girls resembled the Vietnam veteran studies.

Some authorities, notably Elizabeth J. Susman, PhD, and the late Bruce S. McEwen, MD, had hypothesized that major early life stress, such as child sexual abuse, initially increased cortisol levels. But because prolonged exposure to high cortisol levels damages the brain and body, the body responds by "downregulating" the HPA axis and cortisol secretion. This is precisely the pattern that we found for most of the sexually abused girls in the FGDS.

The question now became, what role (if any) did the cortisol attenuation curve play in the health and wellbeing of the sexually abused girls? Another data set provided an answer.

Cortisol and Morbid Obesity

In the early 1990s, I received two papers from a prevention medicine specialist at Kaiser Permanente in San Diego. Both papers reported finding strong relationships between sexual abuse and deleterious adult medical outcomes, especially morbid obesity (Felitti, 1991).

We had at least one follow-up call, during which Vincent Felitti, MD (of later ACEs fame), described running a health and wellness weight loss program for people with morbid obesity. He found that an extremely high percentage of his most overweight clients had histories of childhood sexual abuse. The CSA victims were also the most frequent recidivists, unable to keep the excessive weight off after they lost it. Having heard about the FGDS, Vince wanted to know if we were seeing higher rates of eating disorders among our subjects.

We weren't. But then we had only looked at our DICA data for evidence of eating disorders. The DICA data missed disordered eating, because it only rendered binary – you either have it or you don't – DSM diagnoses. It turns out that the disordered eating symptoms were largely "subclinical," meaning that they did not reach the threshold required for a DSM psychiatric diagnosis (Li et al., 2018).

The relationship between a history of child sexual abuse and morbid adult obesity, first described by Dr. Felitti, continued to be reported in cross-sectional studies by other researchers investigating samples, ranging from the general population to gastric bypass surgery patients. In general, subjects reporting more extreme abuse were more obese.

What the longitudinal FGDS was able to do, however, was identify a critical biological process by which the sexually abused girls as a group, became heavier as they aged. At every visit, we recorded the subjects' heights and weights and calculated their body mass index (BMI).[1] We then compared the rates of change in the abused and comparison girls' BMIs over time.

At every evaluation time point, the abused girls had higher BMIs and were gaining weight faster than the comparison girls (Noll et al., 2007b). The average linear slope of BMI increase was significantly steeper for the abused subjects than for the comparison subjects, after controlling for minority status and history of pregnancy.

Around age 18, the average abused girl in the FGDS crossed the 75th percentile for BMI, meaning their BMI was greater than 75 percent of 18-year-old US females. As young adults, women with a history of CSA were more than twice as likely to be obese (i.e., BMI ≥ 30) than their non-abused peers. Even more striking was that the sexually abused subjects continued to gain weight at significantly faster rates than the matched comparison subjects. If this trend continued unabated, they were likely to become morbidly obese later in life. In contrast, the comparison subjects tracked the US population's 50th percentile over the same age range.

The critical question was, what was driving this accelerated weight gain? Was it depression, which has been linked to increased risk for adult obesity? Was it due to a high intake of calorie-laden food and snacks? Was it the result of inactivity or sleep disruption? Stress and trauma are associated with depression, post-traumatic stress disorder, and eating disorders, all of which affect diet, sleep, and activity levels.

Furthermore, it was not uncommon to hear CSA victims describe deliberately gaining large amounts of weight to make themselves "unattractive" or "too large to be easy targets of rapists."

Given the well-studied, powerful effects of cortisol on metabolism, we wondered if there could be a causal relationship between the cortisol attenuation curve and the abused girls' increased susceptibility to gaining excess weight. A mediation analysis would be the most appropriate way to test this[2].

We used two analytic methods to test the extent to which the cortisol attenuation curve mediated the effects of CSA on the abused subjects' accelerated BMI growth trajectory (Li et al. 2021). In both, we controlled for minority status, parity (number of pregnancies), steroid medication use, depression history, and disordered eating history. Each approach showed that high resting cortisol in childhood, followed by an attenuated cortisol curve during adolescence, significantly mediated the CSA subjects' accelerated BMI and adult obesity.

This discovery held important implications. First, screening for elevated resting levels of cortisol (the starting point of the attenuation curve) in traumatized children could improve early identification of those at risk for morbid obesity in adulthood. Second, interventions and trauma treatments that normalize the HPA axis may not only prevent morbid obesity but also improve or prevent a host of medical problems associated with obesity. Last, but just as important, consider the effects of rapid, excessive weight gain and obesity on the self-confidence and body image of adolescent girls coming of age in a society obsessed with the female body.

Our findings, like all scientific results, will require independent replication before they become established facts. But the FGDS has moved the field beyond simply linking CSA with obesity, to a deeper understanding of how a specific biological stress response (the cortisol attenuation curve) mediates obesity by early adulthood.

Multigenerational Effects and the Intergenerational Transmission of Risk

The multigenerational results from the FGDS (e.g., Figure 4.1) along with my experiences as director of a CAC, scientific director of Every Child Succeeds, and as a therapist working with traumatized children and their families, have led me to the conclusion that a serious reduction of child maltreatment and family violence must be approached from an intergenerational/multigenerational perspective. Most US cases of child maltreatment are tragic repetitions of multigenerational cycles of family violence and dysfunction.

Whenever possible, therapeutic interventions and prevention programs should address multiple generations simultaneously. The good news is that multigenerational interventions are extremely powerful. They tap the strong reciprocal attachment instincts that exist between most parents and children. For children, the most reinforcing reward is positive attention from their parents. For many parents, the most gratifying motivation is their children's love and respect. Indeed, most parents raised in extreme adversity want a better life for their children, and they view being able to provide it as one way they can "fix" what happened to them when they were children.

As a therapist, I've seen the immense power that positive parental attention has on children's behavior. Consistently using a few simple positive responses, parents can transform out-of-control misbehavior into willing obedience and eager cooperation. Perhaps the best-studied treatment model is Parent Child Interaction Therapy (PCIT), which has repeatedly been proven to bring about manageable and enjoyable parent-child interactions in a relatively short time.

Conversely, treating trauma in children leads to a large reduction of trauma symptoms in their parents (Hahn et al., 2019). Most proven child trauma treatments include parental/primary caretaker components, although to different degrees. As with most prevention and remediation interventions, the sooner they are applied, the better the outcomes will be.

Government policies that support family financial stability (for example, the tragically short-lived expanded child tax credit), would go a long way toward reducing global family stress and distress, which, in turn, would lower the incidence of maltreatment and family violence.

For us to bring about meaningful, sustained reductions in child abuse and family violence, we will need a multigenerational perspective backed by unwavering persistence and patience. It may require several generations of rigorously applied prevention programs before we can see a measurable difference in national incidence and prevalence of child maltreatment.

Old Before Their Time

The FGDS finding that child sexual abuse accelerates puberty in females, led us to ask whether there were other examples of accelerated biological aging in the sexual abuse group. In the case of puberty, the Tanner scale measured the rate of sexual maturation. But how would we measure the rate of biological aging elsewhere in the body – in one's eyes, knees, hearts, or minds?

An increasingly accepted measure is "epigenetic aging." "Epigenetics" covers any heritable chemical modification that affects gene expression without changing the genetic sequence. Epigenetic age acceleration is biological aging that is not attributable to chronological aging. Although a number of biological processes qualify as "epigenetic," empirical measures of epigenetic aging (called "clocks") are most commonly based on variations in DNA methylation across cytosine-phosphate-guanine (CpG) dinucleotide sites in the genome. Epigenetic aging clocks are integrative biomarkers that broadly reflect the health of multiple bodily processes and biological systems (such as activity in metabolic pathways, proportions of stem cells in tissues, immune competence, and levels of systemic inflammation).

Using four different clocks, we compared the amount of epigenetic aging at midlife (mean age 36.8 years) in the sexually abused versus the matched, non-abused comparison women. Each clock provided four indices of epigenetic biological age acceleration. The four epigenetic aging clocks were moderately correlated but largely tapped different regions and functions in the genome. Consequently, they reflected "aging" across a wide range of biological processes and systems. As such, they provided a window into just how broadly and deeply early traumatic experiences, such as childhood sexual abuse, biologically embed themselves and are expressed over the lifespan.

Although there were stronger effects for some clocks and indices than others, collectively, they supported the finding that there was significantly increased epigenetic age acceleration in the CSA group (Shenk et al., 2021; Felt et al., 2022). Indeed, an accelerated rate of aging is the ultimate "score" that the body keeps.

Aging is the single most powerful risk factor for the leading medical causes of chronic disability and death. The science of aging is exploding, driven by new molecular biological techniques that scientists use to estimate the ages of individual organs and specialized cells. These studies find that aging is not a simple linear process that affects all body parts equally. In different people, their heart may age faster than their brain or their pancreas age faster than their muscles. Age-related molecular profiles have been developed for about 15 organs and bodily systems. They enable scientists to assign people "ageotypes," based on the patterns of biological organ aging that deviate from average chronological age profiles across the lifespan. Researchers categorize subjects as "brain agers" or "heart agers" or conversely as brain "youthers" or immune system "youthers," depending on whether the biological age of organs or systems is significantly ahead or behind a person's birth age.

There is emerging evidence that older biological ages of certain organs lead to earlier illnesses in that organ, such as heart disease or dementia. Younger organ ages correlate with a decreased incidence of disease in those organs. Risky lifestyle choices, especially poor diet and tobacco, alcohol, and drug use, increase biological aging in certain organs and systems. Healthy habits notably decrease biological aging when genetic risk is controlled for. Commercial kits that can categorize ageotypes have already made their way onto the market.[3]

Diverse examples of accelerated aging have proven to be the most broadly replicated, long-term, meta-finding of the FGDS. But, of course, one can only appreciate that from the perspective of 35+ years of multi-measure evaluations.

From Penny and my very first conceptualizations, we shared a concern that child sexual abuse accelerated puberty. This was central to informing the FGDS design, methodology, and choice of biological and behavioral measures. Subjects were Tanner-staged, had their sex hormones measured, and were blindly rated in standardized behavioral scenarios to test for accelerated biological and behavioral aging against the matched comparison subjects.

Throughout the study, we saw additional types of data that indicated the sexually abused subjects were aging more rapidly: accelerated BMI, increased autoimmune activity, and lower cognitive peak performance, followed by cognitive decline. Test results repeatedly indicated that the abused subjects were aging faster and less gracefully than the comparison girls. The results of the epigenetic studies extended this observation to yet another domain.

When one extrapolates this trend of accelerated biological aging, it leads to the sadly inescapable conclusion that the sexually abused subjects will, on average, die at younger ages than the matched comparison subjects. Fortunately, as a group, the FGDS subjects are not yet old enough for that tragic outcome to become apparent. However, there are data from the original adverse childhood experience (ACE) research group to support this hypothesis.

Designed to investigate the long-term relationship between ACEs and a variety of adult health outcomes, the well-regarded original ACE study has greatly influenced the public's and policy makers' understanding of the lifelong costs of childhood trauma and adversity. In a follow-up study, over a 9- to 11-year period, the ACE research group prospectively looked at the risk for premature death in a large sample (Brown et al., 2009). Adults with six or more ACEs died approximately 20 years earlier on average than those with no ACEs and were 2.4 times more likely to die before the age of 66.

Interestingly, there was no single specific cause of death; in fact, most fell somewhere within one of the five leading causes of death in the US (vascular disease: heart disease and stroke; cancers; nervous system diseases; respiratory diseases; and digestive diseases). Without a doubt, preventing child maltreatment and associated family violence would significantly reduce these, typically older-age-related, causes of death in younger adults.

Recent epigenetic aging research supports the FGDS's multiple biobehavioral findings of accelerated aging linked to stress and early life trauma. Trends emerging from this still limited number of studies implicates both early socioeconomic adversity and childhood maltreatment, especially CSA, as major risk factors for accelerated epigenetic aging (Palma-Gudiel et al., 2019).

As these early epigenetic results are further replicated and refined, they will open up a new window on understanding the nature of biologically embedded trauma. We will have multiple, easily obtainable, biomarkers that are altered (starting in infancy and perhaps even in utero) throughout the lifespan. Since there is evidence for reversibility of epigenetic processes, such as methylation, we may be able to measure not only increased risk for a variety of medical and mental health outcomes, but also therapeutic responses to targeted interventions.

The bottom line is that the FGDS found numerous, significant, lifelong negative impacts on the mental, physical, and social health of the sexually abused girls. The common thread across these seemingly dissimilar effects was that the abused girls were growing older in mind, brain, and body much faster than the comparison girls.

In some respects, we've always known this. An archetypical understanding of the aging effects of stress and trauma is implicit in popular sayings that express the sentiment that traumatic life experiences will "make one old before one's time" or "will be the death of me."

The Present and Future of the FGDS

In 2006, Jennie Noll joined me at Cincinnati Children's Hospital, where she continued leading the FGDS, while initiating innovative research on uses of the internet by sexually abused teenagers.[4] Seed funding from an anonymous donor to OhioCANDo allowed us to pilot new methodology to continue following the FGDS subjects, now increasingly scattered around the US. These preliminary data provided the basis for major grants from the National Institute of Child Health and Human Development extending the FGDS re-evaluations to Times 7 and 8.

In July 2012, I accepted a part-time position in the department of psychiatry at the University of North Carolina at Chapel Hill. Not long thereafter, I was diagnosed with Stage IV prostate cancer. As a result of my illness, I was forced to withdraw from clinical and teaching activities, but I was able to continue to work on research from home. In terms of the number of scientific publications, this has been one of the most productive periods of my career.

Jennie left Cincinnati Children's Hospital Medical Center in 2013 to set up a large-scale, comprehensive child sexual abuse program at the Pennsylvania State University (Penn State), funded in the wake of the Sandusky child sexual abuse scandal. She named it Center for Safe and Healthy Children. At Penn State, Jennie assembled a group of distinguished international collaborators and mentored a promising cohort of graduate students and junior faculty, who continue working with FGDS data. Jennie and colleagues were awarded the very first NIH-funded center of excellence in child maltreatment research and training. The focus of that P50 grant was the biologic embedding of early life stress and maltreatment. After a decade of building the P50 program at Penn State, the center was renewed, a testament to the increasing support that NIH now gives to the study of child maltreatment.

Like me, Jennie says that, because of her work, it has become her passion to improve the prevention of child maltreatment. She developed a program for parents called *Smarter Parents Safer Kids*, and also worked with the state of Pennsylvania on a three-pronged, place-based, community-wide intervention in five counties that successfully lowered rates of sexual abuse at the population level (Noll et al., 2025).

In 2023, Jennie left Penn State to become the executive director of the Mount Hope Family Center in Rochester, New York, originally directed by Dante Cicchetti, a founder of and leading contributor to the field of developmental psychopathology. Jennie and I and, really, all who work in the area of child maltreatment, know that so much more could be accomplished by just using what we already know, if only there were a greater public and political will.

Sadly, our long-time friend, esteemed collaborator, and co-founder of the FGDS, Dr. Penelope Trickett, died in 2016 from complications of her chemotherapy. We dearly miss Penny. Jennie and I cherished the abiding, harmonious, and productive collaboration we shared. I believe we pulled it off because the FGDS was never about us, it was – and still is – *always* about the children.

More than any other research study anywhere, ever, the FGDS has shown how early trauma becomes biologically embedded within individuals. How CSA dysregulates biological stress systems such as the HPA axis. How it can change victims' bodies in a multitude of ways, accelerating puberty, increasing obesity, and speeding up epigenetic aging. CSA affects multiple organ systems and dysregulates a variety of biological processes, including systemic inflammation. It degrades cognitive functioning, potentially increasing the risk for early dementia. CSA shapes victims' social responses to interpersonal situations, confounding the development of their behaviors and sense of self. All these dimensions combine to dramatically increase the occurrence of mental and physical illnesses and of risky and self-destructive behaviors. The ultimate statistical, long-term outcome of severe CSA is premature death, although the fate of any given individual, abused or comparison subject, is not determined by their trauma history alone.

The FGDS continues to be productive, publishing landmark papers on the pernicious embedding of the lifelong effects of childhood sexual abuse in critical biological systems, impairing cognitive capacities, and inducing negative social behaviors. There are still more seminal FGDS findings percolating through the peer-review pipeline.

Today, many professionals, and the public, readily accept the fact that traumatic and aversive early life experiences alter a person's biology. But when Penny and I first met in the NIH clinical center cafeteria and sketched an initial version of Figure 2.1, this premise was considered scientific heresy.

Bringing it All Back Home

The other day I told Karen that the hardest thing I have ever had to do is get through the pain, inconvenience, and infirmity I experience morning after morning, showing up at my desk and putting in some solid work. Yet, I'm eternally grateful for the opportunity and remaining ability to do so. I know how much worse it could be.

What I have learned from living many years beyond the few months I was told I had left to live (by a doctor I never saw again), is that you never know when it is going to be "your time." Over these years, I've known many seemingly hale and hearty people who unexpectedly died. Whether we wish to acknowledge it or not, we live day-to-day.

Pushing past the daily struggles and indignities of living with stage IV cancer, I have come to regard my illness as just one more obstacle to work around and through as best I can.

I feel fortunate that we, collectively – the FGDS team and the much larger field of child maltreatment – have made important gains since my epiphany in the parking lot.

Many essential facts are now firmly and scientifically established.

We have undeniable proof that child abuse, especially CSA, profoundly affects the health and wellbeing of survivors. It seriously disrupts the normal biology of growing children. It changes neuroendocrine responses to stress and the timing of sexual maturation. It alters children's brains, bodies, and even their genes. None for the better. All of this adds up to premature aging, poorer health and functioning, and, often, an earlier death.

In big and little ways, CSA compounds the risks for individuals to do poorly in life, and heartbreakingly, of passing on an insidious, multigenerational curse to their children.

The revved-up, hyperactive, hypersexual, aggressive, behaviorally disorganized children like Jodie (see Prologue), and the shut-down, semi-catatonic, emotionally constricted children hiding deep within their fantasy worlds, are but two sides of the same coin. While the child mental health professions continue to debate how to best to diagnose these children, at least they no longer deny that they exist.

We have begun to connect dysregulated biology with dysfunctional behaviors and subsequent deleterious adult outcomes. This allows us to detect, track, and target the underlying psychobiological processes at an earlier stage. Evidence indicates that the younger the child is and the quicker we can intervene and ensure safety and security in caretaking, the better the child is going to do.

Understanding the long-term effects of child maltreatment on child growth and development provides an essential window into understanding how the mind and body are damaged by trauma and chronic stress.

While funding for research on child trauma is minuscule relative to its long-term costs to society, we know more about the psychobiological mechanisms and developmental pathways by which child abuse and neglect harm children and contribute to the adults they become than about the causal chains underlying other major adult mental health problems.

Arguably, child maltreatment is the largest preventable cause of certain major mental illnesses, interpersonal violence, and much hard substance abuse. Meaningful reductions in the rates of child maltreatment would yield greater improvements in the mental and physical health of our nation than any other single target of prevention.

Although individuals vary, of all the common childhood abuses, traumas, and adversities that have been systematically investigated, CSA is the worst. Especially father-daughter incest. CSA has been shown to alter neuroendocrine stress responses, accelerate reproductive biology, and impair the immune system. It is most closely tied to serious mental illnesses, in particular depression, anxiety disorders, PTSD, and dissociation.

CSA is uniquely associated with the outcome of "traumatic sexualization," manifested by sexual promiscuity, early teenage pregnancy, adult sexual revictimization, sexual dysfunction, and, primarily in males, sexual offending (Noll, 2021).

In addition, other forms of maltreatment, trauma, and adversity are more likely to co-occur with CSA than with other common childhood traumas and adversities. CSA is also the trauma most strongly associated with later revictimization, compounding risk across the lifespan. Finally, it is the form of maltreatment that is most likely to interact synergistically with other trauma, that is to combine with a second type of trauma to produce an outcome that is worse than the statistical sum of the two different traumas' separate effects (Briggs et al., 2021).

One lesson that transcends both clinical and research domains is the uniqueness of each case. Despite an emotionally numbing sense of déjà vu that sets in after working with thousands of cases, each victim, each family, and each survivor, is unique in meaningful ways.

Another lesson learned: *Values trump scientific data.* The only way around this determinative hierarchy is to elevate the concern for children's health and safety to a highly prized, widely shared value and not merely give it lip service (as is so often the case). The worst thing that could happen is for CSA to become further politicized; the knee-jerk reaction of some to call every political opponent or troublesome critic a "pedophile" or "groomer" trivializes these evil crimes, and it has got to stop.

When we started the FGDS in 1987, little was known about treatment of traumatized children, nor was much distinction made among types of maltreatment. Generic child treatments, largely adopted from adult models, were aimed at individual problematic symptoms: aberrant behaviors such as hyperactivity, aggression, hypersexuality, conduct problems, self-destructive behaviors, depression, and mood swings. The very existence of PTSD in children and adolescents (and how it might manifest) was a hotly disputed question. Many child psychiatrists mistakenly viewed the confusing plethora of abuse-related symptoms as a prodrome to later schizophrenia or bipolar disorder.

Not infrequently, antipsychotic medications were prescribed off-label, because pharmaceutical companies were not willing to hazard the long-term liability associated with proper clinical trials of these powerful drugs in children. Beyond scattered single case reports and small case series, there were few outcome data by which to judge the success of one child trauma therapy over another. As is often the case in medicine, adult treatments were applied to children, with little sensitivity to developmental and biological differences. Children are not miniature adults.

Today, the child trauma treatment field has advanced considerably, in large measure thanks to the NCTSN. We have rigorously tested, readily trainable, youth trauma treatments, and we have a better understanding of who they will benefit most. Much remains to be done, but there are templates for what works (Hoppen et al., 2024). It is unrealistic, however, to expect that the profound biological dysregulation, cognitive deficits, and social dysfunction in survivors suffering years of incest and maltreatment can be normalized by 15-session PTSD therapies.

Two decades of NCTSN science-informed support, training, and resources, have provided us with important guidance as to what is required to go to the next level and reach children and families on a national scale. We have an array of evidence-based trauma interventions, and we know how to adapt them for special populations and a diverse array of traumas. Needless to say, because of the enormity and ubiquity of child maltreatment, family traumas, and adversity, a much-expanded version of the NCTSN is necessary to move the national needle.

While we have promising models of how to improve CPS services (for instance, alternate response and child advocacy centers), the entire system needs a complete overhaul.[5] We have ample evidence that the current community-level hodgepodge of child protection systems is failing many children and families, especially boys.

First and foremost, there must be a greater degree of standardization, enacted at a state level but in compliance with federal best practice guidelines. The current degree of variability from jurisdiction to jurisdiction in CPS investigations and decision making is far too great to ensure equal justice under the law.

A high-quality, real-time, national child maltreatment surveillance system, equivalent to that deployed for cancer and flu, can give us more accurate numbers, identify regional hot spots, and enforce standardization in definitions and responses. In times of economic hardship, it can focus support on the neediest regions. It would also be a critical source of valuable data for evaluating the success or failure of local policies and practices and for training AI programs to aid in decision making.

More support is needed for psychology and social work graduate students, psychiatric residents and pediatric fellows, junior faculty, and others interested in research and treatment of child maltreatment and family violence. The powers that be in academic departments, government funding agencies, and child-oriented foundations must recognize that population-based and clinical research on these problems, while methodologically and ethically complicated, holds the promise of enormous payoffs in public health.

Prospective, longitudinal research, such as the FGDS, is essential to further our understanding of the complex interplay of biological, cognitive, behavioral, and social development in maltreated children, especially in long-neglected males. The fledgling science of developmental traumatology is coming of age. It seeks to understand, and thus identify, opportunities for intervention and prevention – how childhood traumas and adversities lead to the array of pernicious outcomes now strongly associated with them.

If you have followed me thus far, I hope I have broadened and deepened your understanding of how pervasive and injurious child maltreatment is, especially sexual abuse. There are unfortunately many other traumas impacting the development of children that I haven't addressed, some of which include sex trafficking, school shootings, internet sexploitation, community violence, war, racism, poverty, cyber- and other bullying, parental mental illness and addiction, and parental separation and loss. All our children need our love, care, and protection, and this "takes a village."

Notes

1. BMI is a person's weight in kilograms divided by the square of their height in meters. BMIs of 30 or higher are classified as obese.
2. A mediation analysis is a statistical approach that breaks down the effect of an intervention into direct and indirect effects. It's used to examine the relationship between an independent variable and a dependent variable.
3. One can expect the commercial ageotype business to take hold like the mail-in personal DNA analyses did. To date, no ageotype kit has received Food and Drug Administration (FDA) approval and many only determine the biological age of a single organ, assigning that value to the person as a whole.
4. In another CSA sample, Jennie and colleagues found that sexually abused girls were more likely to be cyberbullied and sexually propositioned on the internet than non-abused comparison girls. Even though the two groups spent approximately equal time on a range of internet activities, including visiting pornography websites.
5. When the child protection services system was first conceived and implemented, it was based on the untested assumption that the total number of US maltreatment cases was limited to a few hundred a year. No one foresaw that CPS would serve literally millions of children and families annually.

References

Briggs, E.C., Amaya-Jackson, L., Putnam, K.T., & Putnam, F.W. (2021). All adverse childhood experiences (ACEs) are not equal: The contribution of synergy to ACE scores. *American Psychologist*, 76:243–252. https://doi.org/10.1037/amp0000768.

Brown, D.W., Anda, R.F., Tiemeire, H., Felitti, V.J., Edwards, V.J., Croft, J.B., & Giles, W.H. (2009). Adverse childhood experiences and the risk of premature mortality. *American Journal of Preventive Medicine*, 37:389–396.

Felitti, V.J. (1991). Long-term medical consequences of incest, rape, and molestation. *The Southern Medical Journal*, 84:328–331.

Felt, J., Harrington, K., Ram, N., O'Donnell, K., Silwinski M., Benson, L., Meaney, M.J., Putnam, F.W., Noll, J., & Shenk, C. (2022). Receptive language abilities for females exposed to early life adversity: Modification by epigenetic age acceleration at midlife in a 30-year prospective cohort study. *The Journals of Gerontology: Psychological Sciences, Series B*, 78:585–595. doi: 10.1093/geronb/gbac158.

Hahn, H., Putnam, K., Epstein, C., Marans, S., & Putnam, F. (2019). Child and family traumatic stress intervention (CFTSI) reduces parental posttraumatic stress symptoms: A multi-site meta-analysis (MSMA). *Child Abuse & Neglect*, 92:106–115. https://doi.org/10.1016/j.chiabu.2019.03.010.

Hoppen, T.H., Wessarges, L., Jehn, M., Mutz, J., Ahike, K., Schlechter, P., Meiser-Stedman, R., & Morian, N. (2024). Psychological interventions for pediatric post-traumatic stress disorder: A systematic review and network meta-analysis. *JAMA Psychiatry*. doi: 10.1001/jamapsychiatry.2024.3908.

Li, J.C., Hall, M.A., Shalev, I., Schreier, H.M.C., Zarzar, T.G., Marcovici, I., Putnam, F.W., & Noll, J.G. (2021). Hypothalamic-pituitary-adrenal axis attenuation and obesity risk in sexually abused females. *Psychoneuroendocrinology*, 129:105254–105279. https://doi.org/10.1016/j.psyneuen.2021.105254.

Li, J.C., Noll, J.G., Bensman, H.E., & Putnam, F.W. (2018). Childhood sexual abuse increases risks for eating disorder symptoms and eating disorder-related health problems in females. In: S. Negriff (Ed.), *Child Maltreatment Research, Policy, and Practice*: Springer Briefs in Psychology, Springer, pp. 11–26. https://doi.org/10.1007/978-3-030-04561-6_2.

Noll, J.G. (2021). Child sexual abuse as a unique risk factor for the development of psychopathology: The compounded convergence of mechanisms. *Annual Review of Clinical Psychology*, 17:439–464. https://doi.org/10.1146/annurev-clinpsy-081219-11262.

Noll, J.G., Felt, J., Russotti, J., Guastaferro, K., Day, S., & Fisher, Z. (2025). Rates of population-level child sexual abuse after a community-wide preventive intervention. *JAMA Pediatrics*. doi: 10.1001/jamapediatrics.2024.6824.

Noll, J.G., Schulkin, J., Trickett, P.K., Susman, E.J., Breech, L., & Putnam, F.W. (2007a). Differential pathways to preterm delivery in sexually abused and comparison women. *Journal of Pediatric Psychology*, 32:1238–1248.

Noll, J.G., Shenk, C.E., Yeh, M.T., Ji, J., Putnam, F.W., & Trickett, P.K. (2010). Receptive language and educational attainment for sexually abused females. *Pediatrics*, 126:e615–e622. doi: 10.1542/peds.2010-0496.

Noll, J.G., Trickett, P.K., Long, J.D., Negriff, S., Susman, E.J., Shalev, I., Li, J.C., & Putnam, F.W. (2016). Childhood sexual abuse and early timing of puberty. *Journal of Adolescent Health*, 60:65–71. http://dx.doi.org/10.1016/j.jadohealth.2016.09.008.

Noll, J.G., Trickett, P.K., & Putnam, F.W. (2000). Social network constellation and sexuality of sexually abused and comparison girls in childhood and adolescence. *Child Maltreatment*, 5:323–337.

Noll, J.G., Zeller, M.H., Trickett, P.K., & Putnam, F.W. (2007b). Inordinate obesity risk for female victims of childhood sexual abuse: A prospective study. *Pediatrics*, 120:e61–e67.

Palma-Gudiel, H., Fananas, L., Horvath, S., & Zannas, A.S., (2019). Psychosocial stress and epigenetic aging. *International Review of Neurobiology*. doi.org/10.1016/bs.irn.2019.10.020.

Putnam, F.W. (2016). *The Way We Are: How States of Mind Influence Our Identities, Personality and Potential for Change*. IPBooks.

Shenk, C.E., Felt, J.M., Ram, N., O'Donnell, J.J., Sliwinski, M.J., Pokhvisneva, I., Benson, L., Meany, M.J., Putnam F.W., & Noll, J.G. (2021). Cortisol trajectories measured prospectively across thirty years of female development following exposure to childhood sexual abuse: Moderation by epigenetic age acceleration at midlife. *Psychoneuroendocrinology*, 136:105606–105644. https//doi.org/10.1016/j.psyneuen.2021.105606.

Trickett, P.K., McBride-Chang, C., & Putnam, F.W. (1994). The classroom performance and behavior of sexually abused females. *Development and Psychopathology*, 6:183–194.

Trickett, P.K., Noll, J.G., & Putnam, F.W. (2011). The impact of sexual abuse on female development: Lessons from a multigenerational longitudinal research study. *Development and Psychopathology*, 23:453–476.

Van der Kolk, B. (2014). *The Body Keeps the Score: Brain, Mind, and Body in the Healing of Trauma*. Viking.

EPILOGUE

Being There

I am not religious in the conventional sense.

I feel spiritual – wonderstruck by the extraordinary beauty and complexity of the natural world. For me, there are two ways to appreciate this infinitely wondrous intricacy: science and "being present" in the moment.

In that dual context, my experience in the parking lot *is* an epiphany. It stopped me in my tracks with an indescribable mental image of the countless interconnected realms in which child maltreatment harms children, coupled with an unambiguous feeling about the rightness of opposing this unmitigated evil.

Once I had seen it, felt it, I couldn't turn away.

To this day, that image and that feeling, although dimmed by time, inevitably recur during moments of indecision and travail.[1] Together, they have kept me going. And increasingly, data set after data set, the science has come to support them.

The disturbed behavior, dysregulated biology, and accelerated aging of the children I evaluated for possible dissociative disorders, proved to have scientifically traceable biobehavioral life trajectories. But it required time to see these, often tragic, outcomes play out. Many terrible things were indeed happening to these children.

DOI: 10.4324/9781003593928-8

The FGDS is at the heart of what I have tried to do – reveal, repair, and prevent those terrible things happening to children. Humbly, yet proudly, I have watched the ethos of the FGDS, especially our respect for our subjects and our commitment to science, pass from generation to generation of students and scientists. Sadly, Penny is not here to share some of the most important discoveries.

There is more to come, but that will be someone else's story to tell.

I have seen sufficient results to feel gratified.

Note

1. In his masterwork, *The Varieties of Religious Experience*, William James opines that the proof of the power of an epiphany lies in the manner in "… *which* [it] *lives itself out within the private breast*" (p. 262).

Reference

James, W. (1958). *The Varieties of Religious Experience*, New American Library.

INDEX

Note: Locators in *italic* indicate figures and in ***bold-italic*** indicate boxes

For Product Safety Concerns and Information please contact our EU
representative GPSR@taylorandfrancis.com
Taylor & Francis Verlag GmbH, Kaufingerstraße 24, 80331 München, Germany